C000163404

BOMB ALLEY–
FALKLAND ISLANDS
1982

Bomb Alley – Falkland Islands 1982

Aboard HMS *Antrim* at War

David Yates

Pen & Sword
MARITIME

First published in Great Britain in 2006.
Reprinted in this format in 2007 and 2009 by
Pen & Sword Maritime
an imprint of
Pen & Sword Books Ltd
47 Church Street
Barnsley
South Yorkshire
S70 2AS

Copyright © David Yates, 2006, 2009

ISBN 978 1 84415 624 5

The right of David Yates to be identified as Author of this Work has
been asserted by him in accordance with the Copyright, Designs
and Patents Act 1988.

A CIP catalogue record for this book is
available from the British Library

All rights reserved. No part of this book may be reproduced or transmitted in
any form or by any means, electronic or mechanical including photocopying,
recording or by any information storage and retrieval system, without
permission from the Publisher in writing.

Typeset in Palatino by
Phoenix Typesetting, Auldgirth, Dumfriesshire

Printed and bound in England by
CPI Antony Rowe, Chippenham, Wiltshire

Pen & Sword Books Ltd incorporates the imprints of Pen & Sword Aviation,
Pen & Sword Maritime, Pen & Sword Military, Wharncliffe Local History,
Pen & Sword Select, Pen & Sword Military Classics and Leo Cooper.

For a complete list of Pen & Sword titles please contact
PEN & SWORD BOOKS LIMITED
47 Church Street, Barnsley, South Yorkshire, S70 2AS, England
E-mail: enquiries@pen-and-sword.co.uk
Website: www.pen-and-sword.co.uk

Contents

Acknowledgements

I should like to express my sincerest thanks to all those people who knowingly or unknowingly inspired or helped me to write this book. To those closest to me: my children, Adam, Elizabeth and Daisy, my mother and Michael, my brother Martin and my sisters, Helen and Brenda, and my late father and grandparents. I should also like to offer my greatest thanks to all those who so painstakingly critiqued every word: Martha Bottrell, Mike Morgan, Mark Palethorpe, Brian Humphries, Andy Findlay, Eric Paterson, Eve Townsend and Jane Baker, and last but not least my publishers, Pen and Sword.

Finally, I wish to dedicate this book to the immortal memory of my old boss and dearest shipmate on HMS *Antrim*, 'Whisky' Dave Osborne. Cheers to you all.

Foreword

D avid Yates was born on the banks of the Thames at Taplow in September 1957 and was raised a son of Berkshire in the leafy village of Waltham St Lawrence, in the Thames Valley between Windsor, Ascot, Henley and Maidenhead.

Bored with country life and yearning for global travel, at eighteen, David joined the Royal Navy at HMS *Ganges* in March 1976. In a first stint of service, as 'Rowdy' Yates he served on HMS *Salisbury* and then HMS *Antrim*, where he saw active service during the Falklands War of 1982. He left the Navy in March 1985 to pursue a career as a Catering Manager, but when invited to return, rejoined in 1987.

He again visited the Falklands on HMS *Nottingham* in 1988, and saw further active service on HMS *Exeter* in the Gulf War of 1991. Suffering from ill-health resultant from this conflict, he eventually left the Royal Navy for a second and final time in 2000.

David's autobiographical account covers the period from his birth right up to his return from the Falklands War in 1982, where his earliest and last naval recollections were of fairground Laughing Sailors. The book draws heavily upon the diary he maintained before and at the time of the war, the letters he wrote home, and the three large scrapbooks he produced on his return.

Most of the characters described in this book have been granted anonymity through the use of the enormous range of traditional ancient and modern nicknames used in the Royal Navy, a loose index of which is included. However, not all names have been fictionalized. After all, who ever heard of a female British Prime Minister called 'Baggy Snatcher', or an American president named 'Ronnie Raygun'?

Apologies to anyone I offend in this book, but I had to record our actual feelings and sayings at the time.

The strong language used between the men on the lower deck on board was discouraged when ashore, and certainly never used in the presence of women – at least not in the Royal Navy in 1982. An extensive glossary is also included so that civvies can understand what we matelots were on about.

CHAPTER ONE

The Laughing Sailor

Three nightmares disturbed my sweeter childhood dreams. The first two were based on the unknown fears of falling from a high-sided ship into the sea, and being buried alive in a dark metal coffin. My third however, was based on a real experience as a curly-haired three year old, when I had a terrifying confrontation with a coin-operated 'laughing sailor' in an amusement arcade on the Isle of Wight. It did not make me laugh – no sooner had I dropped my old blackened copper penny into the slot than the hideous puppet burst into a barrage of hideous laughter. I screamed in terror, wet myself and ran towards my mother. I was not to know then that one day I would become a laughing sailor myself and that in the Falklands War, my first two nightmares would almost come true.

I first heard of the place they called the Falkland Islands on Friday, 2 April 1982. I had climbed into bed as normal at 0815 after finishing my night watch in HMS *Antrim*'s main galley. I was so tired that I skipped my usual shower, and just stripped off my boots and my flour-encrusted chef's whites, grabbed hold of the thick overhead bar, and slung my tired carcass up into my pit. Hopefully I would sleep away the remaining daytime hours until my next shift. I felt much better now than I had on 29 March when we had sailed from Gibraltar. Then, my body had been full of booze from the weekend runs ashore. A terrible hang-over racked my brain. In the choppy conditions that lay just outside the breakwater, my usual bout of first-day seasickness had soon followed.

Now I felt thankful the seasickness was behind me. After reading several pages of Sven Hassle's *March Battalion*, I flicked off the yellow-glazed bunk light and drew the cotton sleeping-bag liner over my head. Thoughts of Jackie, the naughty hairdresser I had seen on my last night ashore in Portsmouth ran through my mind. I would see her again when we were back in our base port in six days' time and I wondered if we would reach the same intimate climax together.

Suddenly my attempts to drift off were disturbed by the muffled sound of the commander making an announcement over the ship's radio broadcast. Half asleep, and with my head nestled deep in my sleeping bag, I could not make out the content of the 'pipe', so I just yawned and buried my head even further. Then the door started repeatedly opening and shutting – each time louder and noisier than before. Another 'pipe'. This time I could just about make out the captain's voice – but my left ear was still too tightly clamped below my armpit to make out what he was saying, so again I tried hard to switch off. Then the lights were turned on, and a voice yelled out, 'Keep the bloody noise down. Get that fuckin' light off.'

No one responded. There was more opening and closing of doors and more clumping feet, the sound of steamy boots being hurled into the pile by the door, and people noisily wrenching open metal locker doors. I was about to call out myself, when the voice I could now recognize as Paddy Flynn's, boomed out, 'KEEP THE BLOODY NOISE DOWN, AND GET THAT FUCKIN' LIGHT OFF.'

This time there *was* a response, and I was conscious of my curtains being swished open before someone shook my shoulder, and I recognized Barry Big Ball's voice mouthing something at me. I could not take in what he was saying, so I moved his hand from my shoulder and groaned, 'Barry – bugger off and leave me alone. Get that light off – I'm a nightworker and I'm trying to get some bloody sleep here.'

Barry ignored my protests. 'Come on Rowdy. Up you get, mate. You heard the skipper's pipe. You've got to get out of bed right now.'

'What are you on about? What skipper's pipe? What's happening?'

'Come on Rowdy. Out of bed. We're going down the Falklands, mate.'

'I'm not going anywhere. I'm a bloody nightworker and I'm staying right here.'

'No Rowdy, you don't understand mate. We're going down the Falkland Islands to fight a war and you've got to get up and write home and make your will out.'

The mention of making my will out was chilling enough, but the thought of writing home made me think of my family in Waltham St Lawrence.

I arrived in the world on 29 September 1957 in the small Thames-side village of Taplow on the Berkshire-Buckinghamshire border. David William Yates shared the birthday of Lord Horatio Nelson, who had been safely delivered exactly 199 years before, without the aid of a whiff of gas and air for the mother or father – but no doubt aided by a tot of rum or two!

The eventual oldest of four children, I started life in a caravan and large wooden shed at the back of a great aunt's house in the sleepy village of Waltham St Lawrence, 6 miles from Taplow on the old back road between Maidenhead and Reading. Our 'outback' homestead had been acquired the year before for Mum and Dad's wedding and remained our cosy little home until we were allocated a local council house when I was two.

Other than my early encounter with the laughing sailor, I knew nothing of the navy, although as I grew older I learned that when I joined the armed forces I would be continuing a family tradition going back several decades.

We stayed in our first proper house until my father's mother died in 1962, when we moved across the village to stay next door to my grandfather, who shared the same name as myself. Grandad David Yates had not been well for some time, suffering from leukemia – the strain of which probably put paid to my poor grandmother. He was not expected to live much longer himself, so we moved in next door to care for him in his final days. But Grandad was a tough old Scottish boot, who defied all the odds to live a further eleven years.

My earliest recollections of him were of his strange-sounding tongue and the missing little finger on his right hand. He used to play games with us, pretending to lose the finger in his pocket or behind his back. In reality, as he told us from a very early age, he had lost it during the First World War when he had been shot by a sniper at the Battle of Loos in France on 25 September 1915. The German bullet hit him in the shoulder and knocked him clean out on the battlefield, and when he came to, he just managed to crawl back to his own lines. The wound somehow damaged the tendons in his hand and the removal of his right 'pinky' resulted in an honourable discharge from the Army in 1916. Thereafter, he received a weekly war pension for his injury, but often told us how he could have got an even bigger award had he also had the next finger removed. However, although it was almost entirely useless, he did not want the look of his hand to be spoilt too much – besides, he said, it would have looked a bit funny when waving to people with only two fingers!

Despite his injury, a lifetime of hardship and his later severe illness, Grandad always came across to me as a bit of a joker. I remember one of the earliest tales he told about his life in the trenches. A Scottish soldier had single-handedly attacked a trench full of Germans, shooting and stabbing all of them bar the last one, whom he wildly slashed at from a distance with his bayonet. 'Ha ha, Tommy, you mizzed,' said the German.

'Oh yeah?' said Jock 'Just wait until ye shake yer heed!' Playing war games at school, minus the bayonet, I always used that gag to win 'you're dead' arguments in the dry shallow ditches that we used at the bottom of the large, green, school playing-field.

Grandad also showed us his old army photographs and told us many other stories of his life before, during and after the war. He had left school at fourteen to follow in his father's and grandfather's footsteps in the Lanarkshire coal mines. At sixteen he joined the Territorials of the King's Own Scottish Borderers, so that he could get an annual holiday away with his pals – which he could not get from the pit.

After returning from the war with his 'Blighty wound' he was billeted and then discharged from the army at Brighton, where he obtained a rehabilitation job suitable for someone with his disability, as a diamond polisher at the local Oppenheimer diamond works. Romantically, he met my grandmother whilst sheltering from the rain in a shop doorway overlooking Brighton pier, and later they moved back to a small hamlet called Ash Gill near Larkhall in Lanarkshire, Scotland, where my father was born at the start of the great depression in September 1922.

From all his old army stories and pictures, I learned at a very early age that the Great War must have been terrible, but that there had also been some funny moments too. I never forgot the tales he told me, and the memories proved inspirational when I eventually came to fight my own battles. He and his brother survived the First World War and my father and his brother later survived the Second, so I always hoped that family luck would be on my side.

My father was seventeen on 6 September 1939, three days after war broke out. Whilst he did not actually see any hand-to-hand fighting, he did lose his formative years in the defence of his country, serving as an armourer in the Royal Air Force almost continuously throughout the long conflict.

His father-in-law, Bert Wilkinson, had also served in the Second War, in the Royal Navy. Grandad Wilkinson told me a few of his old navy stories – but they weren't half as gory as Grandad Yates's tales of the trenches! So all my immediate forefathers had served in the forces, and during the 'swinging sixties', corrective military advice was never too far away. 'They should get their bloody hair cut.' 'They should do a stint in the forces like we did.' 'Put the buggers up against a wall and shoot the bastards!'

Despite the family background, I never really hankered for a service life myself, although I knew I might have to join up, and I would want to do my bit if called upon. Instead, I fostered boyhood dreams of playing rugby for England and winning the heavyweight boxing championship like my hero Muhammad Ali – or even being an archeologist like Howard Carter. I was told I was pretty bright at school but that my education was hampered by my interest in sport. If there was a school team I was invariably in it, and the amount of time devoted to the various sporting activities inevitably affected my studying. Not that I worried about it then – or subsequently, as my sporting attributes often came in very handy later on, during my extended stay at the 'naval university of life'.

I left Cox Green Comprehensive School in the spring of 1974 aged sixteen and a half, and got a job as a trainee quantity surveyor with a local building company. The work was all right – everything in fact that one could expect as a new spotty-faced 'irk' – but, the money and resultant spending power was not very good at all. Whilst still at school I had been picking up £20–£30 a week doing a paper round, gardening, farming jobs on old Mr Pike's Beenham's Farm, plus the odd bit of babysitting. Now, dressed in my donkey jacket, shirt and tie, and wellies, I was earning £13.50 of which I now had to give my mother £5. So things were pretty tight financially – and socially, stuck in a small village miles from the beaten track I started dreaming of stretching my legs further afield.

I first thought of joining the Royal Navy after my best friend at school joined up and started coming home with over twice the wages that I was getting. Alf told me wild tales of the things he had been up to. He referred to his naval career as his 'life in a blue suit' – a term used to describe his matelot's life in naval uniform.

Whenever Alf came home on leave we popped out for a couple of beers. Although these outings did not lead to any real trouble, they always seemed to involve some scrape or other. 'Doing a runner' from Indian restaurants, relocating early-morning milk bottles and swapping front gates were all part of our drunken repertoire. It was all pretty harmless fun, which never got us into any trouble because we never got caught – well, only once or twice.

The first few months in my job ticked by and then Christmas passed, and in spring 1975 my feet were getting decidedly itchy. So, one day I popped into the Royal Navy Careers Office in Reading and sat down with a crusty old Second World War veteran to be told the options open to me. The navy was recruiting heavily at the time, and he said there were several trades I might be interested in. All I had to do was sit an aptitude test and pass a medical, and that would be it – or so I thought, as I left the office clutching a large wad of glossy naval brochures.

I returned the following week for the aptitude test – a lot of dumb maths and logic questions and a perforated board with corresponding wooden pegs, all of which I managed to squeeze through the right holes. A medical followed, the classical military examination, full of deep breaths, covered eyes, touching toes and large coughs. I passed that easily as well, and the following week I received a letter to say I had been accepted to join the Royal Navy, but that, as I was under eighteen, I would also have to get both my parents' consent before I could actually join up. Unfortunately, owing to his own war memories, my father was reluctant to sign the papers, so I had to wait until the end of the summer when I was eighteen, and then sign myself in.

Anxious to spread my wings before joining the navy, I gave up my job and left home in June, riding a yellow Suzuki 100cc motorbike, carrying a tent, with a little over £20 in my pocket. I wanted to hit the road like David Essex in the film *That'll Be the Day*, where he ended up bedding a stream of young girls by 'riding the whip' on a fairground waltzer with the ex-Beatle, Ringo Starr. Unfortunately, my attempts to gain red coat, bar and funfair work all ended up in under-age failure. Instead, I toured the sunny south coast from Bournemouth to Lyme Regis, camping out under the stars. It lasted a week, until my money ran out and I had to get a job washing dishes at a transport café near Yeovil in Somerset. It was not the best job, but it was a lot of fun, and it gave me the springboard to enlist at the Taunton careers office a few miles away, and I eventually joined the navy, at HMS *Ganges*, on 2 March 1976.

CHAPTER TWO

Where The Hell Are The Falklands?

B arry's words finally got through to me. With squinting eyes and a dry, sticky mouth I asked, slowly, 'What – are – you – on – about – Barry? What do I need to make a will out for? I've never heard of the bloody Falklands. Where the hell are the Falklands? They're up near Scapa Flow aren't they? What are we going up there for – the sea's as rough as ten and it's always freezin' and pissin' down with rain.'

With other men now cramming into the mess and the noise level rising further, Barry raised his voice slightly.

'It's not *up there* Rowdy,' he explained. 'It's down near the South Pole. They're British islands and the Argentinians have captured them!' Trying to sound as idiot-proof as he could, he said, 'So – we're – going – down – the – Falklands – to get them back. We're leaving today. You're coming with us, and we've all got to fill in one of these Will Forms before mail closes in an hour.' Thrusting the form into my hand, he shuffled away to join the mêlée in the mess square, our communal recreational area.

Realizing this might not be an elaborate wind-up after all, I started to read the form. Sure enough it seemed to be a pretty authentic MOD publication – not the sort of thing that a matelot could knock up on a photocopier. I swung out of my middle bunk, steadied myself to counter the ship's roll and my giddy head, grabbed my towel off my locker rail and tucked it tightly round my waist. Tripping over piles of 'steamies' and other deck-strewn clutter, I strode blinking into the glaring lights of the smoke-filled mess square – all 9 square yards of it.

The only drop-down bunk-seat and all of the four collapsible single chairs were occupied, so I stood for a while, scratching as I tried to take in what was going on. Paddy, the 'keep the bloody noise down' night-working killick (leading hand) steward joined me, then some of the lads started to tell us what they knew. Frank Carvelli, one of the other killick

7

stewards, told everyone what he had heard in the wardroom, the tall, skinny Cockney steward, Steve Davis, repeated what the skipper had said in his recent pipe, and Jimmy Riddle, the killick writer echoed the points he had heard through official channels in the ship's office.

So, I thought, there's definitely something going on. I'm not going to be able to stay in bed until 1800 as planned. I might as well get cleaned up and sort my life out. Grabbing a tin of 'goffa' (cold drink) from the fridge and recording its removal on the mess drinks chit, I sat down for a couple of minutes to relieve my parched mouth and try to make some sense of the madness that seemed to have evolved on board. An awful lot had happened since I had got my head down at 0815, for in less than two hours we had apparently gone to war – for a reason that was a complete mystery to me!

I eventually managed to get a place on one of the two softly furnished folding chairs, and took a long gulp of NAAFI fizzy orange. Thinking back, a few buzzes *had* been flying around during our stay in Gibraltar, but we often heard buzzes about all sorts of things, and when there was serious drinking to be done we did not pay much attention. But this buzz seemed to have a bit more credence to it than some. Apparently, five days before, a newspaper had reported that a rogue band of Argentine-sponsored Chilean scrap-metal workers had landed and staked a claim on the island of South Georgia in protest at the forth-coming 150th anniversary of British rule in January 1983. One of our warships in Gibraltar had already sailed to support our only other ship in the area, HMS *Endurance,* and the rest of the Royal Navy had now been put on alert and short notice for sea. This morning the situation had worsened considerably when the Falkland Islands had been invaded by swarms of Argentinian troops.

I sat there thinking what this all meant, trying to take in the news and where I would fit in with the Royal Navy's plans to wrest the islands back. I was twenty-four and a half years old and serving in the Royal Navy on Her Majesty's Ship *Antrim*, a twelve-year-old County Class guided-missile destroyer. Five hundred and twenty feet long, 54 feet wide and displacing 5,000 tons, the *Antrim* had recently sailed from Gibraltar under the command of Admiral Woodward. It was the flag-ship of a large fleet of vessels from a dozen or more different countries, conducting a major NATO maritime operation, Exercise Springtrain.

The 'Rock', fortress-sanctuary of Royal Navy Mediterranean ships since it was captured from the Spanish by Admiral Rooke and his forces in 1704, had played host to the volunteer and conscript crews of frigates, destroyers, supply vessels, tankers, minesweepers and other assorted ships from countries as far apart as Canada, the Netherlands, America, Germany, Italy, France, Greece and the United Kingdom. Like most of the crews from those ships, I was still recovering from the booze-ridden effects of the four-day pre-exercise blowout we had all had.

I had shared 1G1 mess with seventeen other junior rates since arriving on board just under a year before in Portsmouth – lugging a heavy suitcase and 'pusser's grip' up a high-tidal gangway, as millions of seafarers had done in the past. Weaving down a maze of corridors and ladders, I detected the familiar smells of engine oil, paint, grease, cleaning materials, cooked food, bathrooms, steam rising from the laundry, and magazine munitions. 1G1 mess was found tucked in on the starboard side between No. 5 petty officers' mess and the officer's galley, below the wardroom and above the workshops and machinery spaces on the lower decks. Wardroom chefs and stewards occupied the mess, together with a couple of writers and me, Rowdy Yates, one of the three killick caterers on board at that time.

The age and experience of the mess members ranged from the young steward, Steve Davis, seventeen and on his first ship, hoping for a bright naval career, to 39-year-old, Paddy Flynn, on his tenth ship – outwardly looking forward to, but inwardly dreading, the thought of leaving the navy at the end of his twenty-two years' 'man's time' in 1985. He came from a large and relatively poor Irish family, and the navy was the only real life he knew. His career had started without ambition and, after a thousand piss-ups in a hundred ports around the world, remained so. The average age of the men on board was twenty-five or twenty-six. In my mess, the average age was twenty. At twenty-four I was sixth oldest – already an old hand on my second ship.

We shared a total mess space not much bigger than the inside of a squash court, an intimately cramped space, which held not only our beds and lockers but also everything else we possessed on board. The bunks were arranged in six stacks of three, surrounded by kit lockers measuring about 3 feet by 2 feet. One of these, plus a very shallow boot locker and whatever we could squeeze in our zipped green bed-bag below the mattress, was all the personal stowage space we had.

There was no room for much clothing, ornaments, plants, records or any other personal effects. The absolute basics were carried on board: daily working rig or No. 8 working dress ('eights'), a couple of changes of civilian clothes, wash gear, the odd book and letter-writing stuff. Despite the limited personal facilities, we quickly learned to make do, adapting to the limited confines, sharing our space, money, beer, thoughts and dreams, and, with the odd exception, getting on fairly well and preserving our tight camaraderie, sanity and sense of humour in situations which would severely challenge most land-loving civvies. It was not my first ship and would not be my last, but with hindsight it was undoubtedly the best.

I had only joined *Antrim* for a year to complete some pre-qualifying sea training for advancement to petty officer, and the past eleven months and twenty-six days had been spent in European waters, with some barn-storming runs ashore in Oslo, Bremen, Lisbon and, of course, Gibraltar. Now, with only four days left on my 'days to go' chart I felt just a little annoyed that my cozy little routine was under threat from a bunch of Argentinian conscripts. Bastards, I thought, how dare they!

I drained the cool 'goffa' and flicked the empty can into the crumpled brown paper gash bag under the television, then gathered my wash gear from my boot locker. With images of a barren rock somewhere deep in the ice-cold South Atlantic in my mind, I flip-flopped my way out of the mess. Bastards. Pick a fight on us would they? Well we had bloody show them a thing or two. I turned right to go for'ard, heading up the main drag for a bath and clean-up, or, as it was more commonly known, 'a shit, shower and shave'. With any sort of privacy at a bare minimum, and with nobody really concerned about someone wandering around a warship in the middle of the day half-naked in a skimpy towel, I took my time towards the for'ard bathroom, chatting to men I met along the way, trying to play down the obvious excitement, and pretending that I didn't care about a possible war. 'Bastards,' I said. 'We'll soon show them bunch of bastards.'

Tall, dark, curly haired, fit, tattooed, street-wise, confident and full of mouth, I actually did not initially think much of going off to fight the 'Argies'. The prospect of war did not frighten me one bit. My father and both grandfathers had all done their bit, and now it was my turn. Bastards, I thought again. I was ready to take on the Argentinians right there and then. We had met some Argentinian sailors ashore in Portsmouth the previous summer at a dive called Beasties down at Southsea, and those greasy-haired characters presented no fears to my rugby-playing ego or, as I quickly found out, to many of my mates on board either. Our professional forces will soon get their own back on that miserable bunch of conscripts, we thought.

I reached the end of the main corridor, and with much-practised skill, slid swiftly down the aluminium handrails in one smooth movement, spanning the 10 foot ladder to 2 Deck without touching a rung. I landed with a heavy but perfectly co-ordinated double rubber slap, but nobody else happened to be around to witness the descent, so on this occasion my impressive ladder-sliding display was wasted. The art of ladder-sliding had occupied much of my impressionable character-building time as a new boy or 'sprog' on my first ship, HMS *Salisbury*, and later on the *Antrim* had resulted in a smashed elbow when the ship rolled unexpectedly; it still weeps occasional bone fragments. You learn by your mistakes, they say – which is probably why I am becoming increasingly brilliant with each error-strewn day!

Opening the bathroom door, I was engulfed by the great rolling cloud of steam and almost knocked over by other disturbed night workers, who rushed around between sloshing stainless steel sinks and spitting shower cubicles. The unwritten rule in these circumstances dictated that, as the newest arrival, I had to wait my turn for a sink. As one became available, I quickly washed my face and shaved, before filling the sink again with soapy water to soak my 'nicks and socks' whilst I took a shower, entering the uncurtained cubicle with a loud yell of, 'Switchin' on.'

Apart from the obvious health and safety risks associated with trying to stand upright or move around a for'ard compartment that is bobbing around like a cork, taking a shower is also fairly hazardous. After getting soaped-up, with eyes temporarily closed, your motion-affected balance goes completely haywire and a bar of soap becomes an object of comical desire. Besides which, when you're in the process of taking a shower, it's not unheard of for your towel to be stolen from the rail, leaving you to wander back to your mess stark naked.

No such occurrence took place that morning and I was able to complete my ablutions in the normal ten minutes, singing along to some of the 'ditties' being sung by the Rod Stewart or Tom Jones sound-a-likes rehearsing live in the for'ard bathroom for our private entertainment. Slicking back my dripping hair and draping the freshly rinsed and tightly wrung 'nicks and socks' to dry on a communal rail, I bid good-bye to the lads sharing the bathroom from other messdecks. Now, much more slowly because of my wet flip-flops, I gingerly climbed back up the steep ladder and walked back to the mess, proud to show off my colourfully tattooed arms on the way.

Most of the boys had by now gone back to their parts of ship so, still with just my towel on, I sat down at the small, square wooden mess table and started filling in the cream-coloured will form. I wondered if there was really any point in making out a last will and testament. After all, I was only in my early twenties, I had no wife or children, and my only major possession was a brand new white Ford Capri parked up in an aunt's garage. But feeling that my parents might appreciate the good intentions, I did fill in the form and then wrote brief letters to the family, Jackie the hairdresser, and a couple of other girlfriends and mates dotted around the country:

I'm afraid I won't be coming home as soon as planned. I can't say why, but common sense will tell you where we've gone! I don't know for how long we'll be away, all I know is it's a couple of weeks at least. Watch out for mention of us on the news, and please, please don't worry. I'll be OK.

Of course, what I did not include in my letters were the details of our runs ashore in Gibraltar the endless hours of drunken oblivion and being an hour adrift on the second morning and getting fined £30 by the commander. I just kept to the basics. After all, what people did not know about, they could not worry about!

I handed the will form in to writer 'Barny' Barnes in the ship's office and slid the letters into the red postbox at the NAAFI before nipping off for a quick bite to eat and climbing back into bed. This time, nobody, not even a bloody war, was going to shift me until my rightful hour of 1800. I read a bit more of *March Battalion*, then hit the sack again, but now my head was racing with all the talk of war and my mind started to drift further and further back in time as I tried to fathom out how I had ended up on *Antrim* in this situation. I also reached back for the moral strength and inspiration I might need for the battles that might lie ahead – 8,000 miles from home and dry land and fresh cow's milk, pints of Guinness and Kentucky Fried Chicken, decent haircuts, and female lips and breasts. And with these sweet images in my mind I finally reached the land of Nod.

CHAPTER THREE

HMS *Antrim*

My dreams took me back to the day I joined HMS *Antrim*. I ended the Easter leave of 1981 staying at an aunt's house near Portsmouth. My uncle, a commander in the navy, had offered to run me in to join my new ship on 28 April 1981. Very familiar with the intricate layout of Portsmouth Dockyard and its maze of dry and flooded docks, pontoons, caissons and jetties, my uncle quickly navigated us to the looming grey side of HMS *Antrim*. She looked enormous compared to *Salisbury*, as she towered above Fountain Lake Jetty on a high spring tide. My pusser's grip and suitcase were lifted from the boot, handshakes and best wishes exchanged and off I trotted up the steep for'ard gangway, case gripped in my left hand, grip slung over the other shoulder. Much to my surprise, a wooden upper deck greeted my feet as I stepped off the gangway and introduced myself to the quartermaster and his bosun's mate. ID card shown and introductions made, the duty steward was then piped to show me to 1G1 mess. Simon Hodges, short, bespectacled, slightly cross-eyed, with short-sided, blond, curly hair, shook hands, then grabbed the case as I cuddled the grip in front of me. We wound our way aft down the port side, through a door, through another door, down a flight of stairs, along a passageway, down more stairs and along a large wide passageway to a wooden stable door with the words '1G1 mess' splashed on the front in large gold Germanic letters.

As for my job on board, because I had changed branches, from a stores accountant or 'Jack Dusty' to a leading catering accountant, I was required by naval convention to complete a one-year period of continuation sea training – six months stewarding and six months cooking. On day one I was told I would start off with the stewards, hence my allocation to 1G1 mess, which was half full of 'platelayers' in a compartment next to the wardroom galley and immediately below the wardroom itself. The chief steward explained that I would be working for Taff Hyde, one of his petty officer stewards up in the cabin flat, and as part of one of the watches responsible for day-to-day wardroom service. Although I had expected this, I still was not too happy about the news. I had joined *Antrim* without making good things to say about stewards in the navy, and the thought that I would soon be temporarily joining their miserable ranks did not exactly fill me with joy.

Just as on *Salisbury*, the first evening and following day were a complete whirl of passageways and ladders and compartments, and names and titles and handshakes and polite greetings, as I met my new shipmates and completed my multi-sectioned joining routine. Armed with masses of forms to fill in and literature to read, I retired to the mess at the end of the day with my head spinning like a top as I tried to take in everything I had seen and heard over the past twenty-four hours. I could just about tell which way was aft and for'ard, and how to get back to the mess, but the rest of the directions, names and everything else were just a tumbling blur in my head. Boy, did I ever need a beer. 1G1 mess filled with men at secure as everyone, apart from the duty watch, finished for the day and either headed off home if they were RA (rationed ashore), or lounged around if they were living on board. A big young fresh-faced steward by the name of Barry Big Ball introduced himself and pulled enough tins out of the fridge for those of us who were left, which included Jimmy Riddle, a killick writer I had previously shared a house with whilst based at the Royal Naval Air Station at Yeovilton. Mac McClaren, another writer, joined us, as did Paddy Flynn, a killick steward, and the oldest member of the mess, Frank Carvelli, another killick steward, and Sharkey Ward, a killick chef, as black as the ace of spades, from somewhere up near Oxford. One messmate, Simon, declined a tin, on account, so the lads said in whispered tones of, 'being a right boring bible-bashing Mormon twat, who's always going ashore in 'Jesus boots' (sandals)'. They added, 'He's leaving the mob soon to go and live in Salt Lake City.'

The atmosphere in the mess was much the same as in HMS *Salisbury*'s 3H mess, but with one big difference – there was no dining table, as *Antrim* was one of the newer ships that had actual dining halls on board. The mess still had a small card table though, onto which was vividly painted an 'uckers' board (a game similar to Ludo) in red, blue, green and yellow paint. It was now covered in a second wave of tins as Paddy marked off another five tally-marks on the mess beer chit, which already resembled a child's drawing of a busy railway junction. 1G1 also had a 'gronk board' like some of the others I had seen in the past, but unlike 3H's, this one did not have any used girls' knickers stuck on it. We discussed the ship's programme and where I had joined up, where I had been, the foreign runs I had had, the guys I had known that they knew, the ship's routine, the good guys. And then we wrapped in to get showered and changed for what was quickly agreed would be 'Rowdy's joining run'. I had never had a run ashore in Portsmouth before. *Salisbury* had called in for a weekend visit once, but I was on duty on three days and visiting an aunt on the fourth, so this was my first run in Pompey.

In 1981, the days of brown suede desert boots and wide flares were trickling to an end. We still wore jeans, but they were now much narrower (and cleaner), and our long side burns had also been replaced. Our heads were now topped off with floppier, less military, 'new-romantic-style' salon cuts. We still were not allowed to wear trainers ashore, so shoes still tended to be more formal, but the platform soles had vanished. All in all, I would say we looked and felt much better now. At sea, as a Scale A killick, money was also no problem. Recent years had seen our naval pay increase fairly dramatically, and with the advent of the 1980s 'loads-a-money' culture, we were hell bent on spending it.

Leaving Unicorn Gate at 1900, we crossed the road to a dilapidated 'dockies' type of haunt, which lacked any visual, or female, attraction, but did sell cheap, but flat beer. Then it was down the road to an old naval gin palace, the Royal Standard, whose interior reflected her long association with drunken sailors. It was covered from head to foot in ships' plaques, pictures, posters and other nautical mementoes. This was much more up our street and the atmosphere was brighter too. A loud jukebox bashed out 'Grey Day' by Madness and 'Muscle Bound' by Spandau Ballet as we shouted to make ourselves heard, surveying the filling bar for women, and telling more and more old stories. After the Royal Standard, we stopped at the Park Tavern, the Shipwrights' Arms, the Mighty Fine and nearly every other pub we 'nearly passed' as we made our way to where the action was likely to be – off Guildhall square in the Yorkshire Grey and then the White Swan, or as it was more popularly known, the Mucky Duck. The run ran its course, we all got drunk, nobody 'trapped', and we all got something to eat from the Kentucky Fried Chicken, back where we started opposite the Royal Standard, before meandering through Unicorn Gate and along the myriad of narrow dockyard roads to *Antrim*, tied securely by massive ropes to the end of the jetty, my new floating home.

Even though I had had a skinful, with so much to take in on my new ship and new base port, I lay wide awake with the dim yellow-tinted bunklight on, reading with spinning eyes the glossy *Antrim* brochure which had been handed to me with my joining routine by the skinny, weasely-looking killick Reg.

HMS *Antrim*'s keel was laid down in January 1966 at the Fairfield Yard in Govan, Glasgow, Scotland, and she was launched in October

1967. Sister ship to HMS *London*, HMS *Fife*, HMS *Glamorgan* and HMS *Norfolk*, *Antrim* was the last to be commissioned in November 1970. In terms of firepower, she had first been equipped with a MkII Sea Slug surface-to-air guided missile system, hence the description 'guided missile destroyer or GMD. Sea Cat surface-to-air guided missile systems had also been installed on the port and starboard waists, and A and B radars controlled semi-automatic dual 4.5 inch gun turrets on the fo'c'sle, although B was later replaced by an Exocet Flying Fish ship-to-ship missile system. *Antrim* was also equipped with an anti-submarine sonar detection system, Wessex Helicopter (nicknamed 'Humphrey') with 'dipping sonar' hunter-killer torpedoes, plus long-range air and surface warning radars. All of which sounded pretty impressive, but as I had gathered from my time on *Salisbury* and my first night in Portsmouth, the Royal Navy had not fought a real war for a long time, and *Antrim*'s guns had never been used in anger – yet.

The brochure went on to explain how *Antrim* was powered by 60,000 shaft horsepower from two steam turbines and four gas turbines, and had stabilizers fitted (which *Salisbury* did not) which provided a stable firing platform. Fifty thousand kilowatts of electric power was produced by steam, gas and diesel generators. She was manned by thirty-six officers and 450 men, plus four NAAFI staff and five Chinese laundrymen.

That was nearly 500 men. Apart from the small handful I had served with before, there were a lot of new faces to take in and compartments to identify around the ship, where they all worked. All of this however, allowing for drafters and joiners, I just about accomplished over the next four or five months. During any trip around the ship, I passed dozens of men and exchanged some form of greeting with them all. To those of the gold-ringed epaulette variety it was, 'Good morning, Sir,' but no saluting – you do not salute on board a ship. To Chiefs it was 'Afternoon, Chief, how's it going?' And to anyone of lower rank it was, 'Evenin' Rab, Florrie, Digger or Ozzy,' or, 'How's it goin' matey?'

Much bigger than *Salisbury* she might have been, but *Antrim*'s daily routine was virtually the same, following timeless rules laid down in the Queen's Regulations for the Royal Navy (QRRNs). The main differ-ence that I noticed was, being a larger ship, she did not bounce around as much, which helped to keep the contents of last night's supper or run ashore in, and made the task of working on board a darned sight easier too.

Within a week of joining, *Antrim* stored ship and went to sea, and over the next year we followed almost exactly the same pattern of visits that I had encountered on *Salisbury*. There was no much-sought-after States trip, and as she'd only been out to the Far East in 1980, there was little chance of any straying out to those mystical waters so soon. Instead, our visits were confined to European ports on the eastern Atlantic seaboard and, of course, my old stamping ground of Gibraltar. The runs ashore, more of which later, went very well, and the vast majority of the men were brilliant, right from the skipper and the wardroom down.

But, I was totally disillusioned with my new job of steward. Not that I got off to a good start. On my first morning as a cabin steward I exploded when Arnie, one of the regular stewards, tried to explain the routines for making beds, handling dirty and returned laundry, rinsing and polishing wash-hand basins, scrubbing heads, vacuuming carpets, and stripping and polishing the wardroom cabin flat. 'You can get stuffed,' I yelled. 'Doing a bit of cleaning I don't mind, but what my long and expensive catering training has got to do with making beds and scrubbing skid marks off officers' bogs I'll never know. No way mate! I'm a leading catering *accountant*, and it's continuation *accounting* training I'm on here for, not, repeat not, playing housemaid to a bunch of lazy grunters (officers) who should be makin' their own beds like I do.' It was not Arnie's fault, but he took the torrent of abuse pretty badly and huffily suggested, that if I wasn't happy with it, I should go and see the chief steward. So I slammed the door and went to find him.

'Look Chief,' I moaned, as I explained my predicament, 'I've been doing a PO caterer's job up in Yeovil for the past six months, I'm passed for my PO's too and Scale A, and there's just no way I think I should be working as a cabin steward.' Although he was a chief steward, he was only small and weedy, looked about twenty and gave the first impression he was purely an officers' 'yes man'. That, by the necessity of his profession, he may have been, but fortunately, he was also a more modern type of leader, and had a simple man-management solution to my complaint. His killick steward in charge of the bar was going on draft in three days' time and he needed someone to fill his shoes. I would still have to work other duties in the pantry and wardroom itself, and do cabin service when on duty, but I would not have to do the cabins every day.

'How would that suit you Rowdy?'

'Suits me fine Chief. You're a miracle worker. I promise I'll give it my best shot.'

Pansy Potter had three days to show me the ropes of running the bar, to teach me all the intricacies of 'massaging' the books to meet the careful scrutiny of the mess auditor's eyes, and fend off any flak from the grunters, who were always suspicious that the bar steward was ripping them off and lining the pockets (or fridge) of the wardroom staff – particularly down below in 1G1 mess. I remembered some of the forms and books from the joke of a killick steward's course, and with a couple of self-made idiot's guides, was happy to take over Pansy's reigns on Friday morning.

At sea, alongside, in the UK or abroad, for the next five months and three weeks (not that I was counting very much) it was my sole responsibility to ensure that enough stocks of wines, beers and spirits were held on board to satisfy the officers' daily needs, and to plan the requirements of any future wardroom dinners, receptions, christenings and cocktail parties. I had been on the other side of a bar quite a few times but being behind it in such a high profile capacity would be a real novelty. And what a person to give the job to – a bit like putting mice in charge of a cheese factory, or Billy Bunter in charge of a tuck shop! With my increasingly renowned taste for booze, and the book-working wangles I had learned so far as a caterer, I had a feeling this job could be right up my street.

The tiny wardroom bar had just enough room for one steward to stand behind, boxed into a tiny square containing two small barrels of beer and lager, and a range of optic-hung and free-pouring spirits, wines, liqueurs, and even champagne. You name it, we had it. If it was not readily available behind the bar, it was almost certainly held below in the tightly secured wardroom wine cellar. The cellar was now my very own part of ship, and a great place of sanctuary when other hideaways were too visible, on days when one needed an extra bit of shut-eye – or the odd illicit tipple of something before going ashore. The cellar was a right mess when I first took it over, with cases and cases of bottles overflowing from every locker, rack, cage or open bay, sprawling over the deck in a giant cardboard and broken-glass pyramid that squeaked and crunched every time I ventured inside. I hated working in such filthy and shambolic conditions, and remembering an old farmer's words from Waltham St Lawrence, 'Where there's order there's success', I set about sorting it out.

Fourteen solid man-hours later the store was completely gutted, all the horrible little soggy corners cleaned out and all the smashed glass shovelled and vacuumed out of the way. Then every case, bottle, tin or other package was replaced, first in a far more orderly fashion, and secondly in a manner that would prevent further damage any time the ship rolled. The following day I buried myself down in the store again, mustering all the stock, then made comparisons with the bar books and expenditure records, and knocked up a list of findings for the chief steward's perusal.

'You're bloody joking, Rowdy! We *can't* be all that much down. Are you sure you've counted everything?'

'Yes, Chief. Come and take a look. I've straightened things out down there a bit. All the stock can now be counted, and this is how much you're missing.' I followed the chief steward at pace out of his office, sliding and zigzagging down the ladders until I unlocked the door and he stood there in wonderment.

'Bloody hell, Rowdy. Where's everything gone? Last week you could not even step inside! Shit, are we really that much down?'

'Yes, Chief, trust me. I'm certain the figures are accurate.'

The figures *were* accurate too, and there was much ranting and raging by the chief steward as he chastised the two PO stewards, and even tried to ring up Pansy on his leave. Luckily for Pansy he was sunning himself abroad. There was nothing else for it, the chief steward had to present my figures, now typed in red, cap in hand, to the supply officer and then the mess president. Again, much ranting and raving, but this time aimed at the chief steward. Several heads could have rolled because of these large discrepancies. However, ultimately a nominated checking officer would also have been dragged into the net, so eventually the matter was dealt with purely in-house.

Despite some pretty miserable, and what I considered to be very demeaning, times, stewarding also had its attractions, not least of all its off-watches. Initially I found the duty-watch system quite confusing, as we were all split into four different watches. The watches rotated using one system alongside, another at sea, and yet another in non-base ports. The best part of this routine was the off-watches. Off-watches followed the day when you were part of the duty watch and could not go ashore. Off-watches for stewards entailed getting up about an hour before the rest of the ship's company, preparing the wardroom and pantry for breakfast, then taking cups of tea around for officers' early-morning shakes. A handover then took place by 0800 and normally by 0900 at the very latest, the off-watch were all off ashore.

Off-watches in Pompey came round roughly every four days, and for victuallies (those living aboard) and RAs, normally involved heading straight for the nearest boozer and spending the rest of the day getting drunk. Some may have started with honourable, decent intentions like going shopping or going to visit a museum, but most off-watches ended the same way – everyone getting drunk. There was one particular off-watch on *Antrim* in the autumn of 1981. We drank from 0900 through to 0200 the following morning.

There were six of us altogether, myself and Jimmy 'Two Dogs' Stewart from the wardroom staff, Chopper Cox, Taff Bevan and Bungy Edwards from the galley, and Jack Frost, an off-watch seaman. We were all across the gangway with signed and stamped watchkeeper's chits at 0840, straight round to Jack's house for slices of toast and tins of beer for breakfast, while his girlfriend was out office cleaning. We left there just after 1000 and walked into the Mighty Fine at 1030, just as the shutter was being raised. From there we took in as many pubs as we could squeeze in before they all shut for afternoon closing at 1430. Then Jimmy left to meet his 'missus' from her work and the rest of us, with an hour and a half to kill before the Home Club opened at four, decided to mark the occasion by getting a tattoo in Taff's place along Queen Street.

We talked about various designs on the way, then spent a few minutes gazing through Taff's brightly coloured catalogues, before making our selections at anything from £5 to £10 a time. Taff made himself comfortable in his little black plastic topped swivel chair, shaved the first limb, applied the required transfer, extracted the drill from the sterilizing unit, dipped the point in indigo ink and set to work tattooing the first black outline. We all yelped a bit at first, the severity varying according to where the drill was initially applied. There are some pretty comfortable places to decorate a human body and some-where the level of pain tolerance is not so high! The tattoos that afternoon varied from the traditional 'The sweetest girl I ever kissed – another man's wife – my mother', to funny little cartoon characters of Road Runner putting his cock away at the entrance to an anal orifice, with a sound bubble saying, 'Now beep-beep you little bastard.' I had a uniquely individual and stupid design etched on my upper right arm which encompassed my favourite saying from Yeovilton, 'Women are OK, but you can't beat the real thing (picture of cider pot). Cheers!'

All five of us were finished by 1550 and stumbled outside Taff's to walk the short distance to the Four O'clock Club. There, standing at the bar was, 'Two Dogs' Jimmy. He had just popped in for a quick one before nipping back on board to cover wardroom dinner. We included him in our round of drinks, showed off the new Vaseline-and-tissue-covered tattoos, and discussed our plans for the second half of the day. We still felt like celebrating, despite the fact there was nothing what-ever *to* celebrate. Eventually, we decided we should stay where we were until 1800, hit the pubs until 2300, and then go clubbing at Ritz's. The only problem with this plan was that they would not let us into Ritz's with jeans and T shirts, so we took the unanimous decision to nip back along Queen Street to Jack Blair's Naval Tailors and buy new casual trousers and crisp cotton shirts.' Two Dogs' even offered to take our old gear back on board. 'Bloody great plan this is,' we thought.

The limp-wristed assistant in Jack Blair's quickly sorted us out with a range of his latest high-fashion clothing. We each topped off our new cotton shirts with a differently coloured silk flower – for the ladies, later.

'Best of luck then lads,' shouted 'Two Dogs', as he carried the bags of old clothes back towards Victory Gate. 'Hope you all get rid of your flowers all right you jammy bastards. Wish I was coming with you.'

The run then followed our plan almost to the exact detail. We drank pints until eleven all over Pompey, then breezed into Ritz's, where we moved on to shorts and set about finding potential targets for our beautiful silk flowers – which we said had been given to us by the owner of the yacht we were crewing down in Old Portsmouth harbour. Most of us trapped by one o'clock, and three of us were lucky enough to get invites to share taxis, cups of coffee, and whatever else was on the menu. I ended up in a dingy ground-floor council flat only 200 yards from Ritz's with a girl called Janet – who only 'after the deed was done' admitted that she was actually living with a man from the *Antrim* – after also going out with three of his mates! When I told her I was in 1G1 mess, she went a bit quiet, not revealing the name of her boyfriend. I felt from her reaction that he might also be in the same mess. I did not want to know his name either, and also did not tell her about the 'flower challenge'. But when I made my early-morning departure, while she was still asleep, I gently tucked my red silk bloom into a bamboo pot of makeup brushes and styling combs on her dressing table.

Back on board, we went round telling everyone of the great run ashore we had had, where we had all got new tattoos and clothes, and three of us had got girls and left our flowers behind. But that was not quite the end of the story, for at lunchtime 'Two Dogs' came back on board with all his gear from his flat, screaming, 'Which of you dirty buggers shagged my Janet? Who had the red flower you bastards?'

Apart from the blissfully drunken and amorous joys of off-watches, stewarding also had the attraction of providing some free drinks, and occasional female introductions on all first nights in foreign ports, where we had the traditional wardroom cocktail party. Although we could swig a few cans down in the mess in the afternoon, any real drinking was supposed to wait until we were ashore. Before my first cocktail party in the German port of Bremerhaven, I was repeatedly told by the PO and chief steward, that, under no circumstances were any of the staff allowed any of the wardroom drink, and all drinks and bottles must be fully accounted for at the end of the evening.

'Right ho, Chief. No problem, I'll make sure nobody touches a drop and everything's locked away before I go ashore.'

With a brightly striped awning spread over the fo'c'sle, any number of tables covered with rows of sparkling, polished bottles and glasses, and all the stewards neatly turned out in full No. 1s, at 1830, the party was ready to begin. Guests started arriving before seven, and all were ceremonially piped on board and greeted by the saluting officer of the day, who in turn graciously passed them over to other senior officers, according to their social status. From that graciously receptive company, they were ushered to the cloakroom and fo'c'sle by a chain of eager young naval officers, all keen to impress their bosses with their Dartmouth-trained social skills, and to make the best of impressions on the more attractive females. These females were shy and demure on arrival, but could soon be livened up with a couple of drinks.

Our stewarding role was much the same as that of any other stewards, although with the occasional thumbs up, wink, nod or circling finger, a form of naval sign language was used to indicate which drinks officers wanted for what guests, and, more importantly, the strength and level in each glass. As this was my first cocktail party Frank Carvelli was assigned to work alongside me and teach me the ropes, which I picked up quickly.

To save time and keep spirit consumption levels reasonable, Frank explained that I should always knock up the bulk drinks in jugs just before the start, put ice in the glasses as the guests approached and pour in the drinks just before the silver trays were carried over to their positions.

'Don't make the first few jugs too strong or you'll put the guests off the bulk drinks and you'll end up mucking around making individual orders. After a couple of glasses each, though, make them stronger and try to get them all pissed. Watch for signs from officers who want more or less drinks for their guests, or want to strengthen or weaken them. If the officer's all right, do what he says, but if you don't like him, do the opposite and make sure his drink is always the strongest. As the evening progresses and empty bottles can be taken away, always slide in a couple of full ones for later on down the mess, but don't let the chief or PO catch you doing it. Oh, and towards the end always write off a couple of bottles of port. The chief and PO always like a bottle for themselves after the do is over.'

And so my first party all went according to plan and I mastered the art of serving, doctoring and pilfering wardroom drinks according to circumstances. We all took it in turns to nip down the mess for 'quick ones' that we had slipped away when refilling the trays of hors-d'oeuvres, making sure the cooks were well looked after too. There was no going over the top, for as long as we all kept a few drunken paces behind the officers, everyone was happy, including the chief and PO steward, with their own personal bottles of Cockburn's Port safely stashed away – and accounted for.

Some guests stayed on board for 'further entertainment', the remainder left around 2100, and half an hour later most of the heavy, valuable or drinks stuff had been securely cleared away, leaving only the bare minimum of cleaning for the duty watch. The chief steward formally thanked us all down in the mess, and let us tuck in to a couple of slabs of beer that the wardroom had kindly donated for our efforts. Most of the tins were drained in less than twenty minutes, and then there was a frantic rush to tear off our hot, stiff uniforms, shower again, throw on the first civvies that came out of our lockers and head off down the gangway. We were the last of *Antrim*'s men to go ashore in Bremerhaven.

CHAPTER FOUR

The Last Runs Ashore

O ur brief stay in Bremerhaven was followed by trips to Oslo, Gibraltar and Lisbon, interspersed with maintenance periods in Portsmouth and some sea training in Portland at the beginning of 1982. *Antrim* was then due to sail on the morning of 17 March 1982, for Exercise Springtrain, a major exercise in the Mediterranean and eastern Atlantic. Expecting busy times ahead, on the Tuesday night Jimmy Riddle and I made the most of my very last steward's off-watch in Pompey, by getting drunk in Beasties, near Southsea Pier. We hit all the usual haunts on the way and drank ourselves into the normal stupor associated with such leaving-base-port occasions – particularly when it came to knocking back a couple of pints of Guinness and Pernod in three seconds. But with early starts in the morning for one last store ship, we started making our way back about 2300.

As we ordered some greasy meals from the densely packed 'chippy' outside Victory Gate, we got chatting to a couple of girls, who revealed they were hairdressers. They were equally drunk and also making their way home, via Portsmouth Harbour railway station, where they said they were getting a train back to Havant and then a taxi to the large housing estate nearby, Lee Park. We chatted for half an hour gorging our soggy pie, chips and mushy peas, then walked them to the platform and stood in drunken 'lip-locks' for ten minutes until their train arrived. Just before I gently lifted mine up into the carriage, she handed me her salon business card and asked me to give her a ring the following day. However, I did not even catch her name, and it was only when the laundry man found the card in my dirty shirt pocket the following morning that I even remembered the encounter at all. 'What the hell,' I thought, 'I can't remember what her name is or what she looks like, but I'll give her a ring anyway.'

I made the call, found out my hairdresser's name was Jackie, and that the other girl's name was Yvonne. Then, after a quick chat with Jimmy, I made a second call to confirm that we would all meet again, this time outside Havant railway station at 1900. I promised that we would be a little bit more sober this time, but I could not guarantee anything, because it was our last night out before sailing. Later that day, just as planned, Jimmy and I had a couple of drinks outside Victory Gate in The Victory and The Ship Anson, then caught the train to Havant. Because neither of us could remember what they looked like, we classed it as a blind date. Outside Havant station, the two girls were waiting for us in all their finery and thankfully recognized us. We exchanged greetings and all went off for a couple of drinks. Drinking as a foursome for the next two hours, Jimmy and I established that these two were quintes-sential-type hairdressers of the day, with their long, fluffed-up hair in the style of Farah Fawcett-Majors, lots of make-up and beautifully trim bodies. However, they were not exactly over-endowed in the brains and flowing conversation department!

They drank Bacardi and Cokes, while Jimmy and I swallowed pints of Guinness, and at the end of the evening we all exchanged addresses and promised to write to each other. Then we bought Kentucky Fried Chickens, and walked them back across Havant Park to catch our train to Pompey. Up till then we had just been 'new friends' – making polite chit-chat. In the middle of the park, the tentative relationship suddenly changed. As if by prior arrangement, our two nice little innocent hair-dressers started tugging our hands in different directions.

Yvonne led Jimmy towards some large rhododendron bushes, and Jackie led me towards a bench by the public toilets.

'Wait here a mo will ya Rowdy,' she whispered in her finest Pompey accent, planting her first full kiss on my open mouth. 'I'm just nippin in to check me' anbag.'

I looked round to see where Yvonne and Jimmy were, but could not spot them anywhere. What I did see though, was an old man hovering around outside the ladies. When I walked towards him, he ran off in the opposite direction. Strolling around outside myself, I heard Jackie call out, 'Is that you Rowdy?'

'Yeah, it's me. What's up?'

'Come in and see me a second. I want a word with you in my office!'

I did not quite anticipate this approach in such surroundings, but imagined what the surprise might be. After I checked to see that nobody was looking, I tiptoed into the ladies to see what my naughty hairdresser had got in store for me by way of a leaving harbour present.

I didn't have to walk far. Jackie was leaning against the door frame of cubicle two, seductively twirling her recently removed red skimpy knickers around her right index finger, licking her lips and calling out,

'Come here you. I've got something for you to take away tomorrow!' We then kissed slowly and deeply, and remained locked tightly together as we shuffled past the door, closed and locked it behind us, and then lowered just enough of my clothing to deliver my own leaving-harbour present. There was not much room in the toilet. So, Jackie was only about 5 feet 2 inches tall and skinny as a rake, I lifted her bare legs up and around my waist. We cemented our brief relationship up against the heavy metal door, with my hands supporting her tiny frame under her slender bare bottom. Jackie wrapped her arms around my neck, using her long blue finger nails to tear nerve-tingling strips out of my shoulders and back, as she forced her wet, slender tongue deep down my throat, and our eager bodies rhythmically ground away against the door of cubicle two.

The ecstatic thrill of the moment seemed to last for ages that last night ashore in Havant Public Toilets, but the sweet memory of the Guinness and the Kentucky Fried Chicken, and the small hairdresser with the Farah Fawcett-Majors hairstyle, all had to last, much, much longer than that. The whole episode frequently occupied my dreams as *Antrim* sailed the following day for Gibraltar.

A little later on 26 March, 'Call the hands' was piped as *Antrim* entered the Straits of Gibraltar, her entire crew eager for their first foreign run ashore of the year – albeit only Gib. However, there were going to be about thirty NATO ships in, so there was a strong likelihood of seeing old mates and getting 'call-rounds', or bumping into the hundreds of foreign sailors off the German, American, Dutch, French and other nations' ships. The prospect of one hell of a weekend was very much to the forefront of everyone's minds. My own weekend had been partially arranged in advance, as I had already received a 'call-round' from Nobby Hall, my old drinking partner from Yeovilton catering office. Nobby was now based in Gibraltar with his wife, Donna, and he was working in the catering office of HMS *Rooke*, the small naval establishment on the Rock.

'Whenever you get into Gib,' he had said when I last saw him, 'give us a ring and pop round for a drink.' As soon as shore telephone lines had been connected, I phoned him to confirm arrangements. 'Just drop round the office,' he said in his familiar cheeky northern accent. 'Soon as I can get off we'll go for a couple of pints – or ten.'

With our own bit of work on board soon completed, it was not too long before leave was granted and I joined the first wave of sweet-smelling matelots heading ashore through the old dockyard, although at the main gate we then went our separate ways. They all stomped off past the old cemetery and governor's residence, and I continued along the dockside road, heading for the cluster of modern buildings that formed *Rooke*, between the inner harbour and all-weather sports field and the town centre itself. At the small catering office, Nobby looked totally different from when I had last seen him over eighteen months before. He was now much slimmer, very tanned and wearing short blue tropical working rig, that made him look like a big blushing schoolboy caught stealing a bag of sweets in the playground. At Yeovilton, he had always been keen on the local married quarters club, where the entertainment – and more importantly the beer – was plentiful and cheap, and the pennies shaved off the cost of each pint could accumulate to several pounds each week. So it came as no surprise when Nobby said, 'Right. Give us a couple of minutes to round up things here and get changed, and I'll meet you in the Families Club across the road.'

I went on alone to the club, and Nobby and Donna finally joined me about half an hour later. 'Sorry, Rowdy.' Nobby apologized, 'The missus insisted on coming along too.'

I didn't mind in the least, as I also knew Donna from Yeovilton, and it was good to meet her again. It was just a shame that she did not have any single or unattached friends of her own she could bring along to make up a foursome. All her friends were also married to men at *Rooke*. But, I was not too bothered by this bit of bad news. I just felt lucky to be away from the absolute mayhem that must now be taking place in the town, where nearly 7,000 matelots speaking different languages must now be ashore drinking as though NATO's very survival depended on it! No, a few quiet pints with a couple of old chums would make a refreshing and reasonably sober change from my normal 'first night' antics.

After a couple of hours of steady drinking and story-telling, Nobby asked if I had like to stay the night at their place. Accepting gladly, I thought this would make the first night even better – no getting completely trashed, and no need to try and stagger back to the ship and spend a night in a room full of drunken bastards who'd be banging drawers and doors all night long and raising their voices because they thought they were still in a club somewhere ashore.

The three of us sat in the club for about five or six hours in total, Nobby knocking back pint after pint of the local lager, Donna sipping long glasses of vodka and orange, and me, after a few pints, switching to my favourite Gibraltar tipple of JCs (a gin drink). We talked over old times in the catering office and up at the Heron married quarters club, about all the rough scrumpy we used to drink, the High Ham football match and the office christmas party. And we spun hundreds of yarns about people we knew, or just about anything we had ever seen or heard. About 1700, Nobby and I started hinting that we might like to join the rest of the 'first nighters' in town. But Donna would not hear of it, and insisted we both join her for a Chinese takeaway and a few tins round at their place. Again, my sensible head took charge and I accepted the second offer without any quibbling.

During the silver-tubbed Chinese meal and endless rounds of 'tinnies' that followed, I was given my third invitation of the weekend – to join the pair of them, with a load of my mates, in the *Rooke* club to watch Shep Woolley the following lunchtime. If it had been anyone else but Shep I would probably have turned them down, but I had had a great time watching him when I last saw him at HMS *Cambridge*. I thought, 'Why not? It'll keep me out of trouble, and Nobby and I can slash even more pounds off another good day's drinking bill.'

It was really nice to climb into Nobby and Donna's spare bed, and even though I was on my own, I slept like a baby, and woke nice and early on the Sunday morning, feeling none the worse the wear for the fairly considerable volume of booze I had tucked away during the first day ashore. Making as little noise as I could, I dressed quickly, used the downstairs toilet, patted my hair into place with a bit of cold tap water and let myself out to start the long walk back to the ship. I could have got a taxi, but it was a lovely blue Mediterranean morning, the air was still, the sun had already seen off the light silver dew and was now starting its daily ground-baking process. I checked my watch, 0705 – forty minutes before leave expired. No problem, plenty of time. A nice gentle pace should easily do it. There was no need for any frantic dash – or was there?

The night before arriving in Gib, as was fairly customary before entering any foreign port, the ship's clocks were put forward one hour to align them with the local time ashore. We did it so often, it was never a problem, as an hour either way did not really make that much differ-ence to our body clocks. So when the ship's Land Rover suddenly screeched to a halt behind me and the driver started tapping his watch, I wondered what on earth he could be on about. I had put my watch forward, I knew I had, and Nobby's kitchen clock had also read the same, so what was the problem?

Leaning out of the open window, Rab Butler, a killick seaman yelled at me, 'Oi Rowdy, you dirty stop-out. What's the matter mate? Didn't your bit of stuff get you up in time or what? Do you want a lift mate?'

'Not really,' I replied, 'but as you seem to think I might be close to being adrift, I suppose I had better hop in.' Sitting in the passenger seat on the short drive back to the ship, Rab then broke the news to me that there had not only been one clock-change that weekend, there had been two – a second, local one the previous night.

'Bugger off Rab,' I swore. 'You must be joking, I never saw a second clock-change on daily orders or heard any pipe made. I can't be adrift –

surely?' But unfortunately Rab was not joking, and his wristwatch and the clock on the dashboard regrettably backed up his story. 'Shit,' I thought. 'How's this happened? I turn down loads of offers to go on crazy first-day runs, I spend a really civilized evening with a couple of old chums and sleep on my own in a warm comfortable bed, and then I get up in what I think is plenty of time to return to the ship.' It just did not add up. Rab went on to explain that I was not the only 'daft bugger' who was adrift in this manner, but that the 'jossman' was having none of it, and we were all getting done! I was totally baffled, but realized there was no way the 'joss' was going to accept any feeble excuses. I did not even bother giving him the full story when I met him waiting for me with his grubby little clipboard at the top of the gangway.

'Another one who failed to read daily orders before going ashore eh, Leading Caterer? Another one who'll be joining the queue to see the commander at his next table eh?'

'Yes, Master,' I replied. 'I guess it'll teach me not to go ashore too early. Sorry about that, Master.'

'Don't worry, Rowdy,' he whispered in his less formal voice. 'The ship is not actually under sailing orders and you're clearly not pissed or anything, so you'll just get done for being a few minutes adrift. What shall we say – thirty-five minutes sound about right?'

Although technically a very serious offence in the navy, actually being adrift is often looked upon very lightly in the messdecks, because it is normally associated with some good dit (story) containing juicy sex, fighting, or getting drunk and ending up on the wrong train. Unlike boring civilians, matelots rarely just slept in, or had a cold, or missed the bus. They always had far more interesting reasons for being late for work!

'Stand by your beds lads. Criminal entering the mess,' Frank shouted as I walked through the door. I tried explaining what had actually happened, but alternative excuses had already been made up before I returned.

'Who was she, Rowdy? Where did you trap her you jammy bastard? Did you get yards? Did her old man come back and catch you at it this morning?'

I gave my side of the story again, but nobody would believe me. After all, what daft idiot would forget to change his watch and then sleep in when they weren't even drunk?

'Nobody's that bloody stupid, Rowdy. Come on mate! Tell us what she looked like. Did you bring her knickers back as a mess trophy?'

The news of my being adrift, and the various rumours associated with it, were soon round the ship like wildfire. The version involving the irate husband was even 'confirmed' in some quarters, as I had apparently been seen being chased down a street by someone brandishing a knife! I did not really care, though, because after a small meal of bread, milk, salad and fruit, I was back in civvies again and heading back to *Rooke* and to Nobby's place, to find out why he had not warned me about the clock-change. But Nobby and Donna had been fooled too – although he was not in any trouble because he had not had to turn-to. 'We only realized the clocks had changed when we turned on the radio at nine and found out it was really ten!'

I nipped into town to send a few postcards to the family, Jackie, a couple of other girlfriends and my aunt – to say I would pick my 'Capri' up from her garage next week. Then I met up with some of the lads off the ship and we made our way back to the *Rooke* club to meet up again with Nobby and Donna, and settle down to watch a bit of Shep Woolley. There were not many in the bar when our group arrived, and after only about fifteen minutes it was clear there were not going to be too many more either. So with an audience of only about forty, this was not going to be one of Shep's biggest concerts. But it did not matter – in fact it made it slightly better, because instead of standing on a stage and singing at us, Shep was now able to clear a small space and sing his popular repertoire of naval ditties virtually amongst us, making us all feel like exclusive members of his band – even though he did not actually have one. In terms of drinking arrangements, it had been decided that we would each put a fiver behind the bar for the bar staff to look after in a little kitty. With prices so cheap in the club, we reckoned that £50 should last a couple of hours, and to make life easier for ourselves and the bar staff, Jimmy wrote down the 'standing order' on the back of a little round cardboard beer mat.

In Gibraltar in 1982 the spirit-based drinks were very cheap and the measures very large, but in the *Rooke* club the prices appeared to be even cheaper and the measures even larger. One tall glass might contain the equivalent of four UK measures, and at only a fraction of the price. Hence the reason we felt pretty confident that £50 would go quite a long way. The only problem with drinking shorts, especially on a hot day when lots of singing is going on, is that they do not last very long. So we got into the routine of passing the beer mat on to the next person like a baton between runners. As one person delivered the drinks, the next grabbed the mat and went to the bar, and when he returned about ten minutes later the mat was passed on again – and again, and again, and again. Using this clockwork resupply method, drinks arrived at the table in an almost continuous stream, and when Nobby and Frank changed from pints to JCs, the pace became even quicker. On average (because we timed it) there were about nine minutes per round. Nine minutes may sound a long time to consume a drink, but when you consider the strength we were all knocking back, you will understand how quickly the machine-gun regularity took its effect.

Within an hour, we were all singing along to Shep's songs with great gusto, and a few faces amongst us were reddening and swaying – particularly Donna, who, although married to Nobby, was not quite used to this *Antrim* pace of drinking. Half an hour later she could hardly speak, let alone sing! Shep made constant reference to our group in his funny dits and silly songs, and we were quickly known as 'Nobby's Crazy Gang, who are drinking like there's no tomorrow – and it's only one o'clock'.

Shep took a half-time break, joining in with us and our round (and putting a fiver behind the bar), and then the second half kicked off. With the second assault on the bar stocks underway, Donna fell asleep on a bench, while the rest of us really went at it hammer and tongs – glass after glass. We lost all sense of time and surroundings, other than the fact that we were drinking together in some club where this guy called Shep was singing his 'Rammit Mate' and 'Oggy' songs, and we were the best backing band he had never had. Shep's last half-hour, however, was not as raucous as the first two sessions. It still ended with one final round of the 'Oggy' song and 'Rammit', but before that he sang a short collection of slow, emotional anti-war songs. There were Irish tales of woe in the potato famine, hard-luck tales of the Boer War, Great War and Second World War songs, and finally some hippy songs from the anti-Vietnam era.

Some of these less familiar songs we could sing along to, but most of the last session was sung by Shep on his own. He stilled the atmosphere and added a touch of real thought-provoking serenity to the previously wild drunken mayhem, and despite my state, I particularly remembered some of the words from one of the last of these sobering soul-searchers, something from the old Country Joe McDonald and Fish record, 'I Feel Like I'm Fixing to Die':

> And it's one, two, three, what're we fighting for?
> Don't ask me, I don't give a damn – next stop is Vietnam
> And it's five, six, seven, open up the pearly gates
> Well there ain't no time to wonder why. Whoopee! We're all
> gonna die.

As I have said, Shep finished on a high note, and there were several encores of 'Rammit' to finish off the session but as we left the bar I think I was not the only one who felt a slight feeling of premonition. This was strange, because other than the troubles in Northern Ireland, our country had not been in any serious conflict since Korea, some twenty-two years previously. Very strange, I thought, as we tumbled out of the *Rooke* club, bid good-bye to Nobby, who had the blind-drunk Donna under his arm, and set off for the town and some big eats. It had been a long time since the breakfast that hardly any of us had had that morning.

Three o'clock in the afternoon is still only the middle of the day, but we were truly drunk, so rather than head back on board and get into a lot of bother, we decided we would get something to eat and find a nice place to sunbathe for the rest of the day – one of the local beaches perhaps. But as we bounced out of *Rooke*, across the road and in between the sports fields, we all knew there was no way any of us were going to make it anywhere near the sand and sea today. Somehow we did make it in one piece to the central piazza, where we staggered into a 'chippy' and started trying to order some food. But when you've drunk well over a bottle and a half of spirits at lunchtime, a simple task like ordering some food can take on a whole new meaning. 'Shish' – hi – ships chiss matey.'

'Shicken for me mate chiss mate.'

'Shicken for me chiss mate, and don't – hic – bovver to wrap her up – hic – mate.'

The order that day included three whole chickens straight from the large rotisserie; Barry had one, Chuck had one, and I had one. Crashing into tables and chairs, walls and cars, we eventually made it back across the very narrow road into the piazza, where a man served us with a round of bottled beers. We ripped open the bundles of paper and started devouring our food with our fingers – which had not touched clean water for hours. We were so ravenous and drunk, the meals just seemed to disappear in front of our spinning eyes, and it was not long before we all staggered back across the road to place repeat orders.

Back in the piazza, the next chickens were eaten as part of a developing 'challenge' – to see who could eat the most in one afternoon. The second emaciated-looking birds quickly following the same quick path as their earlier cousins! With the others all declining further meals and starting to nod off in little crumpled heaps here and there, new faces took their place. The new arrivals formed a ring round the one remaining table left in the game.

Despite the previous lack of food, our stomachs had quickly swollen. How on earth the contents stayed down I'll never know, but stay down they did – even after the third bird and part of a fourth. The contest was finally declared a three-way draw and we all crashed onto the concrete benches to die.

After a matelot has been to a lunchtime Shep Wooly concert, drunk well over a bottle and a half of gin and half a dozen bottles of beer, and eaten three chickens; in the absence of any willing females the next thing he desperately needs is a good kip. And right there in the baking hot piazza, the seven of us spent the late afternoon and early evening, while a pack of mangy dogs chewed the chicken bones and licked the greasy papers dry – then licked our fingers and faces too. Not that we knew much about it. Even a steam train running through the middle of the piazza would not have disturbed us from the depths of our slumber that day.

We must have lain there like the victims of battle for well over five hours, as swarms of thin flies scoured our cheeks and paws dry. The sky was dark and full of distant stars by the time we were eventually shaken awake by the piazza's bar owner. He wanted to tidy up the place a bit so that the next band of drunk matelots could use the space and drink his beer. Slowly raising our bodies from their mortuary-slab positions, we looked and felt like what we were – absolute shipwrecks. We eventually managed to stand upright enough to regain the use of our legs, but we were in no fit state to continue the run ashore for much longer. So we battled our way back through the crowd of bodies pouring in the opposite direction, and called in for a few pints in the various mobbed bars on the way. Finally, we stopped for a traditional piss in the old graveyard and downed a couple of nightcaps in the Tabac Bar. We must have got back on board sometime after midnight, then slept like the tired old mangy dogs that had licked our faces eight hours before.

As I had experienced many times before, once started on a weekend binge of this nature, especially in Gib, we found it extremely difficult to stop. I had no duty or patrol commitments that weekend, so there really was nothing else to do but carry on getting drunk. The best way to avoid hangovers, as we used to say, was, 'just stay pissed!' So after somehow turning-to for just long enough to refresh ourselves and do whatever else it was we were meant to be doing, it was a case of having another quick shower, another change of clothes and going on yet another run ashore. With all the ships sailing the next day, we knew this really would be the final run ashore.

The last night in any port is almost as bad as the first. Everyone has completely acclimatized to the local drink and the frantic pace of consuming it. Now, with a head full of new dits to tell and a far greater alcoholic tolerance, the fun and consumption levels could reach truly incredible levels. Every conversation was a dirty or Irish joke, or a dit about some poor unfortunate event over the past three days. And every pint, JC, or whisky and Coke was drunk even faster than before, with almost no effect whatsoever, for we were all now riding the crest of an unreal dream-like wave of intoxicated adrenalin and euphoria, where we were the funniest clowns on earth and could easily drink the entire universe dry.

That day I went ashore with Rattler Morgan and Shady Lane, but in the rugby-scrum conditions in the first few bars we quickly got separated. It did not matter because there were just so many other people we recognized, and after three days even the Germans and Yanks had familiar faces and were as high on life as we were. There were, however, uglier moments and the occasional sounds of breaking chairs and tables and glasses and windows, and the screams of terrified barmaids yelling, 'Get the patrol quick.' The naval patrol vans were busy, and seemed to be parked on every narrow street and alley in town. With so many lads in town, the run ashore was just like one massive NATO naval reunion. I even met up with Bomber Mills from Yeovilton, a guy whose No. 8s I used to pass in his girlfriend's kitchen on my way to work when he was on duty on board. After shaking hands and buying him a beer, I asked him how Stella was.

'That bloody slapper,' he replied in disgust. 'I found out she was shagging other blokes when I was duty. Now she's married to some booty [marine], and bloody good luck to him as well.'

Bomber looked and sounded pretty drunk, so rather than keeping my little secret to myself anymore, I gripped him round the shoulders tightly and said, 'Sorry Bomber old mate, but one of those blokes was me!'

Bomber stopped drinking his pint and put the glass down on the bar, and I thought he was going to smash me in the mouth, but instead he shook my hand! 'You dirty bastard, Rowdy Yates! You mean to say you were shagging my bird when I was duty? I tell you what, son, anyone who accused you of ever possessing any morals whatsoever is a bloody liar. You dirty, cheating bastard you!' After the initial shock had subsided, we actually had a good laugh about it, and Bomber said he wondered why I had looked a bit sheepish one morning when we had met at work, and why there were two coffee cups in the bedroom and enormous aromatic oil stains on the sheets!

Next, we moved into a bar in Irish Town, adjacent to the police station, where we bumped into a gang of cooks off *Antrim*'s sister ship, *Glamorgan,* or 'the Glamorous Organ' as everyone called her. Bomber and I both knew a few of the men from Yeovilton, including a young cook called Jock Malcolm, whose place we had been to for a party once. So as we waited for our pints we started swapping old Yeovil dits. But just as I took my first sip, my attention was drawn to an argument that was breaking out behind me between two other *Glamorgan* men and a couple of lads from some other ship. Turning round, I could see that they were all pretty drunk and arguing over what looked like some spilt drinks.

The *Glamorgan* boys were sitting at a small, round table, whilst the other lads were standing over them, beckoning them to stand up and 'sort it out'. I could sense that with so many *Glamorgan* boys in the bar, this would probably not be a good move for the lads off the other ship, so without any further ado, and with the odds leaning heavily in my favour, I decided to sort the problem out myself. Putting my pint on the bar, I stepped just two paces forward to where the two *Glamorgan* boys were now starting to get pulled about a bit, then chipped in quietly with, 'You two boys all right – these two giving you any grief are they?'

One of the lads off the other ship asked, 'So what if we are?' They were the last words he managed to speak, because before he had a chance to put his pint down, I hit him with one of my 'Henry Cooper' left-hook specials to the chin. Then before his mate could do anything, I also hit him – with a cracking straight right to the nose. Two punches, two bullies lying on top of each other on the floor, covered in their own beer and blood.

'I know,' I said, to the rapidly approaching bouncers. 'It's all right. I'll just finish this pint and I'll be off!' The *Glamorgan* boys then formed a barrier between the bouncers and me, and after draining my full pint of beer in less than three seconds, I made a quick exit. When they had eventually recovered their senses, staunched their cuts and dried themselves off a bit, the two men in the bar had apparently tried looking for me around town, but by then so many people had heard how I was only defending the two smaller blokes, that I was not worried. Even if they had tried to jump me somewhere, I think I would have had enough support around me to sort them out again. No, I was not worried in the least – in fact I was quite proud of what I had done on the spur of the moment – just what Oliver Reed, Clint Eastwood or Lee Marvin would have done in the same situation. However, I hoped my battles were over for the day, and I was now determined to spend the rest of the run ashore more peacefully.

I never saw Bomber or Jock, or any of the other *Glamorgan* boys again that weekend, but moving from bar to bar to bar and yet more bars, I did see plenty of other old faces from different ships. First I bumped into Dodger Long, who had also with me once at Yeovil, and was now one of *Antrim*'s other killick caterers, in a bar off the piazza called the Captain's Cabin. After getting a few drinks, we were squeezed away from the bar by the surge of men waiting to be served, and we ended up perching on the ledge of an open window overlooking the piazza itself. The ledge was a bit uncomfortable and precarious, but it was also the ideal place to fling abuse at any passers-by we knew – or did not know.

Amongst those who passed by in the roadway below over the next three hours were a small group of lads off the *Sheffield* and *Coventry*, two of whom we both knew quite well.

'Oi, Slammer you lanky streak of piss, what are you doing here?'

'Hey, Ned, what are you doing in town you wimp – get in here and get the beers in, come on.' Dodger and I knew Slammer Dawson from Ganges and Pembroke; like us he was a killick caterer at the time. Ned Kelly was a chef we both knew from Yeovil. The Cabin was by now far too packed to even get in, let alone buy any drinks, so they just chatted for a while from the pavement. Ned told us the *Sheffield* had just completed a five and a half month trip out in the Persian Gulf, and like *Antrim*, was due to get back to the UK straight after Springtrain.

We saw loads of other men who passed the window. Most returned the abuse with interest and then walked on, but others stood trading insults for ages in mock aggression – particularly any Yanks. They were easy to spot, even in the densest crowds, with their square Germanic jaws, big, gum-chewing mouths and weird taste in clothing. They also never appeared to go ashore in mixed racial groups like us; they always seemed to keep in their little separate groups of blacks and whites. This made it easier for us, because we never abused blacks anyway, especially when we were drunk. So the first group of white Yanks we saw ambling along in their short-sleeved checked shirts, with the 'V' of their white crew-neck vests showing, got the typical introductory patter from British sailors to Americans.

'Oi, Yank, want to swap your Zippo with this?' I yelled out, offering a small box of matches in exchange.

'Aw gee, no way fella. Do ya think we're dumb or what?'

'OK then,' I replied, 'Here you are Yank. I'll make it two boxes of English matches for your American Zippo – now come on Yank, that's got to be a bargain, come on mate?' Of course, nobody, not even the dumb white Yanks would trade at those rates, but it did not matter because there were loads of other drunken Yanks in town today, and plenty of Zippos would eventually get traded or 'lifted', so we knew there'd be plenty to barter for on board in the morning.

Yanks, particularly younger, headstrong 'idealistic' ones were always easy to entice into stupid conversations and 'wind-ups'. They swallowed any bait – hook, line, sinker, rod, landing net, the whole fishing tackle. Dead easy they were, especially when we mocked their 'Dumb-d'dumb-dumb-dumb-dumb' national anthem, or mentioned Vietnam.

They took it reasonably lightly though, and dished back their own traditional stuff about the 1776 War of Independence, and fights only occurred when someone on one side had had too much to drink or, more seriously, knocked someone's beer over. There certainly were no women to fight over, for although there were thousands of men ashore that weekend, apart from the usually spoken-for barmaids, there was hardly a single native or any other girl out in the whole of Gibraltar.

The next morning, the ship looked and smelt like a temporary mortuary in a bombed-out brewery. It is truly incredible that *Antrim* was eventually able to sail later that morning in company with the rest of the Operation Springtrain ships. After three solid days' drinking it was a wonder we had enough sober men to untie one rope, let alone navigate and steer and do all the other things that are necessary to enable a British warship to leave harbour without hitting something on the way out.

Although most of us were just about able to turn-to and do a little bit of work, as always, it was not easy as we stumbled around on the moving ship, our heads still full of booze. Like me, even without any further alcohol, most of the lads stayed drunk all morning, just surviving until lunchtime. Then we all had a good sleep. And only then, with perhaps just one or two appropriately timed 'hair of the dog' drinks, did we start to come down out of the clouds and begin to realize fully that our massive run ashore was finally over.

As we started Operation Springtrain in earnest, no one on board could possibly have guessed that, for some of our mates on the other British ships, Gibraltar would not only be their last run ashore this trip, it would also be their last run ashore anywhere ever again. I remember just how strange it was that the words of one of the last songs I could remember being sung during that last run ashore were old Country Joe's.

Well there ain't no time to wonder why. Whoopee! We're all gonna die!

CHAPTER FIVE

Off To War

So, a few days later, I woke at 1800 to the first war development. Some men had been transferred to returning vessels that afternoon, because they were not British, under age or holding a pretty good physical or compassionate 'get me home card'. One such homeward-bound person was our killick steward Jock Haig, who claimed a terminally collapsing marriage so successfully that he was able to stake his place on Humphrey, our helicopter. He left within an hour – along with over £100 worth of 'beer-boat' profits, with which, as 'beer bosun', he had been entrusted. To say this upset all the mess members would be a slight understatement. Several of the lads were more excited by this flagrant breach of strictly illegal but commonly accepted mess practice than by the prospect of sailing off to war! However, nothing official could be done to retrieve the money, as maintaining a junior rate's 'beer-boat' was distinctly against QRRNs. But, other means of recovery were discussed and plans set in motion to extract the money physically should the proper amount not arrive in the post by the time we returned to Portsmouth. In the short term however, I profited by Jock's sly departure, as I was now summarily elected as the new 1G1 mess beer bosun – a position which carried a great deal of prestige and created endless opportunities for 'wheeling and dealing' and 'ducking and diving' over the coming weeks away.

Rubbing my hands with glee at the prospect, I trotted out of the mess for my second shower of the day in preparation for food and turning to. This time though, because of the hour of day, the bathroom was absolutely heaving with towel-clad tattooed bodies. Although I loathe queuing, on this occasion I did not mind too much, as waiting my turn for a sink also gave me an ideal opportunity to catch up on the news developments of the day.

The next port of call for news was the Supply and Secretariat (S & S) queue for food. We linked up with the main galley cooks and catering office staff in their evening half blues, and were able to exchange news and views.

Once the long aluminium roller-shutters were raised in one great echoing crash, Taff Hewitt behind the counter screamed, 'Come and get it then, you bunch of miserable bastards!' Grabbing their moulded steel platters from the spring-loaded heater, the queue surged forward like a giant caterpillar to scoop the delights from the counter. We filed further aft towards the junior rates dining hall, where we grabbed our utensils and dropped down in one of the sixty or so seats that were provided for the 380 junior rates on board.

First lieutenant's evening rounds took place at the same time as the S & S queued up for food. So being in the queue early was also a good excuse to get out of last-minute mess cleaning. This left the duty mess cooks to give the place a quick blitz. Sometimes, the officer caught up with us in the dining hall, where we sat briefly to attention and gulped our last mouthful.

'Thank you gentlemen. At ease chaps. What's supper like tonight?'

'Bloody rubbish, Sir – usual shit again, Sir – bloody cooks need shaggin', Sir.'

'But you lot are cooks aren't you?'

'Yes Sir, that's what we mean, it's been a long time since we had a decent shag, Sir!'

'Oh very witty, cook Blake. Good to see you haven't lost your sense of humour yet.'

'Take more than a few Argies to do that, Sir.'

'I hope so too Blake. Just watch your good sense of humour doesn't turn into senile dementia!'

'Yeah, okay, Sir.'

'Goodnight, chaps.'

'Goodnight, Sir.'

With the S & S and a handful of watchkeepers finished at the counter, it was the turn of the other 300 or so lads to start making their way past the troughs, always accusing the 'white collared S & S wankers' of taking all the best choices before them. With the meal out of the way, the whole ship's company settled down to watch the commander give his nightly broadcast on the ship's TV. On *Salisbury*, there had only been the occasional 'pipe' made to round off the day's affairs if there was something worth saying, but on *Antrim* the commander made good use of the small TV studio to speak to the ship's company in person every night.

With no daily newspapers, faxes, e-mails, mobile phones, satellite or terrestrial TV in those days at sea, this form of news communication was really all we had to look forward to, apart from the occasional mail drops – which only contained news that was often weeks old in any case. So, at 2000, at the end of our first day at war, the messes were full of craning necks, as anxious men all over the ship waited with bated breath to find out what buzzes (rumours) were true or false, and where we were going, and when we would next get mail, and whether the commander thought we would actually end up fighting.

The commander's first war broadcast was impressive, setting the tone for all those that followed in the long weeks ahead – briefing us, warning us, congratulating us, and above all else I think, inspiring us; sometimes giving us a tingle down our spines, sometimes dis-illusioning us completely; at other times driving us on to raise our dipping spirits. Maybe that was not everyone's view of his nightly speeches, but personally I developed increasing respect for the commander and his individual style of leadership. Whatever different people felt of that style, it certainly seemed to work in my book.

The TV screen flickered, the taped Spandau Ballet music stopped, and the commander's large, jovial Scottish figure was before us. I do not remember the exact words of his first war broadcast, but they went something like this:

> Well, good evening gentlemen. I think I can honestly say this has been a day we will all remember for the rest of our lives, and in view of the situation that I am now going to brief you about, there may well be many more such memorable days to come before we return home. As you will have no doubt realized by now, we will not be returning to Portsmouth as originally planned. I don't know when we'll be going back, and it may be quite some time.

He went on to explain as much as he knew or could tell us about the recent events that had led to today's dramatic change of ship's programme. He confirmed the stories of scrap metal workers on South Georgia, an invasion of the main Falkland Islands and the capture of its Royal Marine contingent. Exercise Springtrain was now cancelled, and all British ships would either be heading south or returning to the UK for urgent repairs. We were also informed that the planned £150 million sale of our newest aircraft carrier, HMS *Invincible* to Australia, had been cancelled. In only three days she, with another older carrier *Hermes*, and the largest task force possible, would set sail from UK ports to launch the main counter-attack. Like most people that evening some way off the north-west African coast, I remained motionless, my eyes fixed to the screen as I drew long deep breaths and the hairs on the back of my neck stood coldly to attention.

The commander went on to brief us as a sports coach would brief a ship's rugby team. He told us in plain English that our first destination was to be a rock in the middle of the Atlantic called Ascension Island,

and that we should start focusing on doing what we had been trained to do and the Royal Navy had always done so well – fighting wars, and winning.

> I want you all to get your eyes 'firmly in the boat' and keep them there. Start getting rid of any unnecessary rubbish and come-in-handy gear, and start getting the ship looking lean and mean. We'll be conducting several NBCDXs [nuclear, biological, chemical defence exercises] over the next few days to sharpen us up, but don't wait until then to think about it. Start thinking about it now. We all want to go home, I know I do too, but we can't until this mess is sorted out, so forget about home for a while and start switching on to the fact that we may now have to fight a war. I have the greatest confidence in all *Antrim*'s ship's company, and I know that none of you will let us down.

There was almost complete silence for some seconds, but it was spectacularly broken, in 1G1 mess at least, by LCK Basher Bates calling out in his best American drill sergeant's voice, in a scene conjured up from a film where a bunch of raw recruits were about to board their landing craft bound for Omaha Beach in Normandy, 'Listen in men. You gotta be brave out there today. It's gone be one hell of a mother-fuckin' son of a bitch on that beach. It's gonna be rough, and it's gonna be tough, and you can bet my arse, some ain't comin back!'

'Gee Sarge,' he replied to himself in a younger, high-pitched, terrified voice, 'Ain't ya afraid Sarge?'

'Nope, I ain't goin!'

The mess fell about laughing, throwing fag packets and empty tins at Basher as he dived into one of the gulches. But soon the tense atmosphere returned. 'Wow, this is real shit,' I thought, as the commander finally faded from view and some bright spark played 'Land of Hope and Glory' from Last Night of the Proms, as details of the evening's video entertainment scrolled up on the screen. But nobody was very interested in watching *Raging Bull* tonight, and despite the promise of being a decent movie, Robert De'Niro and his fist-flying antics would clearly have to wait for another evening, when our minds were not on other more important things.

Swigging back the remains of the tins of beer we liked to savour after supper, Taff Bevan and I grabbed our white cotton cooks' hats and aprons and set off to start our night work, leaving behind a hive of excitement in 1G1 mess. The men started repeating over and over again everything that the commander had just said, going over each point to express their views on why something had happened or might happen in the future. Taff and I encountered the same atmosphere down the main passageway outside the NAAFI, outside the galley, and then inside the chief cook's office, where the duty watch cooks were waiting to hand over to the night watch cooks – Taff and me.

I had been a night-working cook at sea almost from the start of my time in the galley. I had started off in one of the four duty watches working similar shifts to the steward's, but when the chief cook found out that I had been the 'Butcher of Yeovil' and liked baking, but could not cook much else without constantly referring to the Cesarani and Kinton (C & K) Cookbook, he decided I would be better off as a night-worker. This suited me fine at sea because it was easy but fairly interesting and rewarding work, and there were lots of quiet times to read books and sup the odd tin of beer or play a game of crib.

The routine for night-working in the main galley at that time was to turn up after supper when everywhere had been scrubbed out, read the chief cook's list of tasks in the galley night order book and set to work. Taff, being a proper cook, then started off by checking what was left over from supper and what could be used again for the following day's lunch. Meanwhile, I got on with my butchery tasks, which were much the same as at Yeovil, except that on *Antrim* all the chops came pre-cut and, as we did not have a bandsaw, all the steaks and diced meats had to be cleavered by hand with a beautiful, mean-looking weapon called the 'choggie's chopper.' This one-piece shiny metal implement looked as if it had probably been made from part of an oil drum left over from the war – a long rectangle, with a third folded back on itself to form a handle. It was much lighter than the traditional butcher's chopper, but boy could it chop meat.

With all the butchery out of the way in a couple of hours, Taff and I then normally sat down in the office for a cup of tea or a can of something, and a quick hand of cards. When the official time for closing all the junior rates beer fridges came around at 2230, we waited for the inevitable trickle of men coming up to the port and starboard galley doors, calling out in hopeful, almost begging tones, 'Any chance of a spot of grub, chef? Any chops left over from supper mate? Gizza loaf of bread and a hunk of mouse trap will ya Rowdy?' What we gave them depended on who they were, plus of course the gifts they bore in exchange, or invites for 'call-rounds'.

Only the odd straggler popped in after that, and then of course the other night watchkeepers, who called in for milk etc. for the bridge, operation room and wheelhouse. Apart from that, we had the galley, and indeed the whole ship, to ourselves, for everyone else was tucked up safely in bed.

The butchery and any other overnight cooking preparations out of the way, we would then get stuck into knocking up the bread and milk. Of course we had to make our own, with the aid of a few mechanical devices like eight large farmyard milk churns, an enormous Hobart food mixer with a great dough hook, a bread-roll making machine, dozens of baking tins and trays, a warm proving cabinet and some large, red hot ovens. I enjoyed the butchery, but baking at sea was even better. Old cassette tapes of the Stranglers or the Sex Pistols blared out, flour, water and yeast flew everywhere – and then there was the lovely smell of freshly baked bread in the air.

The milk was made first, by whisking powdered Millac into churns full of water, and lowering them down to the main fridges by box-lift to cool down overnight, ready for breakfast. Then Taff used his own secret recipe to knock up the series of massive bread doughs, while I set to work kneading great heaps of the stuff for the bread tins, or smaller balls, with both hands, for the bread-roll making machine. Our routine ran like clockwork, and we were rightly proud of a good batch of bread. We tried our best with the milk, but it was never very good in those days.

The only snags we ever had with our slick routine was when the ship hit a spot of rough sea. Then the 25 kg bags of flour and full churns of milk were much harder to move around, and I had to act like a slip fielder at the end of the bread-roll making machine. The idea of this wonder of bakery science was to feed a roughly kneaded lump of dough in one end and receive a nicely rolled ball out of the other. It worked a treat on a flat, calm sea, but fired misshapen lumps of dough everywhere when it was anything above a sea state 3. I eventually solved the problem. One particularly rough night, my arms were flying everywhere trying to catch the random missiles, when I spotted a small cardboard box. Tearing off bits and sticking them in other places, I reshaped it and taped it over the end of the discharge hole to form a makeshift direction shute – and it worked a treat. In fact it worked so well, I eventually got the carpenter to knock up a more permanent version out of thin sheet metal, which we duly christened the Rowdy Yates Flying Bun Deflector Plate.

With the bread and milk out the way, after yet more games of uckers, crib and other games, we started getting breakfast ready – the traditional 'pusser's breakfast'. This comprised charred grill trays full of fatty bacon, and deep-fried sausages (which should have been grilled in the oven, but rarely were), deep general mess dishes of baked beans and tinned tomatoes, piles of deep-fried bread and box after box of NAAFI medium eggs, fried, poached or boiled. There was also the daily 'special', plus cereals and sliced bread for making toast on a large rotary toaster, but most matelots preferred their pusser's breakfast's.

A nightworker's other main perk was that we were automatically excused daytime duties and exercises, because we were in bed. The only exception to that was when the ship was conducting an NBCDX, and talk of one of those was very much on the lips of the men who headed the queue for breakfast at 0700.

Some tired-looking faces shuffled past the bacon and sausages that morning, a lot of boys had clearly not slept well. But even at that early hour of the morning, fresh buzzes were everywhere.

'Maggie Thatcher's gonna resign.'

'She'll never leave; she'll kick others out, but she won't go.'

'Well, I've heard that the foreign secretary, Lord Carrington, and that "numpty" defence secretary, John Knott, will be the first to stick their heads on the old chopping block.'

'Yeah, I heard that too. How can a bunch of Argentinians invade one of our islands, and nobody know about it? They deserve the bloody sack if you ask me, 'cos now we've got to sort their shit out.'

Other talk concerned the prospect of meeting the Type 42 Argentinian destroyer *Santissima Trinidad*, which had been berthed close to us on Fountain Lake Jetty the year before.

'No wonder they buggered off in such a hurry. Do you remember, Jock?'

'Yeah, I bloody remember all right, tried to sell off a loads of cars and bikes before they went, left loads of them lying on the dockside. You'd have thought someone up top would have thought that was a bit strange wouldn't ya?'

'Hope we do meet the bastards again. Our 42s will bloody murder theirs. We sold 'em a couple of duff ones, did we not, with dodgy spare parts and all that?'

'Yeah, I heard that too, bloody serve 'em right. I've had my draft cancelled 'cos of them bastards.'

Saturday, 3 April should have been a fairly relaxed day at sea, and Taff and I got our heads down all right, but it was difficult to sleep with so many 'pipes' being made and so much foot-traffic passing in and out of the mess. There was not even much point in Taff shouting, 'Keep the bloody noise down.' We both understood the reason why.

Admiral Woodward was still on board, using *Antrim* as his flag ship. He and his team of staff officers had obviously been very busy up in the admiral's cabin since the war kicked off, because it soon became apparent that a vast amount of critical assessments had been made to determine which ships were capable of heading south and which would have to return to the UK. From that starting point, the planners then had to gather key logistic information to calculate what stores could be transferred in the limited time before we needed to be on our way. I only once saw the admiral on board. We got regular reports from his steward of what he had to eat and who he was meeting, but he did not seem to be one for taking the occasional wander round the ship to meet the lads. And we certainly never saw him on the commander's evening TV slot.

Giving up any attempts to get any more sleep as the hands on my fluorescent clock reached lunchtime, I got up and offered to give the chief cook a hand. 'There's not much needs doing here, thanks Rowdy, but you could give the caterers a hand. They've got a bit of a store ship taking place in half an hour or so.' The chief cook was not kidding. I nipped down below to the catering office, and discovered that tons of stuff was coming on board – food, naval stores, ammunition, sweets, beer and soft drinks.

Royal Fleet Auxiliaries (RFAs) were going to be transferring stuff across by heavy jackstay from either side at the same time, whilst choppers would be 'vertrepping' (vertical replenishing) us also at the same time on the flight deck and on the fo'c'sle.

'Cheers Rowdy! Yeah we could do with a hand all right. It's going to be bloody murder this afternoon,' bellowed 'Whisky Dave' Osborne, the barrel-chested chief caterer in his deep, earthy Midlands accent. 'You take charge of the for'ard stores party will you?'

Storing ship on *Antrim*, whether alongside or at sea, was a massive logistical undertaking, and with the lack of sufficient between-deck lifts, relied heavily upon manhandling. A clear lower deck was called for 1330 and the whole ship's company, with almost no exceptions, sectioned off to move the afternoon's stores by hand. I took charge of the for'ard stores party, from where the victualling stores came inboard from the starboard RAS (replenishing from another vessel) and for'ard vertrep – moving up and down the chain of seventy or so men that ran from the points of entry from the upper deck crews, along flats and passageways, through doors and down hatches and steep ladders, and along more corridors to where my chain met up with the main body of men hurling gear down to the catering dry provision stores and fridges. NAAFI, and naval stores and munitions were moved by other routes, as the ship took on more stores in one afternoon than it had ever done in its life before.

All that day, there were some thirty ships in the area, transferring stores back and forth by sea and air. Ships bound for the UK drained themselves of absolutely everything they could spare and rose higher and higher in the water, while the vessels bound for the South Atlantic took on board everything they could possibly lay their hands on, and settled lower and lower in the water as the day wore on. And it was not only the ships at sea that were sending us on our way with full holds.

The sky was full of helicopters transferring urgent stores from airports within flying distance, which had received heavy streams of 'air-bridge' payloads overnight and throughout the morning.

Personnel were also transferred that day, as certain specialists started to arrive on board. Our Royal Australian Navy and United States Navy officers and others with reasons to go home, left. Our Chinese laundry-men were also offered places on a chopper, and two of them grabbed the opportunity; but the remaining three, (with keen eyes on the amount of money they would no doubt make – and a great deal of courage, I hasten to add) decided to stay with us. Everyone was glad they did, too, because the thought of the stokers doing our laundry did not fill us with a lot of optimism!

Storing eventually finished in the darkness of late evening, long after the time when I had had to hand over my storing duties and return to the galley. With the final load on board, *Antrim* was well stored for war. The ship's storerooms were jam-packed with all manner of wanted, and some unwanted, stores, and many of the flats and passageways had been false-decked and still contained piles of boxes. Evening rounds were cancelled and the commander's broadcast delayed until 2200. In a very brief statement, he informed us that a horse called Gritta had won the Grand National. He then thanked his exhausted men for their efforts in the day, and wished a safe passage to the returning ships. Meanwhile, *Antrim* and her escorting convoy gathered pace for the start of the 6,000 mile journey south.

Sundays at sea are traditionally lazy days, when not a lot is done and everyone lounges around and takes it easy. Sunday, 4 April however, was not recorded on daily orders as a lazy Sunday routine, or anything like it. It was the start of our 'shake-down' period, as our own band of planners and co-ordinators set about creating a programme to increase our state of readiness for war.

We were only two days south of Gibraltar, but already the weather was noticeably warmer than it had been in the relatively cool Mediterranean spring – so much so, in fact, that I took advantage of the first real rays of sun of the year to sunbathe. There were plenty of places where one could find space to lie down – any flat, dry surface that was not in a hazardous area or did not cause an obstruction would do. As there were only a handful of dozing night workers on deck, it was easy for me to find a nice little secluded spot where I could strip down to my swimming trunks, read a bit more Sven Hassel and crash out on my towel – to wake two hours later with the start of that year's suntan.

Toasting my back for a pair of hours in the afternoon, with lashings of baby oil, gave me time for some reasonably solitary reflection. It was clear that a war was brewing, but, like nearly everyone else on board, I was confused as to why. I wondered what would happen if it did come to a serious exchange of bullets, bombs and missiles. And, of course, I also searched my own soul to try and anticipate how I would cope in such circumstances. I did not believe in God or any other religious father figure, but I guess I did believe in fate, and in that respect alone I felt I would follow in my ancestors' footsteps and see this war out without too many close calls.

At about 1630, I put on my No. 8s, and made my way back to the mess, where I was confronted by more buff-coloured forms to read and sign. There was a British Forces Identity Card (in case of capture), and a copy of Article 17 of the Geneva Convention of 1949. We laughed about it a bit, but quickly remembered that a contingent of our Royal Marine friends were already under Argentinian lock and key. 'Poor unlucky bootneck bastards.'

The news that filtered through from various sources throughout the day was denied, or confirmed and elaborated upon by the commander, during that evening's broadcast. The tales included how eighty-one booties had been captured at Port Stanley by over 2,000 Argentinians, (which our own 'bootneck' detachment thought were pretty fair odds!), and how another twenty-two had been captured at South Georgia, after they had put up a defiant defence and even shot down an Argentinian Puma helicopter, killing two of the enemy marines. Thirteen British Antarctic Survey (BAS) scientists had also been taken, but two female film makers were still unaccounted for. We were surprised to learn that together with Sir Rex Hunt, the Governor of the Falkland Islands, all the 'bootnecks' were already heading home via Uruguay. Strange kind of war this we thought – can't they afford to feed them?

All civilians on the islands, of which we were told there were only a few hundred, had apparently been placed under house arrest, and several farmsteads had already been commandeered as military outposts. Back home, the Leader of the Opposition, Michael Foot, had been pressurizing the Government to resign and hand over the reigns of power.

'What! Let that commie twat take over,' piped up Sharkey. 'No way, mate, we might as well hand over the keys to the Russians if his mob ever gets in. Leave it to Maggie. You watch, she'll sort this lot out.'

LCK Max Wall then went on to repeat a joke we had all heard several times before, but still seemed very apt for the occasion. 'Did you realize, that in the days when we had an empire, we used to have an emperor? Then in the days when we just had a kingdom, we used to have a king? And now we've just got a country, we've got Maggie Thatcher!'

On the task force front, HMS *Invincible*'s crew of 900 was taking on all the extra manpower they could handle, plus eight vertical-take-off

Sea Harriers and a squadron of Sea King helicopters. Other naval and RFA ships were also gearing up for departure, and even civilian STUFT (ships taken up from trade), had been commandeered to assist the operation. We were not told of any submarine movements, but we were aware that HMS *Superb* was probably already down south – and we also knew that she alone could probably take on all the Argentinian fleet and sink the lot! As the two world wars proved, submarines can be dangerous.

Monday, 5 April was *Antrim*'s eighth day at sea, and the day that the main task force sailed from the UK. We could only imagine the scenes that must have been taking place along the quaysides as our mates sailed to join us, with their loved ones in tears and waving banners. Of course, the crews of Admiral Woodward's flag ship, HMS *Antrim* and her squadron of HMS *Glamorgan*, HMS *Coventry*, HMS *Glasgow*, HMS *Sheffield*, HMS *Plymouth* and RFA *Blue Rover*, never had the chance to say goodbye to anyone. Not a last hug or kiss, nor even a last wave goodbye or a final telephone call. Nothing. And the thought of this was, I am sure, very much on the minds of our crews that day as HMS *Invincible* and HMS *Hermes* and their vast array of ships cast off and our little cluster steamed ever further south.

I stood looking towards the horizon, thinking of all the mates I knew on the ships around us as we sailed in classic convoy formation, no more than 2 miles apart. There were bound to be others I knew, but did not realize were with us. I wondered if I would get to see any of them down south – or ever see them again for that matter. I always thought about them briefly whenever their ship was mentioned, flicking through the names in my mind like an office card index.

That day also saw the start in earnest of our 'shake-down' period, as we started wearing and carrying battle dress. With increasing temperatures the extra clothing was a real pain at first. It was not too bad when we were exercising in the cold North Sea, but it was very uncomfortable in the heat of the West African coast. Our battle dress consisted of our normal No. 8s, which everyone now had to wear all the time – no more cook's whites, evening rig or T shirts or sunbathing thongs. Our shirtsleeves had to stay rolled down, and we also started carrying around our green nylon gas mask bags, complete with a set of white anti-flash gloves and hood.

We had worn this rig on many occasions before during exercises, but never for so long. Wearing it now had to become second nature, and we needed to start wearing it as much as possible, which meant showers now had to be taken as quickly as possible, and changing would take place in the bathrooms. At night, we were allowed to strip off – mainly because of the oppressive heat – but we still had to have our gear ready for immediate donning in the event of an alarm. We were warned that this was only the start of things, and that both showering and sleeping routines would be tightened up even further in the days to come.

To prepare for our NBCDX's the ship received a thorough going over to ensure that closing up times could be brought to a bare minimum – no more unmade beds after turning to, no more loose items sculling around, no more slack securing for sea. Now we really were raising the stakes – to secure for action.

The commander's Monday evening broadcast expanded upon details of the main task force's departure, stating it was the first such operation since the Suez crisis twenty-six years before, and that the Portsmouth ships' next port of call was 'Guz,' where they would pick up as many 'Booties' as room on board would allow. He then read out a long list of some of the ships that were believed to be forming the main task force: HMS *Battleaxe*, HMS *Brilliant*, HMS *Broadsword*, HMS *Arrow*, HMS *Ariadne*, HMS *Auroa*, HMS *Dido*, HMS *Euraylus*, HMS *Rhyl*, HMS *Yarmouth*, and RFA's *Engadine, Grey Rover, Plumleaf, Stromness*, plus several army logistic landing ships from Marchwood in Southampton.

He went on to explain that there would be other task forces too, and that vessels were being diverted from the West Indies and the Gulf, where ships like our *Sheffield* had just finished their tour of duty and were heading for home, after already spending five months away. He also told us we were in this scrap on our own, because it did not look as though the United Nations would get involved, or other Commonwealth countries or NATO or the Americans – who doubted we could recover the islands so far from home (a red rag to a lot of bulls that comment was).

'All the more reason,' he continued, 'to focus on what we're doing, and get it right first time, every time.'

On a lighter, and to most people a totally unconsidered note, the commander went on to warn us that to 'enhance our operational capability' the ship's stores endurance would have to be stretched considerably to minimize the amount of logistical support we would require as we sailed further and further away from our sources of supply. 'We will of course be storing up at Ascension Island, and there-after as required – or shall I say, as the RFA vessels can complete the 8,000 mile supply route. However, rationing of food, beer and nutty [sweets] is now being considered by the supply officer and his team, and the NAAFI manager – who you may have noticed, has now turned into a chief petty officer for the duration of hostilities!'

The word 'rationing' seemed to spread more fear in the minds of the ship's company than the Argentinians. Not so much in 1G1 mess, but in every other mess, panic-buying and hoarding commenced as soon as the chief petty officer NAAFI manager's shutter clattered open following the commander's speech. All the sweets in the shop had gone in seconds, and the other crisps and nuts and other snacks soon followed. 'Nutty' rationing, when the NAAFI had some on board, started from that evening. Food was not of much concern to people, but drink certainly was. The wardroom would still be allowed unlimited drinks, but it would be frowned upon if their bar bills were too high, and in any case from now on they could only drink what they had left in my old wardroom cellar. Senior rates were in principle now entitled to two pints of beer or lager plus three tots, but again there were limited stocks left on board. All junior rates were officially only entitled to draw enough beer for daily consumption from the NAAFI – now based on two (instead of three) tins per man per day (but I was running the 'beer boat'!). However, stocks of NAAFI tinned beer were also very low, and junior rates were not allowed to drink spirits.

In reality though everyone on board had access to as much drink as they could lay their hands on, and everyone knew it. It would have been impossible to regulate it any other way. So it was entirely possible for someone to get rolling drunk, and, as long as they did not cause any trouble, get away with it scot-free. I rarely heard of men getting done for being drunk on board before, during or after the war – although quite clearly, lads often were.

As mess 'beer bosun', I quickly convened a meeting with the lads who were not in the mile-long NAAFI queue. 'Okay lads. Cards on the table. I've got a few slabs stashed down the dry store, but they're now buried under a mountain of flour; I've also got two slabs behind the bulkhead panel by the telly, and a couple more buried behind the starboard lockers. We can't get to the slabs in the store, but what shall we do with the rest. Keep it there and risk losing it when they check our securing for action – or drink it all tonight?'

'Drink the bugger now – lets have a party.'

And so 1G1 mess had its first party of the war. Taff and I popped in for a drink occasionally between making batches of milk and bread, bringing covered trays of pizza and other leftovers from supper. The other messes just got plain bread and cheese and pickles! And we were not partying alone that night either, it was clear that every other mess was partying too – especially next door in No. 5 petty officers' mess. We were making a fair noise but the din coming from next door was something else. Any Police or Madness music we played was easily drowned out by their louder Phil Collins and Status Quo, and when midnight approached and the singing started, our simple little ditties were suffocated by the thirty-strong male voice choir next door. As the hands passed 0200, it was not some witty naval ditty they were singing, but 'WOODWARD IS A PLONKER, WOODWARD IS A PLONKER, LA LA LA LA – LA LA LA LA, WOODWARD IS A PLONKER, WOOD-WARD IS A PLONKER, LA LA LA LA – LA LA LA LA!'

When they heard what was going on next door, those still drinking in 1G1 mess shut the fridge and hid the few remaining tins in their boot lockers. 'There's no way they'll get away with that. The Admiral's cabin is up above the for'ard end of their mess. He'll go bananas!' And from what the stewards told us and the dressing down that all members of No. 5 petty officers' mess were given by the master at arms at 0230, Admiral Woodward did go bananas!

As a result of this little naval singsong, Ziggy Bowie was summarily removed from his position of mess president. Two days later he appeared on the captain's table, where, 'for an act of gross rudeness to an admiral, and failure to maintain order and discipline in his mess', he lost all his three good-conduct badges and picked up a hefty fine. In addition, No. 5 petty officers' mess not only started beer rationing like the rest of us, they were also 'awarded' complete stoppage of beer for ten days!

Looking on the bright side, the row it caused up top was not all bad news, because we started hearing increasing buzzes that Woodward and our skipper were not getting on. One lad even said that one of the radio operator (ROs) had told him that Woodward was so angry, he was looking to transfer his flag to another ship.

'Bloody good job too,' said Paddy Flynn. 'I heard he even wants to scrub "crossing the line"! Him and his bloody miserable bunch of brown-nosed staff officers! The sooner *Invincible* gets down here and they all bugger off the better.'

With hindsight, I think the reasons that Admiral Woodward did not go down too well on board were twofold: our skipper was a very senior and experienced captain, who knew *Antrim*'s crew much better than the 'embarked' admiral – or his staff. And, as a personality, Woodward obviously had everything it took to make it to such a prominent position, but, as a close-contact man manager he was far less well thought of by those that really mattered – the officers and men who served under him. This distinct impression was gained from almost everyone who had any dealings with him on *Antrim* and rightly or wrongly the word spread and the muck stuck.

Apart from the events in No. 5 petty officers' mess, Tuesday, 6 April was not too bad a day. Just about everyone was carrying hangovers and talking of the drinking races, the singing, the games and the other drunken escapades. But the last night before rationing had also served another purpose: it had lifted some of the tension and boosted morale.

As Shady Lane so lucidly put it, 'Bloody good piss-up that, and Woodward might be buggering off too – bloody excellent farewell party for that bastard!'

The day after the party was the day we should have arrived back in Portsmouth with *Sheffield* and the other ships, and I should have gone on draft. Instead, I was sunbathing with my action dress on, in near equatorial waters. *Antrim* was now 3,000 miles from home and still had another 5,000 miles to run. In the evening, with my face and hands increasingly scorched by the tropical sun, I soon caught up with the latest news and buzzes: HMS *Fearless* had now sailed, instead of being scrapped, and was crammed with bloodthirsty 'booties'. Lord Carrington had resigned, but Margaret Thatcher, the Iron Lady, had refused to even discuss surrendering sovereignty. Commonwealth countries had withdrawn their ambassadors from Buenos Aires, and Ronald Reagan had used all his superpower might to call on the Argentinians to withdraw, but would not be sending any troops.

Without any official warning, all our buzzes came true the next morning when Admiral Woodward, unable to wait any longer for *Invincible* to arrive, ceremonially transferred his flag to our sister ship *Glamorgan*. Officially, he had switched flagships because he had worked with their crew before, but unofficially it did not take a new calculator and a slide rule to work out that his style of leadership did not dovetail together too well with our skipper's – and he did not take too kindly to being called a 'plonker'.

The captain made a short 'pipe' to announce the completion of the flag transfer. He let us know he was not sorry to see the back of the Admiral and his flag team. 'Because now I can get my cabin back, and get a decent night's sleep in my own bed which, you may have realized, is directly above No. 5 petty officers' mess!'

Then to the muffled sound of an enormous cheer rippling round the ship, the skipper went on to say, 'And now *Antrim* will fight this war her way – and we'll start right now!' A second great cheer echoed between the lower decks.

Under those difficult, and for him potentially embarrassing, circumstances, this 'pipe' really lifted spirits and won him enormous admiration on board. He did not make many pipes, as he had the commander and first lieutenant to do that for him, but he got around the ship as often as he could and knew the name of every man on board – just as the best Skippers should. Captain Young was a naval captain of the oldest British naval tradition going. He was a very senior naval officer and a gentleman, and he knew his ship and he knew his men, and he knew what made British warships and British men tick. And that afternoon, with no admiral directly above his head on board, we were ready to follow him all the way – to the ends of the earth if necessary.

Later that day the commander added some words of his own to the captain's, and from his tone it was quite clear that things were going to change considerably in the post-Woodward era. 'We've lost the protection that being a flagship gave us. Now we're going to take the flak like the rest of them – so expect some difficult times ahead!' The commander then confirmed that food, booze and 'nutty' rationing would start the following day, and that there was to be no more hoarding and no more parties until 0300 – 'no mess names mentioned!'

'Despite that however, he continued, and contrary to the Admiral's instructions, '*Antrim will* uphold naval tradition, *regardless* of the situation, and formally "cross the line" on Friday, 9 April.' Yet another massive cheer and stamping of feet could be heard and felt around the ship.

That night in the chief cook's office, I finished letters to family and friends, and to Jackie and some of my other girlfriends, for the first time since the rushed correspondence of 2 April.

I hope you got my last letter okay. Sorry it was a bit rushed, but we did not get much time to write before mail closed.

Well, it seems that we are really in for a scrap with the Argentinians! Still, all but two of their ships are Second World War types and they only have two modern destroyers, both of which are greatly inferior in weaponry to ours. It's funny, but one of them was tied up alongside us in Pompey only three months ago, and now it looks like we may be fighting against it!

Everyone on board is obviously feeling a bit scared in case something goes wrong, but we outnumber them something like 10 to 1, so there's no danger really.

Our captain, who lives near High Wycombe [only 10 miles from where I lived], has told us the politicians will probably sort everything out before it ever comes to blows, but we are working up to get ready just in case. Besides, we've got some marines on board who are itching to get their own back!

We haven't had mail for over a week and don't know what the popular opinion back home is; our only contact is with the BBC World Service, but we know they can't reveal the position of our advanced fleet. We all laughed when it was declared that the aircraft carriers were sailing to meet the rest of the ships near Gibraltar, as we are a long way from there and will 'cross the line' on Friday 9th!

We were caught on the hop with the food situation. As a result have had to put everyone on a reduced menu, though not as yet rationing. We have very little fresh veg, no fresh or UHT milk, very little bread, and to be honest we don't have a lot of any of the usual things we had get back home. But, it's so hot down here, a lot of the lads have not been so hungry anyway.

Yesterday I should have left the ship and gone on Easter leave, courses at Chatham and Royal Arthur, and then on draft to my next shore base. However, my promotion will still come through, but I doubt if they'll let me have it because there isn't a billet for a POCA [petty officer catering accountant] on board. Still, I'm not worried, when I do eventually get it my pay will be backdated!

We have nearly all stopped shaving, and the beard-growing competition is going to be judged at the end of the trip. I'll shave mine off before I get home, as I'm not all that fond of them. Because of the very hot weather, I've had my hair cut short, and what with the beard and dark suntan, you'd hardly recognize me!

Yesterday, some dolphins followed the ship for a few miles – really intelligent-looking they were, and I've just been up top again watching the flying fish. Really amazing little things they are. There seem to be swarms and swarms of them; they weigh I would guess about two or three pounds and are capable of flying about one hundred yards! We even saw one 'Paddy' flying fish as well today. Most of the fish are startled by the ship's approach and fly away from us, but this one leapt out of the water and swam straight into our side!

I hope that you won't worry too much about me, I'm sure I'll be okay. The only thing is we're likely to be away for at least a couple of months, so anybody who would like to drop me a line, tell them it would be greatly appreciated. We get pretty bored on here with nothing to read, and so out of touch with what's going on back home. I would also like you to save some of the news-paper cuttings until I get back so I can have a read. We all miss the papers and mail.

Lots of my old friends are on the various other ships in the fleet and I've managed to send messages across with various stores when being transferred by helicopter or RAS (Replenishment at Sea). That's when we use a light or heavy jackstay to transfer stores, personnel or fuel between us and another ship – sailing only about fifty yards apart, at about fifteen to twenty miles per hour, with both vessels heading on the same straight course. First a line is fired across and then all sorts of pulleys and winches follow so we are able to transfer almost anything.

Well, that's about it for now. I'll look forward to hearing from

you soon, and to seeing you when we get back. I shall think of
Grandad Wilkinson as we do the crossing the line ceremony on
Friday, and hope that I have the same good fortune on this trip as
he did on his.

Love and best wishes,
David

CHAPTER SIX

Crossing The Line

Although I had written home, and posted the 'letter' I knew no mail would leave the ship until we reached Ascension Island. However, it was always nice to write down one's thoughts and get them in the bag rather than rushing around frantically an hour or two before mail closed. From the tone of the letters, you will see already that they did not reveal everything that went on on board, for I was always conscious of the need to maintain some security, and minimize the risk of causing too much alarm and worry. From the reports we picked up from the BBC World Service, we could see how different the public's perception of events was compared to our own. I did not know it at the time, but back home my face had already appeared in a local paper, with a short report of who I was, what ship I was serving on, and what I did on board. None of us knew anything about the local and national interest that the Falklands was creating; the whole country was buzzing with excitement, fear, anger and anticipation – particularly in the parent's and loved ones' households, where there was great uncertainty and trepidation.

On 8 April we broke away from the main convoy, and in company with HMS *Plymouth*, HMS *Sheffield* and RFA *Tidespring*, struck out for our rendezvous at Ascension Island. This was also the day the ship prepared in earnest for the next day's 'crossing the line' ceremony. This would be my first time across the line, so I had been warned to look out for a particularly interesting but nasty initiation! Although I was again dozing on the upper deck for most of the day, I picked up the fact that a massive organization was in place to prepare everything in time for the proceedings. The chippy's party had stopped the ship's securing for action preparations, and was now working flat out with a large team of volunteers to create all manner of staging, equipment, props and – most noticeable of all – a large canvas-lined swimming pool on the flight deck! Other teams were busy knocking up costumes on the ship's sewing machine, but most of these creations were kept tightly under wraps to maximize the visual impact.

56

The master at arms, (RPO) (regulating petty officer), killick regulator and ship's office writers busied themselves knocking up over 500 distinctive 'crossing the line' certificates, checking drafting records and quizzing people to draw up extensive lists of all those, like myself, who had not crossed the line before. The 'reggies' were even going round taking statements to present to some court they kept whispering about. As he passed me, stretched out fully clothed but sunbathing on the flight deck, the RPO flicked through a bundle of these statements to find one with my name on it. 'Oh dear, Rowdy, putting the ship's company on rationing and making lousy milk, oh dear! You're right in the shit tomorrow old son. No sunbathing for you matey when the sea bears get you!'

I nodded off for a while, but although I was exhausted and the sun was absolutely blazing hot, I did not sleep too well because of the sound of banging and sawing going on. Eventually, I moved further up the ship, but there was still quite a racket, and besides, I was starting to wonder what on earth they were going to do to me – these 'sea bears' I kept hearing so much about. I had seen photographs of my grandfather's 'crossing the line' on HMS *Slinger* as she sailed to fight the Japanese. But trying to link those old black and white scenes with what was taking place on *Antrim* was not easy, and I started to get the feeling that this might be a naval initiation I would never forget.

I retired to my bed after lunch, and slept through until evening and the commander's TV broadcast. This evening he explained that a new foreign secretary, Francis Pym, had been appointed, and that he had been loudly cheered in the House of Commons when he vowed that Britain would fight if necessary for the Falklands!

'Yeah, Britain will fight all right, but *he* won't have to kill any bastard will he?' chipped in Max Wall, slowly stretching across to the fridge for his second and final beer of the night.

The commander also updated us on the Government's 'external' willingness to hold peace talks with the Argentinians 'for a fair deal', but said that Francis Pym had added, 'If all our efforts fail, the Argentinian regime will know what to expect – Britain does not appease dictators!' This sounded just like words from a ventriloquist's dummy operated by 'Maggie' herself. Apparently the Shadow Foreign Secretary, Denis Healy had responded by accusing the prime minister of letting Lord Carrington take all the blame for their joint mismanagement. But this comment passed over our heads. We were not really interested in the political in-fighting. We just wanted to know if we were going to have to fight or not.

In the commander's, or any other officer's, broadcasts we could always tell that they were treading a difficult presentational path; it was abundantly clear that they were making every effort to be as politically neutral as possible. Two of our oldest naval sayings sum it up very precisely: 'Never talk about politics or religion' and, 'Always leave politics to politicians and fighting wars to fighting men!' Off the record, however, the political scene was widely discussed on board, and whilst the Government had its knockers, the vast majority seemed to be behind the 'Iron Lady' and her right-wing methods of sorting out the 'nation-wrecking' socialists. Staunch trade unionists, miners and a few other dissatisfied groups might hate her, but most people on board and back home were clearly fed up of Britain drifting into Third World status, and her support gathered increased momentum as each day of 1982 passed – although we also took a swipe at her now and again too, when the occasion warranted it.

The commander ended his speech that evening by laying out the plans for the next few days, including our stop at Ascension Island. Then he wished us all a most enjoyable 'crossing the line' ceremony the following day – particularly (reading from a long list), 'Lieutenant Campion, Chief Petty Officer Burns, Petty Officer McNair and Leading Caterer Yates, and all the rest of you who have not crossed the line before. I shall look forward to seeing you at King Neptune's Court on the flight deck tomorrow afternoon. Have a peaceful night gentlemen!'

In the galley that evening, in addition to our normal list of tasks, the chief cook had left a series of instructions to knock up the following items for the crossing the line ceremony:

200 'crossing the line' tablets – any horrible recipe you like

4 large bins of creamy shaving foam

4 half-filled plastic gallon containers of multi-coloured mouth-wash (I'll add the rum tomorrow)

1 large bin of 'innards' – assorted meat scraps, liver, kidneys, baked beans and spaghetti

4 milk churns of 'pusser's limers' (anti-scurvy drink) – put in the freezer to cool down.

Fortunately, Taff had crossed the line already and had some idea of what the chief cook was on about, which was just as well because I did not have a clue. I started on the 'limers', while Taff poured all sorts of ingredients into the large Hobart mixing bowl to knock up the tablets. In went some flour and sugar and margarine as one might expect, but then he added salt, Tabasco sauce, dried chillies, curry powder, blue colouring and anything else he fancied from the herbs and spices rack.

After a good mix in the bowl, he rolled out the dough and cut out 1 inch circles, which, he then baked to produce the tablets. What part they would play I was still not too sure about, but after knowing what had gone in the tablets, I certainly was not looking forward to swallowing any!

After completing our normal butchery and bakery jobs, we set about completing the rest of the chief cook's extra tasks. The shaving foam we knocked up out of a few packets of synthetic powdered cream, and some jelly crystals to keep it fluffy. The mouthwash was basically ordinary 'limers', but each container was flavoured a bit with spices and different food colourings. I then made the 'innards' with the leftover meat scraps from my evening's butchery: straggly bits of bacon rind, 5 pounds of finely sliced liver, 3 pounds of quartered kidneys, and a few large tins of baked beans and spaghetti – complete with their runny tomato sauces.

'This looks bloody revolting, Taff,' I yelled out on completion. 'What do they want this lot for?'

'You wait and see, Rowdy. You just wait and see!'

The prospects for an enjoyable crossing the line day seemed to take a dive on two fronts early in the morning. First, we had reached a belt of tropical mist and drizzle that threatened to rain the whole thing off, and secondly, buzzes were rife that Admiral Woodward had reiterated his desire for his fleet *not* to cross the line in the traditional naval manner. Spirits were apparently a bit low in the forenoon while I was tucked up soundly in bed, but with the weather easing up a little and nothing official being said about the Admiral's views, after lunch the leading players made their final preparations for HMS *Antrim*'s crossing the line ceremony.

The first thing I noticed on rising at 1300, after nowhere near enough sleep, was the fifteen-page Order of Ceremonies and Summons of Court Attendees including, under the 1G1 mess heading with ten of my mates, the name of LCA YATES D159012R – 'for not crossing the line before, and causing gross cruelty and major embarrassment to the ship's company!'

Although not everyone could attend the ceremony, most of the ship's company who were not on watch made their way up to the flight deck by 1345, or perched on one of the upper decks overlooking the aft of the ship. I joined fifty or sixty others on the hangar roof – most of us on the summons list and hoping our lofty position would delay or even avoid our attendance.

As I watched the stage being made ready below, I read through the introduction and order of ceremonies and began to gather what sort of initiation I was about to undergo! The brief explained that:

King Neptune's outlying scouts had sent information to the Secretary of State that HMS *Antrim* had recently left Gibraltar on 29 March 1982 and was now steering a southerly course towards Ascension Island. Thereupon the Secretary of State, in the customary manner, issued instructions to the bears to intercept the ship soon after sunset on the evening of Thursday, to board her, and, in a cautious and nautical manner, to issue the proclamations and the summonses, and to bear back to him such communications as the ship might wish to make. Having bowed low in assent, and grasping the proclamations, the bears had passed from the watery apartment.

Yesterday evening the bears had finally boarded the ship, and declining all offers of assistance, had made their way towards the captain's cabin. There they presented to Captain Young an illuminated letter from His Majesty King Neptune and a greeting from Her Majesty Queen Amphitrite.

I read the finely worded greeting and looked back to the flight deck. There below me the scene was almost set for the start of the ceremony; with a large canvas pool of water, thrones and various other chairs, and a large medieval-looking ducking stool. The chippies' party had indeed been very busy over the past couple of days. Returning to the finely-worded programme, I read:

The large brown furry envoys had then presented the captain with another letter, announcing their majesties' wishes, in regard to the procedures at the morrow's court. To which the captain had written a swift reply and handed it in a sealed envelope to the envoys, who then discharged their duties in other parts of the ship, and, before departing over the side, visited every officers' mess, handing to the president of each a sheaf of summonses for the novices on the list, and to other messes a summons addressed to the senior members, ordering the presence of the uninitiated.

The Equator
Neptune, by the Grace of Mythology, Lord of the Waters, Sovereign of all Oceans, Governor and Lord High Admiral of the Bath and Soap.

Whereas it has pleased Us to convene a Court to be holden on board His Majesty's Ship *Antrim*, on the flight deck thereof, at the hour of 2 p.m. By these presents We summon those contained in Annexes A – P to King Neptune's Proclamation of the Eighth of April 1982 to appear at the said Court to render Us the usual homage, and to be initiated into the mystic rites according to the ancient usages of Our Kingdom.

Hereof nor you, nor any of you may fail, as you will answer at your peril, and to the delight of Our trusty Bodyguard.

Given at Our Court on the Equator this Ninth day of April, in the year One thousand nine hundred and eighty two of Our Watery Reign.

At precisely 1400, there was a 'pipe' of 'Clear lower deck. All hands not on watch muster on or in the vicinity of the flight deck. Prepare to receive on board King Neptune', and finally the ceremony was ready to begin. Following a blast on Bungy William's Royal Marine trumpet, the bosun's mate piped King Neptune and Queen Amphritite up the steep ladder from the Sea Slug quarter deck, where the royal party was formally welcomed on board from their watery realm by the Captain. Initial greetings exchanged, the captain then escorted the royal procession to their glistening thrones, whilst the still was piped and the entire ship's company present stood to attention as their majesties passed regally between them, followed by the judge, the judge's clerk, the king's messenger, the chariot seahorses (riding suitably attired broom handles), and the king's trumpeter. Taking their thrones between the seats of the captain on one side and a 'scantily clad maiden' (who looked awfully like young Pincher Martin from 3E mess) on the other, loud music barked out a few bars of 'A Life on an Ocean Wave', and the ship's company relaxed to listen to the royal address by King Neptune (who looked very much like the chief writer).

Clutching a massive trident, King Neptune read loudly to the audience from a scroll he clasped in his other mighty hand, as his Queen (who looked just like our chief caterer – who, buzzes suggested, had not even 'crossed the line' himself yet!) listened attentively, whilst, like most other people, eyeing up the scantily clad maiden. Being the closest to a female form we had seen since Gibraltar, she was arousing considerable interest! These formalities over, the court settled down to begin proceedings, which began with the award of the Most Exalted Order of the Old Sea Dog to the captain. After briefly calling for 'suitable refreshment' to quench the royal party's raging thirst, the king stood again to address the court:

On this same spot, as you may know, we held a court some
years ago,
Before the days of Scapa Flow, that bleak and barren harbour.
We've heard about the Firth of Forth, and all your gallant deeds
        up north were told us by our barber.
Though seldom 'tis we have a moan, to one complaint we're
        forced to own against the Royal Navy,
Throughout these awful years of war, too many submarines by
        far you sent down to our Davy
Those U-boats' crews we well could spare, they're far from
        popular down there [pointing];
Our realm became disjointed, and then we had like to add a
        word

About that nonsense so absurd, pointless yet fourteen pointed.
There is a 'freedom of the Seas', but the jossman does not hold
    the keys to open or to lock it.
That freedom's found here on our line, the keys as well – for
    they are mine, I have them in my pocket.
And this suggests the treat in store, for those we've never met
    before, we'll have them separated
Before ourself and Amphritite, according to the ancient rite,
    they'll be initiated.
And if successfully they cope, with Order of the Bath and Soap,
    we'll have them decorated.
Then surgeon, barber, police stand by, and order every novice
    high, in order precedented.
And one by one by rule of rank, to surgeon, barber, and to tank,
    they now shall be presented.

A loud cheer and a slightly quieter groan came from the men on the
flight deck, before the captain could read his reply, which was equally
full of fine, regal words. The court took their places on the thrones and
the king declared the court open.

Attention!
King Neptune I the Lord supreme, 'ere there were ships, or sails,
    or steam.
Of all the seven oceans wide, the lord of wave, the lord of tide.
The monarch of the watery deep, whose laws the whales and
    fishes keep;
Here on the flight deck declare, 'fore fellows fine and ladies fair
    [glancing at the scantily clad maiden]
Our Court is open.
And all our honoured rules of court shall be obeyed, let shrift be
    short
To any who shall dare transgress, the proper speech, the proper
    dress.
If one offend a rule of mine, though twenty times across our line,
He's crossed upon our azure main, our bears shall have him
    once again,
And treated worse than novice he, shall by those bears and
    barbers, be,
Therefore beware!
And now our rule of court decrees, the grant of freedom of our
    seas

To all who've not got that rank, by order of the suds and tank
Let them be ready!
And this the order in which they shall be presented here today:
The captain's charming other half (again glancing at the maiden)
The Jimmy and then the staff,
The wardroom officers then bid, the gun room and the mighty
    mid.,
The warrants – few I think of those, [none in fact]
The CPs and the mere POs,
And then the rest until the crew we've worked our weary way
    right through.
So stand by, surgeon!
Stand by, barber!
Stand by, bears!
In order then as we command, before us let each novice stand
Who has that freedom yet to win:
Enough! My trusty men! Begin!

As the King adjusted his trident and robes, his trumpeter heralded the arrival of the doctor, barber, barber's assistant, lady barber (another even more scantily clad young maiden – with the cutest little pair of eyes I had seen all day!), the police, the secret police and the bodyguards. And then last but not least the growling, grumbling head bear and the pack of even bigger and meaner sea bears themselves! 'Shit,' I thought, 'I think I know what I'm in for now.'

While all this had been going on, the weather had closed in again, and though it was still very hot, the rain was pouring down in a concentrated deluge of unrelenting monsoon-style drizzle, soaking everything and everybody on the upper deck. Notwithstanding the appalling conditions, proceedings continued unabated. Not even a war, a grumpy admiral or a tropical downpour was going to stop *Antrim* having her 'crossing the line' ceremony that day!

The first novice to mount the scaffold was Lieutenant Campion from the wardroom who, despite twelve years' service, had let slip soon after leaving Gibraltar, that, he had never crossed the line before. He was dragged from the assembled wardroom huddle by the police and placed before the court to hear the charges.

'Lieutenant Campion, you are brought before this court today charged with the heinous crimes of not having crossed the line before, and also having failed to record two measures of gin on your wardroom bar chit after the cocktail party in Bremerhaven. How do you plead?'

'Guilty, your majesty.'

'Fair enough. It is the considered verdict of this court that you be summarily dealt with – AND FED TO THE BEARS!'

A loud cheer erupted as everyone delighted in the poor lieutenant's misfortune to be the first to experience the wrath of the surgeon, barber, police and bears – all fresh and keen to practise their professions upon the poor unfortunates who would pass their way that day. The stocky lieutenant was thrown into the ducking stool and held firm, while the surgeon examined him roughly with an enormous wooden hammer to test his reflexes. A mock incision was made with an equally large wooden scalpel across his belly, and some of my ice-cold bloody offal and beans was forced down his shirt and trousers. Then, while his mouth was open in horror, one of Taff's blue tablets was thrust into it by the surgeon's assistant, who immediately followed that up with a large tilt from one of the coloured, and now heavily rum-laced, mouthwashes. That in turn was kept down by one of the policemen clamping his jaw shut until he had swallowed every drop. Then, having pronounced him fit to receive punishment, the barber's motley crew jumped forward, smothered him with our creamy shaving foam and shaved him with a massive 2-foot serrated wooden cut-throat razor.

Poor Lieutenant Campion sat there pinned to the back of the stool by two more policemen, coughing and spluttering, and unable to see or hear much for the foam in his eyes and ears.

'What shall we do with him now, men?' screamed the chief of police.

'THROW HIM TO THE BEARS,' we all roared back in unison – loud enough to wake Admiral Woodward on *Glamorgan*. With a massive hinged jolt, the stool then hurled the lieutenant into the middle of the large canvas pool, where six enormous brown sea bears ducked him, flung him in the air, ducked him again and held him under, then flung him in the air again, before finally throwing him out of the pool and onto a pile of coconut crash-mats that awaited those who had completed their initiation.

I thought, 'I'm getting out of here quick.' And I was not alone. Half the men on the hangar roof arrived at the same conclusion at the same time and rushed for'ard to escape the bears. But there was a shock in store for all of us, as the tops of both ladders were barred by two teams of secret police, who had stalked their quarry in advance. They had us all well and truly cornered.

The ceremony carried on all afternoon in the pouring, warm rain, as mess after mess of novices were brought before the judge (who looked suspiciously like the chief chippy). With all senior rates completed, it was the turn of the junior rates. First in line were 1G1 mess, and first in the front of that line was me!

'Ah, Leading Caterer Rowdy Yates. I've been looking forward a great deal to seeing your useless hulk before me today,' called out the judge. 'You are charged with not crossing the line before, poisoning the ship's company on a daily basis with your horrendous churns of powdered milk, and also for bringing great shame and embarrassment on the ship by contracting a 'foreign disease' in Lisbon. You will, of course, be pleading guilty – FEED HIM TO THE BEARS!'

Although I was 6 feet 2 inches and a back-row rugby player, four even bigger guys man-handled me into the ducking stool, where the surgeon, by now covered from head to foot in blood and gore, gave me the once-over and shoved handfuls of my own offal and beans inside my No. 8 shirt and down the front and back of my trousers. Then one of Taff's tablets was poked down my throat (and tasted just as bad as I had imagined) and the attendant moved in with the gallon of orange mouth-wash, the neck of which I tried to keep clenched between my teeth, but which the police swiftly removed! The barber's assistant then ladled thick foaming cream all over my head so that I could not see or hear. All that I could feel was the jagged cut-throat razor being run over my body, before I felt the stool catapult from under me and I flew through the air to be submerged in the pool beneath the feet of the bears. They held me under until I felt sure my tablet – rum – and foam-filled lungs would explode. Up I came and flew through the air again, gasping for breath as I also took in strands of spaghetti and slivers of liver before descending once more into the heavy furry feet of the bears. Then I was grabbed once more and flung up and out of the pool onto the coconut matting. There I felt a rain of Policemen's truncheon blows as I crawled quickly away from the scene, still choking from the awful tablet and spitting out the beans and lumps of offal that, by now, had made the pool look like one of my soups. Thankfully, my initiation was now complete.

I did not need to shower, the tropical downpour did that for me. So I just clambered back up to my position on the hangar roof, where I slumped against the guardrail and witnessed the procession of junior rates that followed me, and their facial and bodily contortions as they succumbed to the dubious professions of King Neptune's court. No novice, or other 'stitched up' offenders, were spared in the tepid rain that afternoon as we crossed the imaginary line from the North to the South Atlantic; numerous secret police made sure of that. Not even the second officer of the watch was spared when he came down from the bridge in his pristine white overalls and clipboard, waving the latest sheet of signal paper at the Captain from the side of the scaffold.

'What's that in your hand Sub Lieutenant Mynott?' shouted the Captain.

'A signal from *Sheffield*, Sir, that I think you should read, Sir!'

'Oh, all right,' responded the Captain, reaching across to snatch the signal from the young man's thin juvenile fingers. 'Judge of the Court.'

'Yes, Sir.'

'While I'm thinking of a reply to this signal, can you see that Sub Lieutenant Mynott gets – er – FED TO THE BEARS!'

'Yes, Sir. Right away, Sir. I'm sure we can accommodate one more customer, Sir,' the judge eagerly replied, as the 'subbie' was put through the same routine as the rest of us – clipboard, pristine white overalls and all. When he had finally landed on the mats and regained some co-ordination of mind and body, the Captain shouted across, 'Sub-Lieutenant Mynott! Respond to the signal as the officer of the watch sees fit, and tell *Sheffield*, it's pretty wet on *Antrim*'s flight deck too!'

I stayed almost to the end, by which time King Neptune, Queen Amphitrite, the captain, the captain's secretary, the judge and all the scantily clad maidens had also been thrown to the sea bears. The bears were looking pretty tired themselves after an afternoon of drinking their own endless supply of spicy mouthwash and after – just being sea bears in a ship's 'crossing the line' ceremony.

The commander's broadcast that evening was suitably flavoured with references to the afternoon's ceremony, and many a joke cracked about the drunken bloody surgeon and the unruly brown bears, who seemed to have taken full advantage of their positions to beat up just about every single person on board!

The serious side of the broadcast however, informed us that that really was the last party we would be having for some time, and that the news from home was not getting any brighter. Pictures had apparently appeared of the captured Royal Marines surrendering their arms in Port Stanley, spreading their big tough 'bootneck' arms, as skinny young Argentinian conscripts 'fleeced' them – no doubt for trophies to take home. With these pictures in our minds, we could just imagine the atmosphere in our own 'booties' mess – they could not have been too impressed by that news item.

We arrived off the coast of Ascension Island as Taff and I were making final preparations for breakfast, and once the meal was over we popped 'up top' to see what the place looked like. There was no harbour large enough to take a ship of *Antrim*'s size, so we lay a couple of miles offshore, anchored to the crystal-clear tropical blue sea that was predominant in those parts. The island itself looked like a volcanic atoll without any greenery, and I quickly took a series of photos to capture the panorama of the island, with all its sandy brown, orange and yellow colours.

Quite a few other men were also on the upper deck for it was, after all, our first sight of land since leaving Gibraltar twelve days before, and although we knew there was no run ashore in the offing, it was still good to see terra firma again. As well as sightseeing, some of the lads had already got their fishing rods out and were hauling in their catch – which they assured onlookers were salt-water piranhas! Looking at the array of needle-pointed teeth as they flicked onto the wooden decking, I was not about to challenge that description, and declined Danny Kaye's offer to get the hook out for him with my little finger!

They soon appeared in their thousands as lads started chucking in all sorts of food or even little balls of paper to attract them. Some even hauled them in using a bit of string and a button – they attacked absolutely everything thrown anywhere near them. I stood around watching the piles of fish mount up for a while then, as I was making my way to bed at about 1000, I was approached to help some of the fishermen 'stitch up' one of the young midshipmen.

As part of our early tasks at Ascension, the chief bosun's mate (buffer) was detailed to paint over the large ship's numbers on the port and starboard bows, to confuse Argentinian ships' recognition. They had to rig up a cradle mechanism and lower someone over the side with a pot of paint and a roller. Enter Midshipman Simpson, keen as mustard and obviously future admiral material. He jumped at the chance to show his team spirit when the officer in charge of the fo'c'sle asked him casually if he fancied giving the buffer's men a hand covering up the ship's numbers.

The cradle was made up of a couple of scaffold planks lashed together and rigged up to ropes and pulley systems that allowed it to be lowered and raised over the ships side, and when tested by one of the young seamen, worked like a dream.

'Righto Buffer,' chirped the cocky future admiral. 'Hand me the grey paint and roller – off we go, tally ho.' A couple of seamen helped the eager young officer over the side, and as he sat on the planks to prepare for his descent, a large crowd of sightseers appeared from all over the ship. I came along with a carefully concealed black plastic bucket full of juicy breakfast leftovers!

'Stand by to lower away,' bawled the buffer to the two teams of men on the ropes. 'Lower away slowly together.' Very slowly, with Midshipman Simpson grinning broadly to the assembled audience above him, the cradle made it's way down the ship's side, reached the top of the number, passed the middle – and kept on going.

'That'll do nicely, Buffer,' screamed the Admiral-in-waiting. 'I can reach the ship's side just fine from here thank you.'

'What did you say, Sir?' replied the buffer.

'I said, this'll be fine here, Buffer – any lower and my feet will be in the water.'

'Righto lads,' the buffer whispered to the hauling party, 'Another 18 inches should do it.' 'Hold on tight down there, Sir. We're just going to make the cradle secure for you, Sir,' he shouted. Then, looking in my direction, he called out, 'Ok, Rowdy, time to feed the fishes!'

A carefully aimed shot emptied my bucket of juicy scraps right next to the cradle 20 feet below. The not so cocky midshipman started screaming, 'Oi, Buffer, what's going on up there? Don't the lads know they can't ditch gash when there's someone over the side?' He continued screaming as first one or two, then ten or twenty, then half the piranhas off Ascension Island moved in for their late breakfast. 'Jesus Christ almighty, Buffer, get me up quick,' he screamed even louder, in a voice verging on desperation. 'The little bastards are trying to eat my steaming boots!'

It was an excellent stitch-up, which had the full approval of the wardroom, and certainly reminded a certain young midshipman, that along his way to the dizzy heights of admiral he should never volunteer for anything!'

While I was asleep that afternoon, the ship took on more stores from the island by Vertrep and boat transfers. There was not a great deal, but coming in such relatively small amounts it took most of the day. Helicopters and boats were also frantically ferrying gear out to the other ships in our group, and the lads in the mess said they saw a lot of fixed-wing flights landing in the middle of the island, no doubt after 4,000 mile trips down from the UK. Those who were awake eagerly waited for mail with each delivery. Finally some arrived in almost the very last helicopter transfer. I had seven letters, including a very naughty one from Jackie saying what she was going to do to me on my return, and quickly scribbled some replies.

The situation with the Argentinians doesn't seem to have changed at all lately, so it looks as if we may still be going down to sort them out. The Government back home sounds pretty disorganized to me, but to get rid of Maggie now might only make matters worse. That bloke Knott sounds a proper weed doesn't he? We haven't got any confidence in him at all.

I'm really missing a good lie-in in a proper bed and above all else some fresh milk – the people back home don't realize how lucky they are to get the stuff delivered to their doorsteps.

We've been told that the censor won't be at work, but we've also been told not to say too much in case 'they' change their minds! So I can't say where we are at moment, or where we're going. I expect you'll know that before we do. I'll try to keep a mini-diary, so when I get back I'll be able to tell you the whole story 'as it was' and not as written in the papers.

Please thank everyone who has rung up about me. Just tell them that our family has a good record in wars, and that I don't want to be an exception to that rule!

As well as stores, fifty extra Royal Marines and a handful of HMS *Endurance*'s crew also arrived on board, and with no spare bunks available, bed rotation or 'hot-bunking' systems started operating. Two of the candidates in 1G1 mess were Paddy the night-working steward and me! A newly arrived brute of a 'bootneck' called Robbie Roberts was allocated my bed; when I was away working, he could get his head down in his sleeping bag, and when I came off watch, we would swap over.

Before turning to that evening, I went up top with my camera and took a couple of shots – one of which was the lonely silhouette of HMS *Sheffield* against the reddening horizon, with her crew no doubt thinking they should have been at home by now instead of sitting off the coast of Ascension Island heading thousands of miles in the other direction. I knew we would be sailing without *Sheffield* in the morning, and as I left the upper deck that evening a strange cold premonition came over me. I stood and stared one last time and wondered if I would ever see *Sheffield*, or any of my mates on board her again.

CHAPTER SEVEN

Heading South

Leaving the lonely figure of *Sheffield* behind us to wait for the pursuing *Glamorgan* group, *Antrim*, in company with *Plymouth* and RFA *Tidespring*, set sail in the morning bound for the Falklands, but with the more immediate objective of linking up with RFA *Fort Austin*. Last-minute mail was landed, and much to everyone's delight a few more bags were received on board although it was still all a couple of weeks old and none of it was in reply to the mail we had dispatched so hurriedly from Gibaltar on 2 April. There was nothing to acknowledge the fact that we had sailed for a possible war. It was a bit of a low point for us as Ascension Island faded into the distance, and we wondered when or where we would receive mail again.

Because of the influx of further new arrivals, more personal items had to be boxed up or thrown away, as we had to prepare to share our lockers. Even a fine set of Chinese mess crockery and coloured glass fish that Frank Carvelli had brought back from a trip was consigned to the deep, as every possible cubby-hole was cleared to make yet more space – and reduce the time needed to secure for action.

Other preparations were made for war, including taking and storing stocks of blood from as many of the ship's company as possible, to use in emergencies or during battles. I was not asked to provide any, on account of a brief stay in Nelson sickbay, but many did; so many in fact, that Albert Ross the 'baby' caterer, started complaining that his large walk-in fridge had no fresh food left, just piles of polythene bags full of alcohol-steeped blood!

In his evening broadcast, the commander summed up the day's World Service reports, rumours and buzzes, telling us that the white P&O cruise liner *Canberra* had sailed from Southampton, heaving with masses of Royal Marines. Thousands of cheering, crying people had lined the docksides to see her slide away into the Solent and make her way round the Isle of Wight. Some of the dockside females even exposed their breasts to their loved ones on board!

Newspaper reports were also starting to pick up on the fact that whilst the Argentinian army and navy might not present too many problems to the task force, their air force most certainly would. 'Experts' were confident that as they did not have a very good anti-submarine capacity, their fleet would not last long if it stayed at sea, but that with several squadrons of modern fighter jets, their air force could cause us problems because of our lack of long-distance early-warning radar. Ships such as HMS *Salisbury*, an aircraft detection frigate, were unfortunately no longer in commission, and *Salisbury* was, in fact, rusting away in Portsmouth dockyard awaiting sale or disposal. What we really needed was airborne early warning that could detect low-flying enemy aircraft at a distance. One set of reports bolstered our confidence, but the confirmation of our lack of early-warning radar caused us all a great deal of concern.

'Bloody great when we're working with the NATO squadrons and can use her bloody aircraft detection frigates and aircraft,' yelled Rattler Morgan at the TV screen. 'What dozy bastard allowed us to get rid of all our own? Fat lot of use the *Salisbury* is sitting in Pompey – we need the bugger down here now with us!'

I agreed. 'Yeah, lads, I told you they should have kept my old ship *Salisbury*!'

One day away from Ascension Island, our little mini-convoy was clearly the most advanced party of the task force, with *Tidespring*, the slowest of the group, making her maximum speed, flanked on either side by *Antrim* and *Plymouth*. It was still pretty warm, with enough sun to continue tanning our faces, but with each hundred miles south, the temperature got colder. The northern hemisphere was in early spring, heading for summer, whilst the southern hemisphere was in late autumn heading for winter. We knew only too well that we should make the most of the sun at this latitude, because there was not going to be much of it further down in the South Atlantic.

The main bit of enemy action that day, did not actually relate to the Argentinians at all. *Antrim* was buzzed by two large prop-driven spy planes from our old Cold War enemy the Soviet Union! Not that *Antrim* ever showed much respect for the Russians, as four stokers showed when they happened to be on the upper deck as the Russians came thundering past. As they came within about 1,000 yards, they pulled down their dirty overalls and 'mooned' at them!

From the BBC World Service and the commander's broadcast we gathered that the press back home were saying that the main task force was making steady progress (although no position was given), and that as of 0500 this morning, a 200 mile total exclusion zone (TEZ) had been declared around the Falkland Islands. Our submarines, we were told, had even been given permission to sink enemy ships entering it! We doubted whether they would actually be given approval to do this at the moment, when political negotiations were still going on. We were not told exactly what boats were already down south already, or which ones were on their way, but we had heard from the press that *Superb* and *Conqueror* were probably already there. We could not imagine that they would not send a surface task force down without a pack of hungry sub-surface killers to protect it. The only problem with any of our craft though, was that they provided little or no advance air warning.

The press also reported that most of the Argentinian fleet had returned to their base port. These ships, we knew, included such vessels as their only carrier, *Veintencino De Mayo* (25 May – Argentina's independence day), the 1945-vintage, ex-British HMS *Venerable*, their only cruiser *General Belgrano*, ex-US Navy, launched in 1938), seven of its eight destroyers, two of their three frigates, and all its submarines. They were now back in their home ports, leaving only one destroyer and one frigate out at sea.

'Bloody chickens,' screamed Smudge Smith. 'Buggered off before we've even got down there. If I was them, I would bloody stay there too, 'cos if they poke their little greasy heads out again we'll bite the bastards off!'

However, despite the apparent reluctance of the Argentinian navy to stand and fight, their army and air force were keeping busy, with reports of plane-loads of troops being transferred from the mainland to reinforce the islands, and repeated dry-run sorties by their fighter jets. We were not so confident of dealing with their air force, and certainly not at all until our small group had some form of carrier protection. Some on board already felt we had been asked to stick our necks out too far, and the level of anxiety and tension was rising. From the reports back home there was clearly a bit of propaganda going on between the two countries, with a few outlandish claims being made by each side. As with the submarine threat, we appeared to be trying to frighten the life out of them before we arrived, with carefully aimed and massaged military statistics. They, on the other hand, had starting making claims of the first sinking of the war, the red ice-patrol ship, HMS *Endurance*. We were on our way to meet her and knew she was very much still afloat!

We also heard that the large white P&O passenger ship *Uganda* had been requisitioned for use as a hospital ship, probably, because she was already white and would only need a couple of red crosses painted on the side. One hospital ship that would not be joining us however was HM Royal Yacht *Britannia*, which, despite repeated assurances over the years that she would be used in such a role, could no longer be utilized because of 'peculiar fuel requirement's! We felt this was a sham, for if young holidaying kids had to be kicked off a P&O liner, then surely the 'cream of the Royal Navy' should be making her way down here as well. Although most of us were royalists at heart, we could not argue that this decision, for whatever reason, probably broke one of the last straws in the argument for maintaining such a vessel – at least manned by the Royal Navy. And as Chopper Cox so quaintly put it in the galley that night, 'Okay then. If they won't send down the bloody ship because it might cock up the gold paint and shag-pile carpets, fine. Just send the bloody crew down instead on the *Uganda* – useless bunch of brown-nosed, daisy-chaining bastards!'

On Tuesday, 13 April, I did probably the hardest and longest day's work of my entire life. Early in the morning we finally met up with RFA *Fort Austin* and set about transferring every last ounce of munitions, naval stores and food from her holds, leaving her with just enough of each to crawl at slow speed back up to Ascension Island. We thought we had filled the ship up on 3 April, but that was nothing compared to what we took on board that day in order to stretch our endurance even further. Again helping the caterers, like just about everyone else on board that day, I worked flat out right from when we started storing at 0900, to when we finally finished at 0100 the following morning. By that time, we could not take, store or secure any more on board. On the victualling front, we cram-filled all the freezers, fridges and dry stores, then we filled up the petty officer's beer store with flour, filled the senior rates' dining hall with tinned meats and vegetables, and laid false decking sometimes two boxes deep throughout many of the ship's passageways.

Boxes and bags were also wedged behind every ladder with enough space, and into any other small area that could take a few items. We even laid a two-foot layer of boxes in the Sea Slug magazine, which ran almost half the length of the ship. There was gear everywhere, and again a 'clear lower deck' was required to shift the stuff around to its different destinations. I had played a few hard games of rugby in my time, worked tirelessly on a farm during the harvest, and often sweated gallons when storing ship before, but nothing was like this.

As we received gear on board by heavy jackstay from *Fort Austin*, stores were also 'vertrepped' across to speed up the storing. And all the time this enormous undertaking was going on, we continued heading south, whilst *Fort Austin* got lighter and lighter and the three of us all got much, much heavier. Not all the gear arrived on board safely or made it to its storage destination in one piece. On a number occasions, bags split or boxes exploded as they hit the deck or were dropped by tired, aching hands, and I personally saw twenty drums of much-needed frying oil, as well as two far more critical Johnson outboard engines lost overboard, as well as lots of smaller items.

We also welcomed on board more SAS troops, who arrived mysteriously by helicopter from somewhere. I was waiting to receive the next under-slung vertrep load by the hangar, when the troops landed on the flight deck – serious, professional-looking men, extremely focused. On leaving the chopper, they were ushered to join us on the starboard waist to await the arrival of the remainder of their gear on the next flight. We stood around chatting while the aircraft came into distant view, its heavy load of SAS equipment slung below in an enormous net. We exchanged brief hellos and passed general chit-chat, but did not ask them what their mission was. That was obvious to anyone.

Then disaster struck the newly arrived SAS boys. We could see the net swaying violently below the chopper and the aircraft losing stability in the air. 'She won't be able to drop that lot on board here swinging around like that,' muttered one of the 'Wafus' (members of the Fleet Air Arm), 'and if she's not careful the net may catch one of the rotors. I think she'll have to ditch the load!' And he was right too, for despite various manoeuvres to counter the perilously swaying net, the pilot eventually had no option but to let his delivery drop into the sea. There were excited shouts of 'Oh bloody hell. What have we lost this time?' from some onlookers, but when it was pointed out to them that the gear was the SAS's, they shut their mouths pretty quick. It had not been a good day for the new passengers of HMS *Antrim* – first the loss of two outboard engines, and then most of their gear, too.

Shaking their heads but not saying much, the SAS boys were escorted to their various dispersed messes. One, whom we knew only as 'Charlie,' was led down to 1G1 mess, where he turned down the offer of hot-bunking with Taff Bevan. Instead, he pulled a hammock out of his bag, slung it up between two pipes in the mess square, clambered in and went straight to sleep. Nobody dared ask to turn the television on with him snoring away, I can tell you!

With these additional troops on board, groups were sleeping in corridors and dining halls and in mess squares, on camp beds, in hammocks like Charlie, or just in sleeping bags on any bit of spare floor space. As we completed storing and left *Fort Austin* behind, *Antrim* was bursting at the seams with all manner of stores, equipment and men. But there were still some shortages on board, as the boys noticed whenever they visited the NAAFI. 'What, still on bloody nutty rationing are we.'

It was getting noticeably colder outside now and the colour of the sea was changing from tropical blue to a much darker and colder-looking blue-green. Inside the ship, however, the heating was working well, and after being granted a bit of a rest day on the Wedneday because of our exertions, we started to get to know some of the new arrivals. 1G1 now played host to Charlie from the SAS, and three Royal Marines; Ollie Oliver, Artie Shaw and the hardest-looking one of the lot, the same thug who was sharing my bed, 'Robbie Roberts'.

Although one of 3N's chefs had covered some of my night work, I was still pretty exhausted after only a couple of hours sleep in the chief cook's office before breakfast. Nonetheless, once Charlie had unrigged his hammock for the day, I stayed out of my bed long enough to join the four men in khaki and some of our boys in spinning yarns, playing cards and uckers, and supping the odd can of beer. We talked about what might happen from here on in and what they thought *Antrim's* role might me, but even amongst secure company like ours, the 'guests' gave nothing away about future operations, and we asked nothing that we should not have in return. Like all unaccustomed or non-regular seafarers, the new boys were still finding their sea legs in increasingly heavy seas, and many was the time that Charlie or one of the others smashed into a locker or overhead pipe that day, as the cans of beer further loosened their knee joints. Cries went up of, 'Another speed-wobble mate?', 'Want a bucket yet?', 'Go and get your swede down – do you a world of good old mate. You lot might be trained killers, but you aren't used to this bobbin' around like us matelots, are you?'

When the troops were not relaxing in the mess or attending briefings in the wardroom or junior rates' dining hall, we were struck by the amount of time they spent cleaning their equipment – particularly their rifles and pistols. For operational reasons, rather than keep them locked away in the small arms magazine, they kept them alongside their beds – fully loaded. Thankfully they had their safety catches on! There had been no commander's broadcast the day before because of the storing, and the captain, commander and first lieutenant had just individually walked round the ship a few times instead, giving us a hand here and there with the odd box or bag, spurring their men on as good senior naval officers do when there's hard graft to be done on board! So this evening, with all our new arrivals on board, and all the different stories they had brought with them, it was with bated breath that we huddled round our tiny TV screens for the dry, Scottish, second-in-command to speak. Stories of continued political impasse were confirmed, and also confirmed was the fact that we were, by some way now, the farthest south of all the task force. The navy and army were emptying every barracks around the world to meet the looming crisis. Even the RAF were reported as doing all they could to support us, setting up an enormous air-bridge that had now made Ascension Island one of the busiest airports in the world!

The following day saw the unmistakable red shape of HMS *Endurance* as she finally met us, turned around and joined our group heading south in mid-South Atlantic. Following naval tradition for such occasions, a 'clear lower deck' was piped. As many men as possible stood to attention on the upper deck and gave three cheers to her crew, who had only narrowly escaped the Argentinians' clutches. She had been the only naval presence down there when they had attacked, as she had been on and off for year – which is why the Argentinians thought we did not care about the Falkland Islands, and why they thought they could take them without any resistance. A heavy jackstay was again established, but this time it was *Antrim* that supplied the sought-after stores. And the crew members who had been captured ashore by the Argentinians only two weeks before were now rejoining their ship to go and get their own back.

We received the news that increasing political gloom had now prompted the prime minister to approve the second (or what we considered to be the third) wave of task force ships. This group of thirty vessels would apparently include HMS *Intrepid* (rescued from the reserve fleet), and a large civilian container ship called *Atlantic Conveyor*. A signal came through, confirming that *Antrim*'s group's first objective was to recover South Georgia, and that to help us achieve this a decoy group of five other ships had been sent towards the Falkland Islands themselves.

'Shit,' I thought. 'The politicians can't sort it out, so we're going to have to sort it out for them.'

I felt a shiver of adrenalin and a heightened awarenes – just as I would before a big rugby game or a fight. I now wanted to make sure I was prepared – not scared, just very, very prepared. We were now only 1,000 miles from South Georgia, and for the Argentinians on that island, the grains of sand in their hourglass were running out. *Antrim*, *Plymouth*, *Endurance* and *Tidespring* and all our embarked forces were coming to start smashing the glass out of their hands.

On Friday, 16 April our small task force completed its very last NBCDX in preparation for the impending attack. We had carried out many such exercises in the past, especially during work-ups at Portland, and during large exercises like Springtrain. But the ones we had been conducting on this trip had a definite extra edge to them, because although we knew they were still exercises, we also knew the sand in our glass was running out too. Soon the time for exercising would be over.

The final NBCDX involved taking the ship to action stations around 0700, then staying closed up until the completion of 'action messing' at about 1400. During that time, the ship exercised as many different battle scenarios as the planning team thought necessary under the circumstances. And it did not just involve methods of attack. We practised all forms of tracking and spotting, evasion and weapon-deflection, damage control, search and rescue, first-aid drills and medical evacuations. We also practised firing our guns and using our other weapon systems, until the ship's company had beaten off every conceivable type of assault, repaired every possible type of battle damage, and survived to devour a well-deserved 'pot-mess' and totally resecure, ready to fight the next attackers. Of course, it was only an exercise. Some things went right and some things went pretty wrong, but important lessons were learned all round as *Antrim*'s team knitted closer and closer together in preparation for the ultimate challenge.

In the afternoon, on a whim, I tried to transfer to HMS *Endurance*. My 'B13' for advancement to petty officer was long overdue. I was getting fed up with chopping meat and catching bread rolls, and I wanted something more meaningful to do. However, the supply officer turned my request down flat, and with hindsight I was glad he did, because although I felt I could have filled a vacant position on *Endurance* quite easily, looking at the way she rolled around in the sea I probably would not have been able to spend much time out of the heads!

The commander's broadcast that day further heightened the tension by repeating some of the news from the BBC World Service and signals from home. Argentina's fleet had apparently sailed from the naval base of Puerto Belgrano, 425 miles south of Buenos Aires, in direct defiance of Britain's blockade. A Ministry of Defence spokesman had grimly said in response to this news, 'We are not playing games now. This is not an exercise!' We also received news that the main task force had reached Ascension Island.

Antrim's South Georgia task force continued to forge her way south, in ever darker, heavier and colder seas. There was certainly not enough sun left to tan us any longer, and as our skin colours gradually returned to normal, upper-deck crews increasingly added layers of clothing. The food we were eating was also changing, continuing the evolution that had started after leaving Gibraltar and then Ascension Island, and then finally after storing off *Fort Austin*. With each day, stocks of fresh foods diminished and then ran out. All that was left were frozen, tinned and dry items as we increasingly tried to cut back consumption and stretch our endurance.

Food was on its way down with the main Task Force, but what there was would have to supply a lot of ships and a lot of men, so our requirements had to be kept to the bare minimum. Storing ship also involved compacting convoys and shipping groups in order to transfer stores, which reduced speed and manoeuvrability and increased the risk of detection and attack. The menus now comprised:

Breakfast   One sausage, one fried egg and a large spoonful of baked beans or a tinned tomato, one bread roll, butter, jam or marmalade, tea and coffee

Lunch   My 'soup of the night' and two bread rolls

Supper   Three choices of main meal, mashed, boiled or baked potatoes, three types of tinned, frozen or de-hydrated vegetables, assorted tinned fruits and home-made sweets.

Strict portion control was also exercised by the cooks, with all serving utensils now in their hands rather than with the lads on the other side of the counter. Breakfast cereals were taken off the menu, not because we had run out, but to conserve milk powder. The cereals were used to make sweets. Breakfast specials were also removed to conserve stocks.

Lunch was most affected by the cutbacks. Out went the range of courses normally provided, and in its place came just soup and two bread rolls. Supper was also pared back to conserve stocks, and was most notable for its almost complete lack of fresh ingredients. On top of all these cutbacks, chips and all deep fried food had to be removed from the menu, in order to reduce the need for deep fat fryers and the resultant risk of accidental or battle-damage fires. The longer the voyage progressed, the fewer fresh vegetables and salad remained on board, and soon only minimal stocks of fresh potatoes and eggs remained. The potatoes could eventually be replaced by tinned or powdered alternatives, but eggs would be a problem. As a result, each egg was treated with tender loving care by the caterers and chefs, who stood by anyone in the dining hall who left one half eaten on the side of his metal platter. There were many others who would have quickly reprimanded them for their callous waste.

Strangely enough, the ship's company did not take too unkindly to these 'endurance-stretching' measures, for they obviously realized that we had a lot of extra mouths to feed and a long way to go to the nearest shop. We still received some of the normal sarcastic remarks, but generally the lads took to the new diet quite peaceably. The revised menu was, of course, much easier for us to prepare, and had the added bonus of reducing the cleaning tasks within the galley, which in turn helped keep this normally difficult compartment much better secured, not only for sea, but also for action.

One last bonus of the new diet was felt in the chief caterer's financial barometer. The balance, which one would normally expect to dive into the red at sea (but recover alongside) began to rise rapidly. And paradoxically, as we passed latitude 50 degrees south and became eligible for additional cold-weather allowances, we had even less food to give the crew.

News came in that Prince Andrew was a co-pilot on board one of *Invincible*'s Sea King helicopters, and that the queen wanted him to be treated in exactly the same way as his shipmates. More realistically and significantly, we heard that some of the eighty Royal Marines captured at Port Stanley were now on their way to join ships heading south again!

Apart from the RO's communications room and senior officers' fraternity, our only contact with the outside world in the mess decks was still the BBC World Service. With its distinctive title music, it was virtually all we had left to remind us of home. No mail, no phones, no television, no papers, nothing – just the BBC World Service, whose broadcasters read reports in clipped BBC English, and were possibly wearing the same evening attire they had always worn. Mock them as we did, their unique voices from a bygone age provided increasingly important lifelines to the real world.

On Sunday, 18 April we were informed that a task unit had broken away from the main task force and was heading south at top speed. HMS *Arrow*, HMS *Brilliant*, HMS *Coventry*, HMS *Glasgow* and HMS *Sheffield* were coming to help us sort the Argentinians out – if *Antrim* could not do it on her own!

The biggest news that circulated round the ship that day concerned the additional personal allowances we were being paid whilst at sea. At the time, the navy paid its ships' crews varying allowances according to the cost of living in their last port of call. For instance, you got nothing extra after leaving the UK, but once you touched foreign soil, the allowance started, and stayed at that level until you reached the next port, and so on. It was a simple system which we all understood, and more importantly at that time, had been banking on collecting at the end of our time away, whenever that would be. But the shocking news that now reached us was that instead of the extra £2.50 or so we were getting per day, we were now going to get the equivalent of the Northern Ireland allowance of only £1 a day! 'Bastards! What a bunch of tight-arsed bastards,' screamed one of the stokers, Dinger Bell, when he read the official signal on the main noticeboard, 'What a brass neck they've got, the bastards. What's up? Have they run out of money already? I bet the civil servants and all the other civvy buggers back home are raking in the overtime while this lot's going on – and they chop our bastard pay while we're out here fightin' their bloody war for 'em – I'm not havin' that, the bastards no bloody way am I havin' that!!'

He was not alone. Several people, myself including, went to see their divisional officer to make verbal representations that day. He in turn saw the first lieutenant, who in turn saw the commander and the captain. But there was absolutely nothing that any of them could do. The powers that be in Whitehall had made their decision, and that was it. A more detailed explanation was eventually sent down from London, explaining that it was fairer for all the task force to be on the same extra allowance rates. We partially understood the logic behind it, but the way it was just thrown into our laps when we were just about to fight for queen and country was, to say the very least, extremely poor and thoroughly insensitively timed.

The following day, we finally completed our work-up and shake-down preparations, and from 0800 the entire ship's company changed from working normal sea watches to full defence watches. So instead of most people working only days, with some working nights and others watch-keeping, we were now all defence watch-keeping. Clocks were brought forward to Greenwich Mean Time, five hours ahead of the local time, in order to maximize every possible hour of daylight, and also to avoid any confusion with operational orders from the UK. Breakfast was served at 0700–0800, which was 1200–1300 local time. As a result, the bulk of the ship's early-morning preparations could be completed before sunrise instead of after it.

To the existing three meals a day, a fourth was added at midnight, so that no matter what hours a person was working, he could always attend at least two meals in any 24 hour period, during the watch change-overs. Under this sytem, the ship's company was divided into four watches, so that the ship could be held at a maximum state of readiness at all times. Most were roughly six hours long, so that at any one time one watch was on watch, the one they were relieving were going off watch and could go to bed, the third watch could be in bed, and the fourth could be getting up, washed and changed and ready to go on watch again. For us non-watch keepers it took some getting used to: not only learning when we had to turn to and secure, but also when the optimum time was to get our heads down. As it was now too cold and dark to go on the upper deck, it was getting very easy to lose all track of day and night.

As a result of going into defence watches, other changes of routine took place. So as not to disturb anyone's sleep, 'pipes' could only be made during watch change-overs, and social activities in all messes ground to a halt, as inevitably there was always someone in bed trying to get some sleep. NAAFI opening and several other administrative and service times also changed, and between watch changes the ship began to take on an eerie silence, as we crept ever further towards South Georgia. The days of exercising and clearing the ship ready for action were at an end. HMS *Antrim* was now as ready as we felt she could possibly be for war!

With perfect timing, the day after the transition to defence watches, on Tuesday, 20 April, *Antrim* and her group had their first real action stations. Without warning, the ship's main broadcast blurted out the deafening, nerve-jangling, claxon-type alarm, and the entire ship's company charged from all corners of the ship to their action stations. The on watch were of course already closed up, but the other three watches were in various states of sleep or, dress. It did not matter; our lives depended on being where we should be in the fastest possible time.

Antrim and *Plymouth* had both detected incoming 'bleeps' on their ships' radar screens, and had both sounded their alarms simultaneously, fearing a dreaded Exocet attack. Both ships' helicopters took off immediately but failed to substantiate the claims any further, so we were quickly stood down. I think all our minds and bodies had been tested, every single one of us; all the sailors in our little task force, all the civvies on the RFA, all the tough boot necks, even our friends in the SAS. Coming under possible military attack for the first time, especially in the claustrophobic atmosphere of a ship, is an experience one never forgets. It still makes my heart race with excitement just thinking of it all these years later.

As well as the obvious air threat, we were increasingly worried about submarine attacks. There were dangers both above and below the waves. As if all that was not enough to keep us occupied, to make matters far, far worse, the weather that day was the most violent I was ever to experience at sea – a horrendous storm force 11! The waves were taller than blocks of flats, and the sea-filled air battered the ship with 90 miles per hour wind. We were all suffering from a lack of sleep and, a large number of men were throwing up. There were also the defence watches and the threat of air and submarine attack, and finally, the ship's alarm when we least expected it. We were not only at war with the Argentinians, we were also at war with the full force of nature!

Besides all those challenges, some of our poor embarked forces on board also had to make final preparations for reconnaissance missions on South Georgia in the morning. There they would also have to face the viciousness of an early South Atlantic winter and, for the first time during our attempt to recapture the Falkland Islands, the enemy as well.

The next time I switched off my bunk light, I began to think about what it might be like if *Antrim* was ever badly hit in these seas, how we would need to react to save the ship from sinking. Instinctively, my thoughts flashed back to the two chilling training exercises at Shotley Barracks and Chatham, where, to prepare us for this ultimate eventuality at sea, we had fought to save our lives inside a damage control tank, a large metal coffin, which floods with torrents of ice-cold water, and is known quite simply in naval circles as 'the tank'.

CHAPTER EIGHT

The Tank

My first encounter with a damage control tank was at HMS *Ganges* in March 1976, during my basic training. The tank was actually designed to simulate a sinking ship and contained the kinds of damage we might experience in such a catastrophe. All we had to do was stop the water pouring through the shattered sections, and save the 'ship' from sinking. Dressed in our navy blue overalls and freshly cleaned white plimsoles, the class of thirty was split in three and hustled, one group at a time, into the tank.

Measuring about 3 yards square, it was full of jagged mock-ups of shell blasts and perforated overhead pipes, and had no lights. One tiny round window or 'scuttle' in the door provided the only illumination and view of the outside world. We were already shivering as the door slammed and locked shut, but when a loud external explosion shook the tank to its foundations and ice-cold water started gushing in, our senses froze with shock and went haywire. The water streamed in from every conceivable angle, blasting us with great icy torrents. At first it completely took our breath away, but then the banging and screaming intensified from outside, as the staff all roared in unison, 'COME ON – GET THEM BLOODY HOLES SHORED UP! COME ON, MOVE IT YOU LAZY BASTARDS OR THE SHIP'S GONNA SINK – AND YOU'RE ALL GONNA DIE!'

Unable to see much because of the lack of light and jets of water, we nonetheless scrambled around in the canvas damage control bags for wooden pegs, wedges and anything else we could grab hold of to bung in a hole or split pipe – ten lads, scared out of their minds, tripping over each other, desperately trying to stop the water, which felt as though it was ripping off great layers of flesh, such was its awful temperature and force. We tried banging square pegs in gashes, and wedges in splits. In sheer desperation we wrapped our hands and bodies around holes – but it was still no good, the water just poured in.

Up and up it went, deeper and colder than before, inch by inch, until it lifted the smaller men off their feet and was licking at the underside of my chin. Then thankfully the water was turned off and our instructor's familiar white-hatted face was at the scuttle bellowing, 'See what happens to ye if ye cannot stop the water? Ye bloody droon!' As we gripped the back three sides wherever we could, the door was then wrenched open and a tidal wave of water, rope, blocks and mallets swept outside and left us standing stunned, and literally drained.

At Ganges, the tank had been a dreaded part of the six-week basic training programme, and we were fully aware of the date and time we would be visiting it. Unfortunately, at HMS *Pembroke* in February 1979, I had no prior warning of an exercise in the tank whatsoever! I was on the very final day of an exhausting six-month leading catering accountant's course, and only found out about the tank twenty minutes before they switched the water on!

The night before, a mate, John Norman, and I had caught the train down to Margate for a last night's leaving run. We got on the wrong train, and only just arrived at the main gate in time to avoid being adrift. It was snowing heavily, and we were both suffering from bad hang-overs, but we did not care because it was our last day and all we had to crack was a bit of boring NBCD.

The taxi dropped us off at the gate and we ran the 200 yards back to our cabins to get changed, passing other men who were going in the opposite direction to the NBCD school.

'Don't forget to bring your towels,' they yelled.

'Towels? What bloody towels?' we thought. 'What do we need towels for in a warm classroom in the middle of winter?'

Quickly getting changed, and grabbing towels without quite knowing why, we sprinted back down the road, arriving at the school just in the nick of time. We left the towels under our chairs and sat there listening to the fat, boring chief stoker lecturing us for two hours. Feeling more than a bit weak-headed after the trip to Margate, it was an immense struggle for John and me to keep ourselves awake, and we used our tried and tested routine of prodding each other with rulers now and again to preserve some alertness.

Ten o'clock arrived, and I thought, 'Another two hours and we'll be getting taxis back to the station.' Then the chief stoker announced, 'Right then, lads, go and have a fag break for fifteen minutes. Meet me back in the changing room with some overalls and your Wellington boots on.' We wondered what we needed wellies for in a classroom. This must be a wind up, surely. All the lads there had been in the Navy long enough to realize that practical jokes were part and parcel of naval life. These were the last two hours of our time at *Pembroke* and we could smell a joke coming up.

Playing along with the 'little game' we finished our break, got

changed and took our seats in the changing room, waiting for the chief
stoker to reappear. 'Right lads,' he shouted as he entered the room. He
was also dressed in overalls, but with the addition of a pullover and
heavy foul-weather jacket, 'Some of you have been struggling to stay
awake in here this morning, haven't you? Well, to keep you awake for
the next hour, you're now going outside to do the tank!'

'You mean you've got a bloody tank in this place?' I thought. 'We did
the tank at Ganges, they said we would never have to do it again.' Our
looks of horror and incredulity said it all. We hardly breathed a word
as we went outside into the falling snow like prisoners in a Siberian
gulag, and there 50 yards away, black, rusting and menacing was a tank,
just like the one at Ganges – only this one had its own water supply
stored in another tank on top. We just could not believe this was
happening and kept looking around expecting one of our former
instructors to peer out of a snow-covered bush or photographers to
come flying overhead. But nothing happened and soon we were inside
the tank, absolutely freezing and shaking our heads in utter disbelief.

'Fail to stop the water by the time it reaches the height of your
shoulder, Lofty, and you can all do it again.'

As at Ganges, without any warning, massive thunderflash explosions
shook the rusting steel structure to its core and torrents erupted from
every jagged hole or split pipe, completely shrouding us in icy cold
water. It might still have been a wind up, but we were not laughing any
more.

It was so cold in the tank there was no way that eight of us could stop
any of the leaks. We shielded our eyes and wrapped arms and legs
around pipes, but at the rate the tentacles of liquid ice were rising, there
was clearly no point in exerting ourselves. The water swiftly rose to my
waist, to my midriff, to my shoulders – and then the water stopped and
the chief stoker's face glared through the 18 inch porthole.

'Right, you dopey bunch of lazy bastards! You weren't even bloody
trying! So let's run it again, shall we? Hang onto something, stand clear,
open the door.'

The water rushed out in one enormous tidal wave, turning the 6 inch
deep snow outside into a massive pool of slush. Then the door was shut
again and we stood there like eight punch-drunk boxers on our last
legs, waiting for the knockout punch. It soon came. More deafening
explosions and the water was turned back on. This time, adrenalin
flowed and we did stop at least some of the leaks, but the water kept on
coming and coming and coming, up to my midriff again, then past my
shoulders. The smaller lads were doggy-paddling, and the water was
up to my chin. We were all thrashing our arms and legs and screaming,
'Switch the bloody water off.' My head was bent sideways against the

twisted deckhead. I was gasping for air. Others were gurgling. The water stopped – only 4 inches left. Thank God.

We found out why we needed our towels, but the twisted chief stoker had gone by the time we had showered and thawed out, and we never saw him again, nor did we find out why we had to do the tank at all. If it had been a wind-up, at least the perpetrator had the sense to make himself scarce when we came out!

Neither tank had been an enjoyable experience, and the freezing cold water had made it even harder at that time of the year. But, we had learned some pretty vital lessons. It is incredibly hard to stop water entering a ship through split pipes and jagged holes. The cold sends you into an immediate state of shock, and the rapidly rising water gives you very little time to react before the ship capsizes and sinks. Back in my warm *Antrim* bed, I wondered how we might cope in the South Atlantic if we hit an iceberg or were damaged by enemy action. The water down here was going to be a lot colder than at Shotley Barracks or Chatham, and there would be nobody to switch off the water when it rose above our shoulders. I crossed my fingers and hoped that we would never have to face a real tank in these waters.

CHAPTER NINE

South Georgia

At 1145 on Wednesday, 21 April, sixteen of our SAS colleagues were landed ashore at a place called 'Fortuna Glacier' on South Georgia by helicopter, in weather that was absolutely appalling. The previous day's storm was still churning the Southern Ocean, and on land the driving snow and howling winds made conditions almost impossible to imagine. Our admiration went out to the SAS in the task they were undertaking – trying to remain undetected in that terrible environment and yet still gather vital information about Argentinian troop positions. It must have tested even the hardest troopers, and in 1G1 mess, our thoughts were all with Charlie. We wondered where he would hitch his hammock, if at all, that night. For the rest of the day, *Antrim* and her group remained out of visual contact with South Georgia, which was not too difficult because of the continuing storm and blizzard conditions. However, we were still very conscious of the threat of air, submarine, and even possibly land-based missile attack, so we were all ready to go to action stations at a moment's notice and, with the important lessons of the previous day learned, even faster and more effectively than ever before. We felt like sprinters in their starting blocks, knowing the gun is going to go off at any second. And there were even false starts too!

When 'pipes' are made on board, a button is pressed on the mouthpiece for the broadcaster to speak. Normally, this barely audible click was not noticed, and certainly never prompted the ship's company to pay attention to any forthcoming announcement. Now, however, that tiny click was the sound we dreaded most of all, each time thinking it would precede the ship's alarm. Times when we heard it and then a longer than momentary pause, now became times when most people were already tugging their anti-flash hoods over their heads and diving towards their action stations. Our trigger-sharp mentality meant we were now always ready to react, no matter what time of day or night it was. In the interests of collective survival, any slackness in our securing for sea and action had completely disappeared. All loose items or equipment were immediately resecured after use to avoid creating dangerous hazards or exacerbate any possible battle damage. Our work-up since Gibraltar, and the continual driving by officers, senior rates and mess-mates, and then the first real action stations had taught us all these lessons, and we knew that some day soon they might save the ship – and our lives.

The commander's briefing that evening described in greater detail what our immediate objectives were, where the SAS had landed and what their mission was. He drove home the message yet again of the different attack threats and the critical need for supreme vigilance and reactions at all times. There was little news from home. Political measures had been virtually exhausted, and apart from the obvious concerns over the task force's progress and safety, we appeared to have reached the lull before the storm. We were also informed that there were believed to be thirteen scientists of the British Antarctic Survey held captive in Grytviken. Two British females, Cindy Buxton and Annie Price, were also somewhere else on South Georgia. They had apparently been making a nature programme for Anglia TV when the Argentinians invaded, and were now in hiding somewhere on the island. Cindy was alleged to have been a former girlfriend of Prince Charles.

The following morning, again very early, Royal Marine Special Boat Squadron (SBS) men were landed ashore by helicopter from HMS *Endurance*. Clearly plans were moving forward and things seemed to be going well. But then later in the morning, developments took a turn for the worse when our own SAS troops radioed for help from the side of Fortuna Glacier, where they had been reconnoitring Leith Harbour, Stromness Island and Grass Island. They had spent the night in extremely cold conditions and now feared their lives were at risk due to hypothermia.

Three helicopters took part in the rescue: our Wessex 3 (Humphrey), and two Wessex 5 aircraft from RFA *Tidespring*, which had apparently been built on the way south from kits delivered at Ascension Island! The violent blizzard was still raging across the stark snow-covered mountainous peaks of South Georgia. In the near-zero visibility the choppers were unable to trace them, and returned to refuel. On the second attempt however, the SAS troops *were* located and the three aircraft landed and picked them all up. But then rescue turned to disaster in the brutal whiteout conditions when one of the kit helicopters crashed into the glacier shortly after take-off. Fortunately, there were no fatalities, and the only notable injury suffered was by one of the SAS men, who received a small cut on his forehead. Humphrey and the remaining Wessex 5 landed again, shared the survivors out between their two craft, and took off again. But once more disaster struck, when shortly after take off, the other Wessex 5 also crashed into the glacier. Fortunately again, however, the occupants of this second crash were extremely lucky, although the same SAS trooper received another cut on his forehead – this time completing the figure of a cross.

With two helicopters down, Humphrey returned to *Antrim* alone. Because of the continuing bad weather conditions, she was not able to launch a rescue bid until 1630, when on her second mission she was fortunate (and the men extremely brave and skilled) enough to pick up all the remaining SAS and aircrew from the two previous crashes in just one very heavily overloaded flight. All the time the rescue was going on, we held our breath, hoping above impossible hope that nobody had been killed and that everyone would return safely. Like all the other rescued personnel, and particularly the SAS who had spent a frozen night on the glacier, Charlie had been pretty badly knocked about, and after being checked out by the medical officer in the sickbay, he staggered exhausted and shivering back into the mess. We were almost speechless when he dumped his kit by the side of the uckers table. What do you say to someone who's just three times escaped the freezing jaws of death?

'How are you, Charlie mate? You look bloody freezin' you bastard. Here lads, give Charlie a hand to get his wet gear off and get warmed up. Want a mug of tea, Charlie? I'll nip up and get a pot from the wardroom pantry.'

'Cheers boys, I did not think I had ever see your ugly faces again after what happened last night and this morning. Boy, could I murder a cup of your pusser's tea alright!'

Charlie tugged his wet and freezing clothes off and put on all sorts of 'donations' instead, then we wrapped sleeping bags around him as he sat, slowly thawing, drinking steaming mugs of rich, dark, sweet liquid. Hot food and soup was also rustled up, which he demolished with the ease of a terribly cold and starving man who was thankful to be alive. He could not reveal everything his team had been up to ashore, but he did give a graphic account of how bitterly cold it was and what it felt like to be in two helicopter crashes on a frozen glacier.

The rescue was the only topic of conversation that day, as all around the ship messdecks received their SAS guests back into their folds – and made even more room for *Tidespring*'s two aircrews. We did not need pulling together as a ship's company: *Antrim*'s steely *esprit de corps* over the past weeks and months had done that already, bonding us all together as one tight fighting unit. But the rescue now gave us a real sense of purpose and focus. We were now totally immersed in the war, and with all our embarked forces included, the bonding glue was setting rock hard.

As if this heroic saga was not enough, the following day the SAS gave us a curtain call of almost equal drama! Unbelievably, the very same men made their way ashore again very early that morning, about 0400 – this time though, through lack of sufficient helicopters, by rubber Geminis. Unfortunately, on the way ashore, through post-stormy but still very heavy seas, two of their five outboard engines broke down. That was the last news we heard of the attempt that day, but again it dominated all our thoughts as, for the second time in forty-eight hours, we held our breath for our SAS shipmates. The news from home was also not very cheerful, it sounded as if all attempts to find a political solution were now evaporating fast. We were still in defence watches, still being tossed around in freezing, stormy seas, and still under threat of attack. This threat came mainly from submarines, one of which, the Guppy Class *Santa Fe*, we now understood might be operating around South Georgia. So little signs appeared on all doors and hatches, with the black silhouettes of submarines and the words, 'SHUT QUIETLY' in big red letters. The political fight might be near an end, but we wondered who would throw the first punch in our more dangerous fight, and with the worries about our SAS friends, they were not thoughts to inspire sweet dreams!

At the crack of dawn on Saturday, 24 April, Humphrey and her crew were again called to rescue two members of the SAS, who were apparently swimming back to the ship. One of them was our Charlie! Once successfully recovered, he staggered back into the mess in an even worse state than before. So we once more refuelled his battered and freezing body, and wrapped him up with every spare sleeping bag we could find. And despite defence watches, there was nobody asleep in 1G1 mess when Charlie told us his story.

Just after three in the morning, we got kitted up in our wet suits and the rest of our gear, and in almost total darkness, clambered into our five Geminis, to be lowered over the side by crane. The sea was pretty rough so we had to hang on for dear life as we trailed each other in a long snaking line towards a place called Grass Island. We were making pretty good pace and had gone about 3 miles, when our motor packed in. We tried restarting it, but the fuckin' thing just would not bite, so we hitched a tow from one of the other boats. Then a second engine packed in and a second tow was established. We began to look like a string of sausages! At that stage the operation was not exactly going to plan, but then it got a whole lot worse when our towrope parted! And this time we had to be cast adrift to let the others try and get ashore on their own without us hampering them any further.

We knew from the briefings beforehand, which way the tide was running – away from the islands – so we thought we might as well just

lie-up at sea until the morning and then radio for help. It was fuckin'
freezin' and it was still bloody rough in the little rubber boat, but we
managed to stay undetected and not give the game away. Just before the
sun came up we felt we had given the others plenty of time to get ashore,
so we contacted the ship for assistance. Once we knew the chopper was
close enough, we had to make sure that the boat was not discovered afterwards, so there was only one thing for it. We could not risk sitting there
like holiday-makers waiting for a bus, so we lit our orange distress flares,
slashed the boat and slid into the water!

We carried on slashing the boat until it sunk, and then started swimming back in the direction of the ship, waving the flares. It was bloody
cold and rough as a bastard, but we had to keep swimming to keep warm
– otherwise we would freeze to death or drown, even with our wet suits
on. The weather was bloody shit too, but we carried on swimming for ages
until that chopper of yours came and got us, and winched us up quick as
a flash – no sweat. Bit of a close call though lads. We really thought we
had had it this time.

We could hardly believe what this young giant of a man was telling us.
The day after coming so close to death three times on a frozen glacier,
Charlie and his mate had spent the night in the South Atlantic in a little
rubber boat, risking their own lives to save the mission. And he was now
sitting in front of us describing the adventure as just a 'close call'! After
that, we started calling him 'Charlie the cat with only five lives left'! That
evening, the news from the rest of Charlie's mates was much better.
They had apparently established a safe recce position on Grass Island
in Stromness Bay, overlooking Leith Harbour.

As our other guests returned from their mid-morning briefings, news
spread like wildfire around the ship; it had finally been confirmed that
Antrim's task force, shortly to be joined by HMS *Brilliant*, would begin
the British fight-back the next morning by attempting to recover South
Georgia. The assault would be called Operation Paraquat – after a
particularly aggressive weedkiller sold in all the best gardening centres!

'Here we go boys,' whispered Shady Lane excitedly, so as not to
disturb those asleep. 'As usual, the bloody politicians have failed again,
so we've got to go in and sort their bloody mess out for 'em. Bloody
typical that bastard!'

And as if this news was not enough to keep our minds occupied, we
also encountered an unidentified vessel when we were in total radar
silence. The main broadcast gave its distinctive little 'click' and within
three minutes we were all closed up at action stations and ready to sink
the foreigner. Fortunately, a star shell or two was fired and it turned out
to be *Plymouth*! This was a very close call and could easily have resulted
in a 'blue on blue' engagement!

After that bit of excitement, our embarked forces went on making their final preparations for the next day's landing. In 1G1 mess we watched Charlie and the three 'booties' strip down their weapons for the last time before they might use them for real.

'How ya feelin' boys? You okay? Ready to go and kick some Argy arse, are ya boys?'

'Oh we're bloody ready all right Frank,' replied Robbie, as always speaking for his two barrel-cleaning 'bootneck' chums. 'We've been lookin' forward to this bastard since the moment we got told we was comin' down here. We're bloody ready for those wankers alright. We'll teach them a bloody lesson for making our mates look like a bunch of doughnuts in Port Stanley and Grytviken.' Charlie did not say anything. He just sat there cleaning his gear and packing it away tightly in his bag. As we had already discovered, Charlie did not need to sound tough, like the other three!

As the rest of the day wore on and more briefings followed and more time was spent chatting quietly in the mess square, the conversation about the impending attack opened up even further.

'Bring us back a souvenir, will ya, Robbie.'

'Yeah, bring us one back too, will ya, mate.'

'And me too Robbie.'

'Don't worry lads. There'll be plenty of souvenirs for all the extra rations you've given us, no problem. What do you want, a shirt, boots, helmet, bayonet, hat, gun – or what about something a bit more tasty like an ear or a finger!'

'Just a helmet will do me Robbie,' I chipped in, scratching my own cauliflowered ear. 'I see enough blood already, chopping up meat in the galley!'

Charlie again just sat there quietly. Deep into one of my old Sven Hassel books, he seemed like a man without a care in the world, while the three 'booties' were now laying bets on who would shoot the most Argentinians in South Georgia!

Sunday began as we had now become accustomed to on *Antrim*: breakfast straddling the watch changeover by half an hour each side, everyone washed or showered, and the ship fully secured for action by 0800 – which was only 0500 local time. However, the routine differed because we knew we would be going to action stations before commencing the landings, so nobody got their head down – not properly anyway.

The captain spoke to the ship's company at 0815, and gave us all a final briefing on what was planned for the day, and how he expected us to react. In his crisp, clear, senior naval officer's broadcasting tones, he then ended his speech by saying, 'I know I don't need to hoist Nelson's famous signal for the men of this ship, or our embarked forces, to let you know what you have to do today – I *know* you will all do your duty as the country expects.'

With most pulses racing, ten minutes later, without any 'click' or alarm, HMS *Antrim* and her task force of HMS *Brilliant*, HMS *Plymouth*, HMS *Endurance* and RFA *Tidespring* went to action stations, not in re-active mode as before, but ready to launch Britain's first counter-attack of the Falklands War!

Humphrey was detailed to fly the first planned reconnaissance, but due to some last minute mechanical problems, took off a few minutes late and ended up flying a different course from the one originally planned. It was as well she did, because otherwise she might have missed the *Santa Fe*, which was leaving South Georgia on the surface having landed reinforcements. Much sooner than expected, the counter-attack had begun!

Humphrey swept in to attack, but being armed only with depth charges on that occasion instead of torpedoes, the damage she was able to inflict was relatively minimal. However, it was significant enough to prevent the *Santa Fe* from diving; instead, she was forced to head for cover closer to the shore. The other reason, we were later informed that the *Santa Fe* had not dived, was because her commander had observed that the next wave of helicopters *were* armed with torpedoes, and had he dived then it might have been for his last time!

The choppers that the commander had detected approaching, from *Brilliant*, *Endurance* and *Plymouth*, swept in like a flock of vultures over the next hour, to peck away at the boat and eventually cause enough damage to stop her diving completely. She managed to return some small-arms fire from her conning tower, but once close enough to Grytviken, the attack ceased as she limped slowly into the old whaling station at King Edward Point. As this news was announced on board, excited cheers rippled around the fleet; our first Argentinian aggressor had been stopped in its tracks.

We were ready now for the next stage of the operation – the landings themselves. This was no D Day or Iwo Jima, but our thoughts were with the troops who from 1415 were packed into Humphrey and Brilliant's two Lynx aircraft and flown in waves to land at carefully selected points on the outskirts of Grytviken and King Edward Point as our invasion force of only seventy-five SAS, SBS and Royal Marines troops made their way ashore. On board, there was nothing we could do but stay at maximum readiness, and listen to the operations room broadcasts.

Like the vast majority of men on board, I had been at my action station below decks during the first action, so like them I had to rely on the operations room commentary to keep track of events and try to visualize what was happening up top. My action messing role on board gave me licence to wander wherever I liked above or below decks, so I decided to try and find a better vantage point to see the next round of Operation Paraquat.

'Just nipping up the bridge with Albatross to check they're all right for hot drinks and No. 3s, Chief.'

'Okay, Rowdy. Check the section bases on your way up, will you?' Albert and I grabbed a full 5 gallon urn of coffee between us by its thin metal handles, and started the long trek past the midship's section base, along the main passage way, past the for'ard section base, and on up the several flights of ladders to the bridge. On the way there, we lightened our load by topping up the section base urns, and also got a good feel for the way the men were reacting to the events going on outside.

'Bloody good news so far, Sir, eh?'

'There you are, Chief, told you they'd run a bloody mile when they saw us coming.'

' Hey, Bungy, you fat bastard, that's three tins you owe me – I said we'd strike the first blow. Give 'em to me later though mate, I'm too busy to drink 'em now!'

Each person we saw on our way to the bridge was obviously happy with the early success, but there was also uncertainty and fear in people's eyes, too – the only part of their faces we could see because of their increasingly dirty anti-flash hoods. We were all learning the age-old problem of fighting wars from the confines of the lower decks. It is terrible not knowing what is going on up top – terrible wondering when something may crash through the ship's side and rip you to pieces. Not being able to hear the outside world also added to the almost spooky atmosphere. We below decks began to get the feeling that black-hooded demons of death might suddenly pop out of the next cupboard.

Albert and I finally arrived at our destination, and in traditional naval fashion sought approval to step on the bridge before climbing the last short flight of steps,

'Permission to enter the bridge, Sir,' I called out to the officer of the watch.

'Permission granted, Leading Caterer. Come on up Rowdy,' whispered the young lieutenant, whom I knew from the rugby team.

'*Plymouth*'s just about to open fire, so you've picked a good time to arrive. Any NAAFI No. 3 biscuits with you?'

The bridge was a hive of activity. The captain sat in his large high chair in the centre, raising and lowering his binoculars, and calling out instructions to the various officers, senior rates and junior rates sitting or standing in their allocated bridge positions. I recognized most of them from the eyes I saw peering out from their hoods, or from names or other distinguishing marks on their anti-flash gear or No. 8s. But I knew better than to engage in conversation with any of them, as they were all far too busy going about their various tasks of navigating the ship, coordinating courses and communicating with the operation room and wheelhouse below, not to mention interacting with their counterparts on the other ships as well.

Albert passed over the small brown paper bag of assorted NAAFI No. 3's to the bosun's mate, and we both made our way onto the port bridge wing where, looking aft, we could clearly see *Plymouth* trailing in our wake, with her 4.5 inch gun trained to port, ready to fire the first naval gunfire support (NGS) salvo.

I knew from my time on *Salisbury* and *Antrim* that NGS is not just a case of pointing your gun and firing. All sorts of computerized and analogue calculations are made to process information regarding range and position, and then to counter the moving platform that a ship at sea provides.

On *Salisbury*, I had even been inside the 4.5 gun during a live firing exercise, and seen how the last stage of the firing process, the physical loading of the shells, was still done by hand, and discovered that the sound inside the gun was not anywhere near as loud as on the outside. As well as the gun aiming taking place on board the ships that day, we had a team of gun spotters ashore – the SAS boys who had landed by Gemini two days before. All these thoughts went through my head as I looked for'ard at our own gun, and wondered how the gun crew inside must be feeling. All their years of training were now about to be put to the ultimate test. I heard a voice call from somewhere, '*Plymouth* about to open fire, Sir.' Then, staring at *Plymouth*'s 4.5 gun, I saw one barrel and then the other erupt in loud explosions and bursts of smoke, as her first shells screamed through the air to the shoreline south of Grytviken. I did not know what they were aiming at, so I did not know where to look, but even at a distance of nearly 10 miles it was just possible to see the tiny bursts of rocks and soil, and a seal colony, as the first shells rained in on the South Georgia coastline.

One of the seamen, Danny Daniels, who stood next to Albert and me, gave us a quiet running commentary of what was going on, passing us his own binoculars occasionally. 'See that big green shed and those smaller buildings to the left? Well that's Grytviken. Now move to the left again and you'll see the BAS jetty at King Edward Point. Further to the left you should be able to see the old whaling station at the top of King Edward Cove, with the submarine a few hundred yards off it. Now swing further to your left and you'll see the area we're trying to hit. Not because there's much there mind you, it's just to prove to the enemy how accurate our guns are!'

After the next hour and a half we stayed on the bridge, watching as our two ships took it in turns to fire over 200 bolts of thunder, blasting great craters around, but deliberately not on, the Argentinian positions, like large puncture marks on a rifle-range target. Then the firing stopped and the rich, sickly smell of sulphurous cordite was all that remained of the first real naval gunfire for decades.

'Okay,' whispered Danny again. 'Now we'll be checking co-ordinates with the SAS spotters ashore and getting ready to really shake them up.' No more than ten minutes passed before the firing started again. This time an isolated wooden shed was blasted to splinters as three or four shells hammered into it in quick succession. 'That should prove we can hit whatever we want,' said Danny, finishing off his running commentary, as Albert and I handed back the binoculars to return below. The guns remained silent then, as the offer of 'surrender or else' was put to the Argentinians. We did not have to wait. It was with great relief that at 1645, within two hours of firing the first shot, a veritable washing line of white cloths was waving from every Argentinian-held building and ground position.

The second great rumbling cheer of the day rang out between decks as this news was broadcast by the principal warfare officer (PWO) from the operation room. Albert and I were back in our stockade of bean tins in the senior rates dining hall when the great news was announced, and the chief caterer shouted, 'Ah bloody good'ho. Does that mean we can all bugger off home now?' The short barrage of deadly accurate NGS had been enough on its own to win the day, not to mention the threat of seventy-five of Britain's most highly-trained killers coming ashore! I would have hung out a white sheet myself if I had known Charlie and his mates were coming after me.

Having recaptured Grytviken and taken about 130 Argentinian prisoners, our forces ashore started creating their own fortified defensive ground positions and checking out all the buildings for possible booby traps. Back on board, the chefs and stewards got ready for their next stage of Operation Paraquat – a captain's dinner party! I still find it amazing to think that one can fight a battle in the morning, and then sit round a table with the vanquished less than ten hours later! But I suppose that is the way we British have always conducted our wartime affairs, and just like the 'crossing the line' ceremony, Captain Young certainly was not going to miss an opportunity of letting a fine old naval tradition slip by!

Captain Lagos, the Argentinian ground forces commander, and Lieutenant Commander Bicain, *Santa Fe*'s commander, graciously accepted the captain's invitation, and were whisked on board at the appointed hour in the captain's boat, which had been ceremonially lowered by grumbling dabbers especially for the occasion. Captain Young, greeted his special guests, and still with his anti-flash gear standing by formally accepted their surrender and then entertained them on finest roast beef and Yorkshire pudding, with spotted dick and custard. They then went on to discuss the local weather and the cricket and rugby – and not forgetting that day's events at South Georgia – just as good British hosts always do, especially after winning a battle!

No fatal casualties were suffered on either side during the capture of Grytviken that day, although one Argentinian, Masias Alberto, had his lower right leg blown off in *Santa Fe*'s conning tower and later had to have a further part amputated in *Antrim*'s sickbay. A 'booty' also nicked his leg on some barbed wire, and of course there were stories of the other Argentinians, who had allegedly suffered nasty cases of shock and 'severe browning' of the trousers! However, the same relatively happy story did not continue the following day.

CHAPTER TEN

Black Day at Grytviken

*A*ntrim spent the next day patrolling off the coast of South Georgia, while *Plymouth* and *Endurance* sailed round to Leith on the other side of the island to accept the surrender of a certain Captain Astiz, and a further twenty prisoners. Captain Astiz was already well known by the world's media for allegedly killing a 17-year-old Swedish girl in Buenos Aires five years before. In the Spanish press, 'Nasty Asti' had even been portrayed as a notorious torturer and murderer of political enemies of the Argentine dictatorship. The Swedish government had asked several times to interview the infamous thug, but had been turned down each time.

Pictures of Captain Astiz's surrender to *Plymouth*'s captain eventually made front-page news back home, which irritated us because it was only the surrender of his little squad of men and not the real surrender of South Georgia itself. That honour had fallen to our captain, the commander of Operation Paraquat, before his dinner party, when he had signalled back to the UK, in language typical of our glorious naval tradition: 'BE PLEASED TO INFORM HER MAJESTY THAT THE WHITE ENSIGN FLIES ALONGSIDE THE UNION FLAG IN GRYTVIKEN SOUTH GEORGIA. GOD SAVE THE QUEEN.'

During one of our early morning patrols, *Antrim* also had the chance to correct someone's oversight by re-enacting the attack on Grytviken for the benefit of the cameras – this time *with* our large battle ensign flying triumphantly, unlike the previous day when someone forgot to put it up, as all the other ships had done! Still, it gave Humphrey something to do after a fairly uneventful few days!

This bit of fun was out of the way and the good news received from Leith, but the rest of the day was unfortunately tainted by a much less cheery account of an incident on board the *Santa Fe*. A prisoner was supposed to have been shot by one of his Royal Marine guards. A jumble of rumours reached us at sea through various channels for some reason, very 'hush hush'. And all the time the facts remained unbroadcast, the buzzes got louder and louder. 'I heard the Argy went crazy and attacked the "booty" guards, so one of them shot him.' 'I heard there were no witnesses at all, and the "booty" who shot him is under arrest!' Somewhere amongst the buzzes lay the truth, but it took some pretty dogged undercover 'information gathering' to find out more of what happened.

That evening the commander confirmed there had been an 'incident' on board the *Santa Fe*, and regretfully that an Argentinian petty officer, Felix Artuso, had not only been shot, but killed. He said he could not reveal any further information because the matter was now the subject of an official board of inquiry, which would be held in accordance with the Geneva Convention. The shocking news stunned us all. How could we capture the submarine and indeed the whole island one day without killing anyone, and the following day kill an unarmed prisoner? Something smelt very, very rotten, and from our 'insider' point of view it did not take 1G1 mess long to find out why the stench of foul play was so bad. The culprit turned out to be none other than Robbie Roberts, the man I had 'hot-bunked' with!

We never saw him again in 1G1 mess; he did not return to collect any of his kit. We heard that he was held under arrest ashore while the board of inquiry took three days to investigate the case. Although no official details were ever leaked from the inquiry, there was no way all the witnesses to the subsequent events could keep their lips sealed. And this is what they revealed, in an account that I feel is the worst bit of the war.

In danger of sinking alongside the old whaling station jetty, the *Santa Fe* was moved out to deeper water where she would not cause a problem to shipping if she did go under. In order to do this, six members of the crew were escorted back on board by a party of Royal Marine guards. Five were dispersed to various key parts of the vessel, whilst Felix Artuso was placed in charge of *Santa Fe*'s control room , under the close escort of two Royal Marine guards.

The guards had apparently been given general clearance to open fire independently as part of the state of hostilities, and although they carried their 9 mm Browning pistols with them on board, the prisoners were totally unarmed, so there should have been no reason whatsoever to use the pistols. The Argentinian submariners were reported as being not in the least bit aggressive. Even if they had tried, escaping from South Georgia was impossible.

So why was Petty Officer Felix Artuso killed? At the end of the board of inquiry, Robbie was cleared of killing him, but that decision left most of us on board, and particularly those who had got to know him so well in 1G1 mess, very angry indeed. The inquiry had apparently revealed that Robbie, his colleague and the petty officer had been in a compartment on the submarine together. The submarine began to lurch suddenly and in the darkened control room there was a great fear that it was sinking. When the prisoner had started touching some equipment, Robbie thought he was trying to scuttle the submarine and warned him to stop. He then shot him four times, killing him instantly. One bullet hit his elbow, one went through the throat, and two entered his abdomen. The mitigation swung the findings of the board of inquiry.

But the question that we in 1G1 mess asked was, why? Why shoot and kill an unarmed man, who by all accounts had not threatened any direct malice to the two fully armed Royal Marines. Why kill him anyway at such close range? Why not wing him, or shoot him in the foot, or even perhaps fire a warning shot away from him, or punch him – or why not just shout for assistance? There were after all two marines in that control room – with only one unarmed prisoner.

I think I know what the answer is, and I know all of 1G1 mess and the vast majority of *Antrim*'s company knew too. I also know that most of Robbie's Royal Marine colleagues past and present that I have spoken to know the answer as well.

The incident itself and then the political and media handling of the board of inquiry left an extremely bad smell in the air around South Georgia at the time. And, may I say, from a subsequent visit and photograph of his small grave that lies so very close to Sir Ernest Shackleton's, still does to this day.

On Tuesday, 27 April, I was finally allowed to leave the galley and start work down in the catering office with Whisky Dave, the chief caterer, Shiner Wright, the other killick caterer (recently demoted from PO caterer), Albert and the other baby caterer, Dick Turpin.

Apart from the recapture and subsequent killing at Grytviken that week, the other big event was the *Antrim* caterers' reconnaissance mission to survey the provisions in the BAS hut, or Shackleton House – the large green hut that I had seen from the bridge. Once all occupiable areas ashore had been security cleared for use, our next job was to sort out independent feeding arrangements for all the occupants of the newly christened South Georgia garrison, – so that they did not have to exist solely on ration packs any longer. Teams of men made their way ashore to start servicing the buildings that had been checked out and made safe. Following in the wake of the mechanical and electrical teams, another team of men went ashore to start making preparations for serving the first meal, which would be supper that night. That was me and Shiner, the wardroom chief cook and a small band of chefs, armed to the teeth with choppers, knives and wooden spoons – and notepads and pencils.

All the teams were taken ashore in the captain's boat, which, in between its ceremonial duties was now used as the largest means of ferrying personnel and equipment ashore. Our catering team was in the third boatload, after teams of seamen, stokers and electricians had gone ashore to start checking out the basic utility services of water, sewerage, power, lighting and heating – all of which we would need pretty quickly, as there were only three hours left before nightfall.

From information already provided on board, we were directed to reconnoitre the hut, which we had been informed had a galley and a fairly large stock of food. Landing on the little wooden BAS jetty at King Edward Point, our intrepid little band advanced past the small post office and up through the centre of the small scattering of sheds and other buildings that formed the little community, keeping only to the roads, 'Just in case we've missed any booby traps boys.'

We passed a few groups of sorry-looking prisoners, sitting around in huddles, smoking foul Argentinian cigarettes under the watchful but not so trigger-happy guard of their other marine captors. We also passed piles of their weapons, which had been collected together for checking in one of the buildings – all sorts of strange-looking rifles and pistols, and other munitions in boxes. There were a couple of civilians ashore as well – the male BAS scientists who had been held captive themselves until only three days before. We spoke to one bright-looking university type, who offered to show us to the hut. 'I'm afraid it's in a bit of a state, lads. The Argentinians weren't exactly the cleanest guests we've had staying in the hut.' And he was not wrong either!

He led our group, now joined by a PO stoker and PO electrician through the front door of the enormous wooden green shed, and into a little foyer, where he started his guided tour. 'Right lads. On that side of the ground floor is the bunkroom, and over there on the other side is the food store. Nothing too interesting in there, I should imagine.' We did not actually look in either area, and just made our way up the central staircase to the galley and dining hall, which our guide explained, 'Doubles as our recreation and meeting room'. The hut was in a bit of a mess all right, with rubbish lying everywhere. The galley looked as though the Argentinians had been cooking continuous meals in it, but never doing any washing up!

Our guide then left us to it, and the chefs and mechanical and electrical engineers set about cleaning the galley up and getting everything working, while Shiner and I went downstairs to start the task we had been sent ashore to complete – mustering all the food stocks to determine what needed replenishing from ships' stocks – or in some cases, vice versa. That was the plan anyway, as we trotted back down the wooden staircase.

Entering the door that our guide had pointed to earlier, we walked into another much larger foyer. We could not help but notice the most obvious feature of the room – a massive pile of full and empty beer tins – which our guide had blindly classed as 'nothing too interesting'! For two men who both had a certain partiality to beer, and had not had a decent drink since leaving Gibraltar, *and* had fought a battle that week, this was a veritable Aladdin's cave, and it was not an opportunity to be overlooked at any cost.

'Bloody hell, Shiner,' I muttered, almost unable to believe my eyes. 'Fancy a tin or two while we start making our inventory out?'

'Bloody right I do, mate – before those bastard chefs and galley spanner-wankers upstairs get to know about it.' Barely surviving on only two cans of beer a day, men will consume vast quantities of tins when confronted by a beer mountain of this stature. Well, Shiner and I did anyway!

The mountain looked as though it had started life as a stack of about 100 cases of twenty-four tins, which the Argentinians had gradually drunk their way down to form a rough pyramid shape. The empties had then just been thrown to the sides, with no attempt to dispose of any of this or any other rubbish in the foyer. Like our predecessors, though, Shiner and I took our places on top of the heap and tugged off the first ring pulls. The first cans went down in two draughts, and were followed in quick succession by another two before we started the more serious task of cataloguing the contents of the store – which we had not even entered yet on account of our slight diversion!

'No way am I putting this bloody lot on the list Shiner,' I said, taking another can from the pile. 'We'll have to give some to the Chefs and them other prats upstairs, but if the other bastards ashore get to hear about this lot, it'll be gone in seconds. I reckon we should try covering it up and camouflaging it somehow, and then re-box what we can and get it back on board.'

'Bloody good idea Rowdy. I'm for that plan you bastard. I'm 'beer bosun' down 3N mess, so we could split it between the two messes eh?'

The deal was struck by tapping our two tins together, then we set about hiding all trace of our mouth-watering discovery using a broom and shovel to sweep up all the empties and bag them up for ditching. We found some large tarpaulins that we draped over the pile of beer, and wrapped rope around to secure them in place. The first stage of Operation BAS Hut successfully accomplished, we then started on the less interesting task of cataloguing all the food stocks. Not knowing what we would find in the shed, the ingredients for the first meal were already being sent over by boat from the ship. So we knew we had a couple of hours to survey what we could and radio the information back to Whisky Dave, who could then send more gear across for the next day's meals before the boat stopped running for the day. There were a couple of boxes of tinned goods in the beer foyer to record, then we ventured into the large dry store where we saw rows of wooden racking round the outside with filled pallets and trolleys in the middle. The whole store was as dirty and untidy as the rest of the hut, but we had a quick look and decided to start by the door and work our way round the outside, then survey the middle aisles.

It was pretty mundane work, twisting and turning boxes to check their contents, then recording what we had found on our note pads.

'Oh well, Shiner, at least we don't need to bring any more baked beans ashore. There are bloody tons of them in this corner.'

'Yeah, Rowdy. I've found loads of stewing steak and corned dog, and it's even Argentinian stuff – just like the shite we've been using on board for the last four years!'

Once we got into the swing of it however, the counting went well. The wardroom chief cook even came down once he had got the galley sorted out, and gave us a brief hand. But we had hidden our latest opened tins of beer, and did not let on about our secret find in the foyer – which he had just been sitting on! He concentrated on the items that we had already recorded, and started examining them to see if they were fit to use and what menu he could make up with them. Then, armed with a list of stuff he was going to radio to the chief caterer, he left us to continue our work – which was just as well, because as we started examining the third side of the store I made our second important discovery of the day. We had already found some items that had been shoved behind others below the racking – non-food items like spare plates and cutlery, fronted by tins of potatoes and such like. However, behind some boxes of tinned veg was a cardboard box filled with twelve bottles of Lamb's Navy Rum! 'Bloody hell, Shiner, I've hit the bloody jackpot this time, matey. Come and take a look at this little pot of gold.' Shiner was as amazed as I was by this latest find, and together we stopped counting for a while, to concentrate on pulling out all the ordinary food boxes under the racks – to reveal ten cases of red and white wine. We had deliberately slowed down our pace of drinking during the food counting, but these latest finds were cause for a quick break and a further celebratory drink. So I twisted the top off one of the bottles of Lamb's, took a large swig and passed it across to my mate, who also took his turn at the neck of the bottle.

'Right, Rowdy. How are we going to get this lot back on board?' We sat and tossed a few ideas in the air, then decided our best bet was to start re-boxing the rum and wine, tackle the full cases of beer, and leave all the opened beer packs for the chefs and mechanics upstairs, who we now knew were going to be sleeping next door and might appreciate a nightcap later on. To cover our tracks for the next stage of Operation BAS Hut, which would be the journey back to the ship, we started stacking the contraband into large trolleys and we topped them off with boxes of stuff that would also be quite useful on board – good 'caterer's currency' like ground coffee, sweet biscuits and a couple of boxes of chocolate bars.

We did not want to leave them without any goodies in the hut, but we needed some 'currency' to make sure the rest of the operation ran smoothly. Once all the counting and packing was done, I radioed Whisky Dave via the bridge to give him the news of our highly successful visit. 'Chief, we've found a bloody mountain of beer, rum and wine, and it's all re-boxed ready to be shipped back on board. How soon can you send the boat?'

There was a bit of a pregnant pause, then Whisky Dave whispered back, 'Rowdy, for Pete's sake be careful, mate – but get the stuff down to the jetty and I'll get the boat in to pick you up in about half an hour!' It took a bit of arranging on his part, because we had already missed the last planned trip back. But it is amazing what 'caterer's currency' will buy you, especially when everyone has their price, no matter who they are – or how high up! Just before leaving the hut, Shiner and I got the chief cook to come down and look at the remaining pile of loose beer tins that we had pushed to one side and re-covered.

'Here you are, Chief,' Shiner said. 'A little present for you and your boys from me and Rowdy – we found it in the middle of the last pallet we pulled apart. I expect some Argy bastards had hidden it there eh? If I were you, Chief, I had hide it again somewhere a bit better after we've gone. We're going back on board now with these four trolleys of food that'll come in handy down the dry stores!'

The chief cook was delighted with his generous present, and so too were the rest of the lads upstairs, who willingly gave us a hand to push the trolleys back to the jetty and load them on the boat. 'Eh, cheers for those tins, Rowdy,' called out George Formby, as the last heavy box was passed on board to the waiting seaman. 'I hope you kept a few crates for yourselves, mate?'

'Oh, don't worry about us,' I replied – 'Trust us, my friend. We're caterers. We know what we're doing, my boy.'

'Yeah, I know you two buggers! I bet hardly any of those boxes had food in.' And how very right he was!

After the short trip across Cumberland Bay, which was now in complete darkness, we were met by the chief caterer, and a small band of 'volunteers' he had bribed to give us a hand. 'Have you got all the gear, Rowdy?' he called out as we drew near. 'I've promised the Jimmy and DSO here some good coffee and chocolate biscuits for persuading the skipper to let us have this one last trip in the boat.'

'Yes Chief,' I called back as I slapped a couple of the cardboard boxes I was sitting on 'Loads of nice coffee and chocolate biscuits under here, Chief.'

'Oh marvelous, Yates,' yelled back the DSO. 'I've promised some choccy biscuits to the captain as well.'

And so, with our bellies full of tinned beer and finest rum, the two intrepid smugglers from Operation BAS Hut made it safely back on board with their haul of contraband. After our 'currency' was paid out, Whisky Dave, Shiner and I finished off storing the 'fresh supplies' in the dry store, for use at a later date.

I kept the caterers' little secret safe from the mess when I eventually returned, but the boys could tell I had been drinking. My breath stank of booze, and I crashed out on my bed without going for a shower, or eating, or reading a book, or anything else. Just dreaming sweetly of what a wonderful war this was so far! In the morning though, I had the hangover from hell.

CHAPTER ELEVEN

The 'Three Bears'

After the recapture of South Georgia, *Antrim*'s little force had expected some reprisals from the Argentinians, but as we were now quickly realizing, we were actually pretty safe off Grytviken. South Georgia was over 800 miles from the Falklands, well out of the range of any Argentinian fighters. Although repeated 'bleeps' had been picked up from suspected Argentinian Hercules spotter aircraft flying high above us, by the time London gave us permission to shoot them down, they had stopped appearing. The Argentinians must also have realized that they had better not mess with our surface fleet or our submarines – which were probably gathering in ever-increasing numbers.

In 1G1 mess the mood was quite upbeat. We still had no mail or other direct contact with our folks back home, but we had been briefly 'blooded' in the art of warfare, and two days later gathered round the uckers table to raffle off Charlie's and the two 'booties' souvenirs. There were about ten altogether, from various items of clothing to spent cartridges and bits of crashed Puma helicopter. And then there was the first prize – a smashing helmet. I won that, with the aid of Charlie's sleight of hand in the hat!

Charlie and the rest of his SAS troop left us shortly after that to join *Brilliant* for whatever their next mission would be. We were sad to see him go. He had only been with us for a few days, but in that short time we had got to know one hell of a human being. He was not 'cool', or flash, or loud, or temperamental. He was just very pleasant, mild mannered, extremely dedicated, and physically and mentally tough – incredibly tough. We all stood and shook hands as he left the mess for the last time, and although we did not even know if Charlie was his real name, we knew that we and the battle for the Falklands were in safe hands with men like him around.

On 30 April, the funeral of Petty Officer Felix Artuso was held ashore in the tiny cemetery that flanks the old whaling station chapel. On a clear, cold, still day, *Antrim*'s ship's company provided everything for the burial, from chaplain to gravedigger, coffin and a rifle-bearing honour guard who fired three blank volleys over the grave. The chief caterer went along in his capacity as an ex-submariner, and I am proud to report that he told me Felix was buried with full military honours and the greatest possible human respect – just as if he had been one of our own shipmates.

The infamous 'Nasty Asti' was brought on board the following day, and kept under lock and key in a small officer's cabin next to the wardroom pantry. An armed seaman stood on watch over him at all times, and any time he left the cabin to use the heads or showers he was always accompanied by two armed seamen. I saw him on one occasion as some food was passed into his cabin, and he looked the epitome of an arrogant blond-haired Nazi.

Without much prior warning, I also became a prison warder that day. The master at arms piped for me go to his office. 'You're a big lad, Rowdy. You can look after yourself, can't you? Since you moved out of the galley down to the catering office, you haven't got a proper job on board because you're just a spare hand aren't you? So I've spoken to the Jimmy and supply officer, and they've agreed that you're just the right man to move down the bootnecks' mess with the assistant canman and guard the three Chilean scrap metal merchants who are coming on board today.'

'Yeah, sure, Master,' I replied. 'Do I get a gun as well?'

'No, Audy Murphy, you don't get a bloody gun. They're non-military personnel and we're not allowed to stick them under armed arrest. That's why we've picked you, because the way you behave on a rugby pitch and ashore you shouldn't need a gun!' Clearly, I had no option, so I took the decision on the chin and got on with it, grabbing my sleeping bag and a few bits and pieces and making myself comfortable in 3P mess.

The three Chilean scrap metal merchants were actually the men who had triggered this whole war off by 'invading' South Georgia back on 19 March. They had been duped by the Argentinians into making this move, and that incident had led to one thing, and then another, and now instead of just arguing about scrap metal, two countries were fighting each other. I had heard about them briefly from some of the buzzes going round the ship, but did not realize that they would be coming on board.

Later that day my prisoners arrived, along with the thirteen BAS scientists and the two female film makers who had been hiding away together in their little wooden hut at St Andrew's Bay during the Argentinian occupation, filming penguins. I had been briefed by the master at arms that the three men could not speak any English, and he had told me what I could and could not do with them'. I had to stay with them at all times, starting from the very first moment they stepped on board. I expected them to arrive with lots of personal effects, but climbing up the ladder from the boat were three of the dirtiest, scruffiest creatures I had ever laid eyes on, with not even one suitcase between them. I shouted down at one of the seamen in the boat, 'Hey Billy! Where's all their gear then, mate?'

'They ain't got any gear, Rowdy – all they've got is in those little plastic carrier bags. They bloody stink, too, mate. Right bunch of crabby bastards!'

Fortunately, one of the BAS men spoke a little Spanish, and with the aid of a few hand signals, the three prisoners were told that they would be following me down to their accommodation. I knew no Spanish whatsoever, so once the scientist had finished his introduction, I motioned them to follow me. Polly Pearce, the young canteen manager, took up the rear of the party as we set off for the marines' mess. 'Oi Rowdy! How much are they paying you to look after them dirty bastards?' 'Cor, they bloody chuck up, Rowdy!' 'Get 'em in the bloody shower will ya, mate.'

The observers throughout the ship were not wrong – the Chileans smelt – and even looked – like three dead black sheep!

'Right,' I said as we entered 3P mess. 'This is where you will live, and now you will go for a wash, yes?' My first speech met with absolutely no response. 'Oh, bloody hell, Polly,' I shouted in frustration, 'If they can't understand even basic English, how the fuck are we meant to get them to do anything? Here, pass me that bloody writing pad, will ya? We'll just have to draw pictures of what we want them to do instead!'

Under the circumstances, drawing little pictures, even in my untrained hand, was not such a bad way of communicating. The first three little pictures I drew were of a bed, a shower, and a plate of food, with the numbers 1, 2 and 3 alongside them. Then pointing at the bed I said,

'BED – THIS BED – YOU SAY BED.' Two of the Chileans just stood there, but the oldest one cottoned on to what I was trying to achieve, 'Si, BED – THIS BED.'

'Yeah, yeah that's right, BED, BED,' I kept repeating, 'BED, Señor, BED, Señor.'

The next stage of the lesson was to explain why I had drawn the bed. Pointing to the three beds with the rolled up sleeping bags and pillows on, I said, 'this your bed, this your bed, and this your bed.'

'Ah, BED – BED – BED,' they replied one after the other like three Spanish bears! 'Now I've just got to get them to say "porridge", I thought, "and we're home and dry!"'

Once the prisoners got the hang of my very individual style of instruction, things started to run quite smoothly. Next I pointed to picture number 2 – the shower. But as soon as I did so I realized it was no use taking them for a shower because they had no soap, towels or clean clothes.

'Bloody hell, Polly,' I whined. 'This is going to be a bloody long day, mate. Right, I'll hold the fort. You nip down the NAAFI and see the canman for some soap and razors and stuff – oh, and lots of smellies – and get it charged to the Welfare Fund. The Jimmy said it would be OK.'

Polly went off on his errand, while I sat the 'three bears' down at the mess table and continued my scribbling and English language course. I told them that Polly had gone to get soap and razors, then when he returned I would nip next door to the laundry to get them some clean clothes and towels. After getting that through to them, I explained they were on the ship to be taken north to another ship, which would then take them to an island, from where they would be flown back home. When I got them to understand that plan, they grinned broadly and reached for their wallets to pull out pictures of their wives and children and Jesus on the cross. We were getting on well I thought.

'Here,' I said, pulling three tins of soft drinks out of the fridge, 'You have a drink, Señors?'

'Si – Si – Si,' replied the three bears.

Polly eventually returned with the soap, razors and smellies, then, a little nervously, he stood guard while I nipped next door to see if I could find something for them to wear from the laundry.

'Ah No. 1,' I shouted into the noisy, steaming laundry. 'No. 1, I need a big favour.' I went on to explain to the leader of the team of four Chinese laundrymen exactly what my problem was, and how he could help me out. For anybody but a caterer, this request might have been met with a swift 'rebuff', but caterers and laundrymen always got on well together. We gave them lots of extra free food for them to cook in their woks and rice steamers, and in return they gave us free laundry'! No. 1 laundrymen were also pretty switched on, and like caterers knew a thing or two about ducking and diving, wheeling and dealing, 'currency' and spotting an opportunity, when most other people would walk right over it. As soon as I mentioned I needed shirts and the words 'Welfare Fund', I could see that No. 1 had spotted one such prime opportunity!

'You see the Jimmy, Rowdy, you tell him No. 1's got plenty trousers, but no shirts. You tell him only have *Antrim* T- Shirt – lots of *Antrim* T-shirts. Only £3 each.' As he pulled out pairs of trousers from a large mattress cover of old leftovers, I could see lots of old No. 8 shirts that would easily have served my purpose, but I knew instinctively what No. 1 was up to, and what I stood to gain out of it too. I said, 'No problem

No. 1, I can see you've got no shirts left, so I'll just have to take twelve of those *Antrim* T-shirts instead. Oh and give us three pairs of your flip-flops and twelve pairs of nicks and socks too will you – they've got no spares of those, either!'

A short phone call to the Jimmy confirmed the deal. Then, armed with the second-hand trousers and brand new white T-shirts – with 'HMS *Antrim*' and the ship's crest stamped on the front in large colourful print, I returned to my prisoners to escort them to the showers. I did not actually go in with them, but hung around outside while they did their stuff. The other men in the bathroom at the time all made quick exits. Watching Chilean scrap metal workers strip off and take their first shave and shower in four weeks is not the sort of sight I had expected anyone to stomach.

Their washes complete, and their appearances brightened almost beyond belief, I bagged up all their old clothes and on the way back to the mess, dropped them in to the laundry.

'Here you are, No. 1,' I called out. 'Three new Chileans reporting for duty in your finest clean clothes, Sir!' I asked if his boys could try and clean the trousers, jumpers and jackets, but to forget the underwear and socks and anything else they found. 'Just ditch that bloody lot before they start running round the ship on their own and biting people!'

The Chileans were clearly impressed by the fact we had Chinese laundrymen on board. They were also impressed by some of the other sights I was able to show them on a brief tour of passageways as we made our way up to eat. I could not show them any of the sensitive weaponry or communications compartments, but with the aid of my little notepad and pencil I was able to explain how nearly 600 people were currently living on board and, in the case of 1G1 mess, precisely how they lived. The lads in the mess mocked me something rotten when they saw the 'three bears' in their new attire. 'Bloody hell, Rowdy. How the heck did you arrange that mate? They only came on board two hours ago, and now you've got them looking better than the chimps down the stoker's mess!' 'Some bloody prison officer you are, Rowdy. You're meant to get 'em breaking bloody rocks, not lashing them up to new clobber!'

It continued wherever we went, with me leading, the 'three bears' behind, and diminutive, fresh-faced Polly trailing in their wake. As we finished our meal in the packed 'Junior rates' dining hall, I wondered how long they would be on board for, and what I would do with them all day and in the evenings. They were not allowed to go to most places, they were not allowed to drink – what could I do with them. 'Oh well,' I thought, 'the commander will be on the "box" soon, then I'll teach them how to play uckers – that'll do for the first night anyway. They are, after all, my prisoners, not long-lost soul mates!'

The commander's broadcast that night was full of goodbyes and hellos. Goodbye to the SAS who had flown off for their next secret mission somewhere. Goodbye to the other embarked forces who were now garrisoning South Georgia. And a temporary goodbye to our own 'booties', who were now guarding the main bulk of Argentinian prisoners on the *Tidespring*. Hellos went out to Cindy Buxton and Annie Price, the thirteen BAS men, my three scrap metal workers – and two ducks that the BAS team had brought on board to take back to the UK for research!

'Bloody ducks,' I yelled at the screen. 'First we're a bloody warship, now we're a bloody floating zoo! I wonder who's got the job of looking after them two? I bet it's not the Choggies next door, because they'd bloody turn them into crispy ducks!' Polly laughed at these comments, but the 'three bears' just sat there, unable to understand my coarse brand of sarcastic naval humour.

The commander went on to update us on events over the past couple of days and plot what lay ahead next for the ship. We heard that the main task force was now fast approaching its operating area between the Falklands and South Georgia, and that back home more ships were leaving to follow them down, including the massive *Atlantic Conveyor*, which had been converted in just one week to bring down loads of crucial heavy-lift items. Politically, despite our recapture of South Georgia, things still seemed to be going backwards.

As a result, the commander informed us that early this morning, Vulcan bombers had flown, with mid-air refuelling, from Ascension and inflicted the first damage on the Falklands itself by bombing Stanley airfield. Sea Harriers had also flown in from *Hermes* to add a few of their own bombs and anti-personnel devices in order to hinder the Argentinian repairing the damage. And our ships had also been in action, with *Glamorgan*, *Alacrity* and *Arrow* all bombarding positions around Stanley. In response to this the Argentinians had launched their first air attacks on our vessels. As a result, the first 'dog-fights' had also been reported, and several Argentinian kills claimed – the first such British claims since the Korean War. Thankfully, no British losses were reported.

Despite the talk of continuing political manoeuvres, the world's attention was now focused on the real struggle escalating before our very eyes, deep in the freezing South Atlantic. As I said to Polly after the commander had stopped talking, 'There's no bloody way the people in suits are going sort this out. You watch now, matey, this is gonna get bloody nasty – you mark my words!'

As well as the commander's invaluable broadcast, that Saturday also saw the launch of a personal initiative by the commander in charge of the marine engineering department, who started dishing out his own hand-written situation report. They were primarily produced to enlighten his own department, but once 'on the streets' the clearly written 'sitreps' were eagerly read by all who could get hold of a copy. They were not meant to compete with the commander's TV broadcasts, but being released a couple of hours later, they included details that had not previously been available, and gave us all the very latest information as each day drew to an end. The personal touch of hand writing each sitrep in plain English was also greatly appreciated at a time when increasing reliance was being placed on bland, unappealing, typed text messages. Like the captain's occasional broadcasts and the commander's nightly TV shows, they demonstrated a very human and caring touch. The first sitrep ended with the words: 'Two salvage tugs are on their way to Grytviken to tow out our submarine into deep water and allow it to sink. Tomorrow we say farewell to South Georgia having made our contribution to modern history.'

My Chilean friends of course understood nothing of what was said or read. And after more soft drinks and an introductory game of uckers, they all stripped off and crept into bed for their first night's sleep in what was now being called the three bears' den.

On Sunday, 2 May, we sailed north and straight away hit rough weather. Two of the three prisoners were seasick, but I was quite enjoying the break from routine in looking after them. The 'joss' made it clear that the Chileans were not to drink any beer, but he did not say anything about Polly and me, and when you are sharing a mess with the person who holds the NAAFI beer store keys and the laundry man next door owes you a favour you would be silly not to take advantage of it. I did not drink much that day, though, because of the weather, but I was starting to stash some away in the ventilation trunking for a party when we got a bit further north.

Before turning in for the night we heard that the Argentinian cruiser *General Belgrano* had been sunk by one of our submarines. No casualty figures were received, and at the time the news seemed to be taken fairly lightly, but we all knew that the stakes had been raised much, much higher. I broke the news to the 'three bears', but they didn't believe it was true. On board, we knew nothing of the political storms that had erupted as a result of the sinking. To us at that time it was merely a natural progression of events.

The following day the weather eased slightly, and all the 'three bears' were able to stay out of their beds longer. In the morning we met up with RFA *Tidespring* again, then in the afternoon we both met up with

HMS *Plymouth*, which had been sent to relieve us as South Georgia guard ship. We knew that *Plymouth* was carrying mail for us, which caused great excitement and anticipation.

Normally, we would see on daily orders that mail was due at a certain time by boat transfer or 'vertrep', and people would be watching the clock. But that day, after having fought our first battle, and still not having had any responses to our rushed letters of just over one month ago, the sense of anticipation was almost unbearable. From the Captain down to the most junior man on the ship, we were all desperate to get some mail. And in the hour or so it took to sort the mass of mailbags into their respective messes, the tension increased greatly.

Each mess assigned runners to collect the mail. This was normally a bit of a chore, but that day it was a prized role indeed. 1G1 mess sent up Chopper Cox and Jim Davidson, plus Rattler Morgan to grab the wardroom mail. Other, larger messes, had to send up three or four men, such was the volume of mail to collect. Back in the messes, everything came to a halt. Every person not on watch was wide awake and absolutely desperate for their runners to return, like Father Christmas, with their big sacks of goodies. Then Chopper and Jim returned and forced their way to the centre of the mess square, where the hand out of mail started.

Quite a lot of the mail came through stinking of perfume from some wife or girlfriend (or both), and often the smell permeated to other letters, so that one from the bank manager might come through smelling of Estée Lauder, or the announcement of an old relative's death might come through with an aroma of L'air Du Temps! With all the mail handed out, we sat on the floor or climbed into our bunks, or went away to offices or other compartments to read our mail and cast our minds back to our families, friends, girlfriends, bank managers, car insurance companies, and all the other people who had written to us from back home.

Then there were the intermittent shouts or groans. 'Bloody hell, boys, I'm going to be a dad!' 'Shit, my uncle's died!' 'Jesus, this bit of stuff is gaggin' for it, boys.' There were all sorts of letters, bundles, packages and parcels, and even thin cardboard tubes with naughty posters or maps in them. There was even clothing and food.

My mail contained a range of letters like everyone else's. There were letters from home, letters from my Aunt Carol, letters from an old girlfriend and new, like my hairdressing friend Jackie. There were letters from old school friends, neighbours and people who had only seen my name in the papers and wanted to give their support. And there was also a 'good luck' message from the quite remarkable sports commentator, David Coleman, and even a signed photograph from the ex-matelot Danny La Rue!

The mail had the same effect on me as it had on everyone else that day. It bowled me over and lifted me up, then dropped me down again with a mighty crunch. It made me miss my family, my friends, my car, a nice walk to see the butterflies in the countryside, a nice walk anywhere on dry land again. It also left me full of doubts. Would I ever see home and butterflies again, would I ever feel a woman's touch, or a cool pint of Guinness, or a lovely box of Kentucky Fried Chicken? Or would it just be mail drops like this from now on, and then nothing. I was so thrilled to receive that mail, but it cut me up in so many ways I was glad none of my friends were around when my chin trembled and my eyes glazed over, and I pushed the bundle into my locker and climbed onto my bed and closed my eyes. To dream I was home again.

Despite, or probably because of, the mail, morale on board the next morning was noticeably lower than it had been for some time. Most of the men had been jarred back to reality by their messages from home, and in effect our eyes had been taken off the ball. However, no matter how high or low our emotions were at the start of the day, we all received a massive sledgehammer of a blow late in the afternoon. For buzzes erupted all over the ship that HMS *Sheffield* had been hit by an Exocet missile and was in danger of sinking. By the time the commander made his TV appearance a couple of hours later, most of the buzzes had turned into strong rumours and then a framework of facts – very alarming facts indeed, which the commander more or less confirmed in a very sombre and then very angry broadcast to the ship's company.

> I should imagine that all of you have by now heard of the attack on HMS *Sheffield* just a few hours ago. Details are still a little hazy, but the facts as we know them so far are as follows. *Sheffield* had been operating with the main task force, when two Argentine Super Etendard aircraft attacked the carrier group from the west, each launching Exocet missiles from a range of over 25 miles. Other ships in the vicinity of *Sheffield* managed to launch enough 'chaff' to deflect one of the missiles, but unfortunately, no 'chaff' appears to have been fired, or any other countermeasures taken, by *Sheffield*, which as a result, took a direct 90 degree hit midships.

Around the ship, messdecks were almost completely silent, apart from the occasional 'Bloody stupid bastards.' The commander continued: 'It is understood that although *Sheffield* was not sunk by the Exocet, she was extensively damaged and I regret to inform you, that there have been a considerable number of fatal and other serious casualties.'

He then gave what I felt was his best broadcast of the entire trip. Not everyone read it that way, but coming from a very sporting and partic- ularly physical rugby background, I could see exactly where he was coming from. The five-minute torrent of aggressive dialogue he then spat out reminded me so much of a half-time changing-room talk, when the team has been well and truly beaten in the first forty minutes, and the coach is determined it will not happen in the second half.

Giving us some of the other details that he knew of the incident, but without revealing everything that perhaps he could have, his report confirmed the news that had already leaked on board: that despite the tragedy of the incident, HMS *Sheffield* had been 'caught napping with her trousers down!' There were clues in the carefully selected words he used.

He made no accusations about anybody on *Sheffield*, but he did not dish out any praise to anyone on *Antrim* either. The whole theme of his talk was about being more prepared, about being more ready to react even faster than we had already, about not being caught out semi-clothed in daylight or absent for any length of time from our places of duty while on watch without full cover – no matter who we were. He ended by saying, 'You have had your warning. Not from me, or anyone else on board, but from what happened to *Sheffield* this afternoon. Keep up your morale. Work hard. And don't let what happened to *Sheffield* happen to us! Goodnight gentlemen!'

In the Royal Marine mess, Polly and I sat shaking our heads, deep in our own thoughts. I think that like many other people, Polly was shocked and distressed that *Sheffield* had been hit, whereas I felt the same as the commander and most other men on board: sadness as we had friends there who might now be dead, but also great anger. I hate losing, whether it be on a rugby pitch, in a drinking race or at a game of cards. But what I hate even more, is losing when we had not played well. And many of us felt that although *Sheffield* did not deserve to be hit, however brutal it might sound, she also did not do enough *not* to be hit.

The 'three bears' just sat there, staring at the blank screen, then at our blank faces. They knew something had happened. They had seen the commander's face redden with rage as he tore into us in a language they could not understand. And they saw me fling the fridge door open and drain a tin of beer in one short burst, and then spit out words of my own. 'OK, so they really want a fight eh? Well they've bloody got one now all right!'

I never told the 'three bears' that one of our ships had been lost, and when walking them round the ship, I warned everybody, including officers, that I would like to keep it that way – not because I was afraid of how they might react, but because I so hated losing. I went to bed that night a very bitter young man.

Details of *Sheffield*'s fatalities arrived on board the next morning, and copies of the signal were placed on all the main noticeboards. When I eventually got my turn to read the list of names, it was clear exactly where the missile had struck: a large percentage of those lost were chefs from the galley, midships. And I knew nearly every one. Our first Harrier pilot was also reported lost, which added further to the gloomy news.

Although we had fallen out of true defence watches since reaching a safe latitude, as a result of the previous night's talk we now started living an even more strict routine on board. Regardless of the wider belief that we should now be in safer seas, and despite the fact we had reverted to normal cruising watches, a number of tightening-up rules came into immediate effect. All showers were banned during daylight hours, and irrespective of the temperature, we had to sleep fully clothed. We still had to wear our anti-flash hoods around our necks, and carry our battle bags containing our anti-flash gloves, gas masks and sea-survival suits. We might have been back in cruising watches for a few days, but this was certainly no cruise for *Antrim*.

Sailing as suddenly as we had from Gibraltar, and only being able to take on board stores that were already available on the surrounding ships, we noticed that we were getting very short of a certain key item – anti-flash hoods. The whole idea of these hoods is to reflect the intensely bright light that flashes as the result of an explosion during battle. They are also impregnated with fire-retardant material, so they cannot be washed for fear of weakening their ability to reduce facial burns.

Not being able to wash them though, was becoming a real problem, they were starting to smell a bit! Replacing them each day was not an option, as the ship could not carry enough to meet our needs. So we just had to grin and bear it, spray them now and again and hope no one was offended by the smell. A directive also arrived reminding personnel that they should not mark their hoods in any way as this would also reduce the anti-flash and fire-retardant qualities in those areas. The trouble with this perfectly understandable instruction was that it arrived six weeks too late, as by now virtually everyone had their names and other graffiti scrawled on their hoods, usually to aid recognition.

Tags were also in short supply. Our dog tags had of course been issued along with the rest of our kit, and we were meant to carry them around with our kit at all times. But like a lot of other 'shoulds', this did not always happen. So now many men could be seen in messdecks and corridors emery papering coins to make their own versions! The navy-issue tags were also fire retardant, but we strongly suspected that the coin ones were not. Still, who really cared if the tags did melt? We were pretty sure that if it got that hot there probably would not be much left of us to identify anyway!

Despite the previous day's low point, life with the 'three bears' was

Captain B.G. Young DSO RN, Commanding Officer HMS *Antrim* 1981-83. 'Our Skipper'.

A successful Seaslug firing just prior to the Falklands War.

The crippled Argentinean submarine *Santa Fe*, moored alongside the old whaling station in Grytviken, South Georgia, sometime after the re-capture of the island, 25 April 1982. Scene of the infamous POW shooting.

Shrapnel damage caused by 30mm cannon shells during the attacks in Bomb Alley, 21 May 1982.

DANGER
SEASLUG MAGAZINE
O.S.

The ship's helicopter, '*Humphrey*', returning to Fortuna Glacier, South Georgia, in June 1982.

The view for'ard over the Exocet launchers and 4.5 gun during some rough seas on our way home.

Port Stanley, the capital of the Falkland Islands. Prior to the war.

Summertime at the old whaling station, Grytviken, South Georgia. Prior to the war.

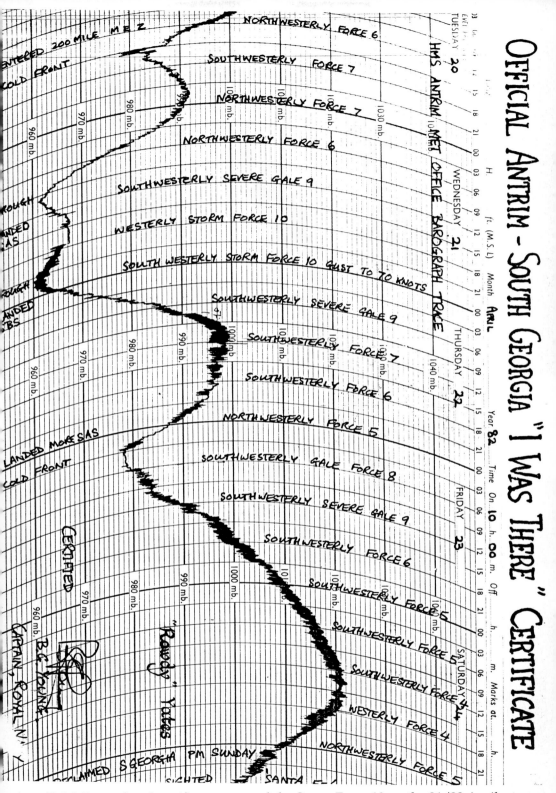

An official 'I was there' certificate to record the Storm Force 10 on the 21/22 April 1982. At the same time as we launched SAS and SBS reconnaissance operations against South Georgia.

HMS *Endurance* at South Georgia, 2 May 1982.

Anchored off Ascension Island, 10 April 1982. The last time I saw HMS *Sheffield*.

HMS *Sheffield*, 4 May 1982. Our first great loss of the war, and a major wake-up call to us all.

HMS *Sheffield*, displaying the shocking effects of an Exocet missile strike.

The Falkland Islands. When we first sailed south, most of us hadn't even heard of the place and had to trace images like these from newspapers to familiarise ourselves with the geography and record any significant events.

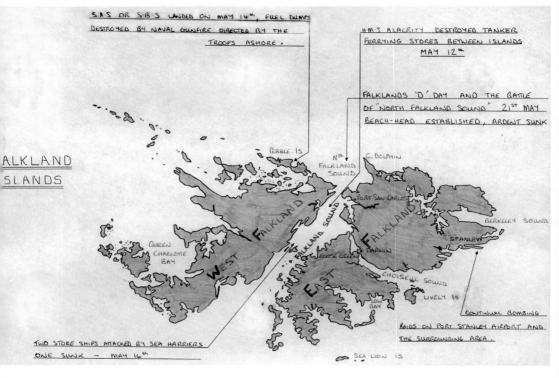

A 30mm cannon shell hole in the officer's heads, Bomb Alley, 21 May 1982. The square piece of 'damage control' wood is four inches square.

A similar hole just below the Captain's position on the bridge.

A rough sketch that I drew to illustrate the bombs and bullets that struck us in Bomb Alley.

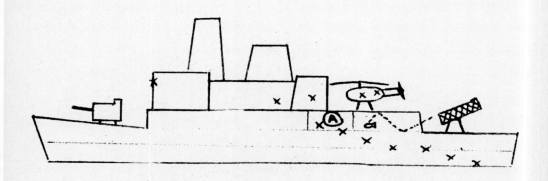

POSITIONS OF BOMB AND BULLET HITS

(A) = MY ACTION STATION!

FROM A SKETCH DRAWN AT THE TIME

A RAS(L) (replenishment at sea - liquid fuel), from an RFA (Royal Fleet Auxiliary). May 1982.

A Vertrep (Vertial replenishment at sea) from an RFA, May 1982, bringing all kinds of stores and mail.

My mate, 'Albert Ross', in relaxed anti-flash and very glad to be alive. 22 May 1982.

The author in full action dress with anti-flash, also carrying my respirator and life jacket. 22 May 1982.

The author braving the rapidly increasing colder elements at South Georgia, 28 May 1982.

Cumberland Sound, South Georgia,
22 June 1982.

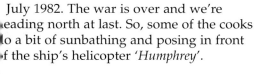

Cumberland Sound, South Georgia, 22 June
1982, and the sea is starting to freeze over.

July 1982. The war is over and we're
heading north at last. So, some of the cooks
do a bit of sunbathing and posing in front
of the ship's helicopter 'Humphrey'.

Humphrey's battle honours

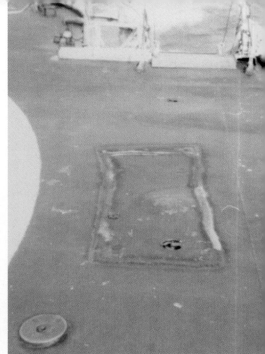

Humphrey sunbathing and enjoying the passage home.

The bulge where the unexploded bomb hit the underside of the flight deck and the patch where it was lifted out.

The view aft over the Seaslug and quarter deck, leaving the South Atlantic behind us.

The view up the starboard side as we head for the North Atlantic.

17 July 1982. The day that HMS *Antrim* finally came home and the massed holiday-making crowds at Southsea went wild.

Alongside at last and our families wait to pour over the gangways.

The author with his parents. A laughing sailor very glad to be home again.

The author in October 1982. Petty Officer Catering Accountant David (Rowdy) Yates, aged 25.

HMS *Antrim* enters Portsmouth harbour, and the crowds on the Gosport side get their chance to cheer us home.

HMS *Antrim* safely alongside in HM Dockyard, Portsmouth.

More families stream onboard, to join over two thousand 'celebrating' between decks.

not too bad. Some of the men had a few digs at them for starting the war, but I think most of us realized that they were only puppets in a much grander scheme of things. I certainly never took it out on any of them. We played endless games of uckers and crib, and drew pictures on scraps of paper to describe to each other anything from our lives at home to our thoughts on football, even to telling Irish – or in their case Peruvian jokes. I started by drawing a swimming pool with a blank sign on the bottom, and asked them what should be written on such a Peruvian swimming-pool sign. Three blank faces stared at the picture and could not come up with the correct answer, which is 'NO SMOKING'. Then I drew a ladder and asked what Peruvian sign should go on the top of that – again blank faces. Answer: 'STOP'.

There were visual jokes as well. Standing up, stretching one leg out in front of me and tapping the floor with my toes whilst closing my eyes and sticking both fingers in my ears I said, 'What's this?' Again, three blank faces. Answer: 'Peruvian Mine Sweeper'! And also, putting one steaming boot on the table and reaching down to the one on the deck, I explained that this was how a Peruvian did up his shoelaces!

We had a good laugh, and I wished I could have given them a beer or two and had a real party, but I knew that might be stretching the rules of the Geneva Convention a bit too far! So I had a couple of tins, they drank soft drinks and coffee, and despite the war that was going on around us, life in the 'three bears' den was quite peaceful.

The weather became noticeably warmer as we continued our watery path north – not warm enough to go on the upper deck or sunbathe, but warm enough to take the biting chill out of the air. In the morning I took it easy in the 'three bears' den and decided to catch up on my letter writing, which had taken a bit of a back seat because of recent events. I had diligently completed my diary each day, but since 10 April, with no mail coming on board until 3 May and none due to go off, I had not bothered to write home. However, I now wrote a long letter explaining what had been going on over the past four weeks.

Thank you for all your letters, they arrived two days ago. I am very well myself, although getting a little fed up of the endless hours of sea time and the close confines of the ship.

After leaving Ascension Island we arrived undetected near South Georgia on the twenty-first of April – after meeting up with HMS *Endurance*. Soon after, we landed a small group of SAS on the island to find out the Argie's numbers, but the weather was so bad down there at the time that we had to bring them back again. Unfortunately, two helicopters were lost in the rescue attempt, but everyone eventually made it back on board alive. They are really tough blokes those SAS boys, and nice people as well.

The following day another group managed to get ashore in small boats and they helped when we came to retake the island a few days later. In the meantime, we knew there was a submarine lurking around somewhere so everybody tried to stay alert in case it found us.

We had to sleep in our clothes, and a couple of times we went to action stations because we thought we had found the submarine, but there are a lot of bergs around and every time it was one of these. Eventually, though, we decided to take back the island on Sunday, 25 April.

It all began about lunchtime when, by sheer luck, our helicopter found an Argy submarine on the surface, and dived straight in and hit it with mines and torpedoes. The sub was badly damaged and had to limp back into the small harbour at Grytviken – unable to submerge because of its damaged state.

Then we got ready to land our troops (about seventy-five in all from the three ships), but first we had to make the landing zone safe. So at about 1.45 pm the *Plymouth* and ourselves began bombarding close to their positions with our 4.5 guns. I was lucky enough to be on the bridge at the time and could see a line of shells landing along the shore. Actually, the shells weren't meant to hit the Argies, only to get them to see that our ships could hit them if they wanted to. After about half an hour, the three ships started flying in the troops, and about two hours later, at around 5 pm, the Argies hoisted the white flag!

The whole incident took only five hours and not one person on either side was killed, which was very fortunate. Only one of their submariners was badly injured in an accident during the day, and a Royal Marine cut himself climbing over some barbed wire.

Something you may have heard about was the shooting of the Argy PO the following day. That happened when he tried to scuttle the submarine, which was listing heavily in the harbour. He was shot before he could actually do any damage, and the Royal Marine who shot him was actually living in our mess at the time, so I know how that happened.

We took about 200 prisoners, and the surrender document was signed the following day. After that the cleaning operation began. The Argies had raided and looted every building and left the place in an awful mess.

I managed to go ashore there on Wednesday to see things for myself, and managed to see Shackleton's grave, which is marked quite near by. After staying there for the week, we started heading north again in company with our supply ship, and between us we are carrying all the prisoners away from the island. Two days ago all the mail came on board, and that was the first time we had had any mail since the 11 April, so that should explain the long delay in writing.

I was never really scared during my time down there, though after what happened to *Sheffield*, I suppose I should have been. It's just that I was so busy and everything happened so fast, I did not really have time to worry about anything. Still, we are away from any danger zone now, and with the mail on board, I now have a bit of time to relax.

I've been keeping very well on here lately. It's surprising how fit one can keep, just going up and down all the ladders during the day. I'm still managing to have a good laugh, and I know I'm on a good ship, so I'm sure everything will turn out all right in the end.

P.S. Please empty the swimming pool before I get home – I never want to see water again!

It was finally confirmed that we would be meeting up with HMS *Antelope* on Friday, 7 May and that all our British civilian guests and prisoners would be leaving us. So I quickly finalized plans for the 'three bears' leaving run! I knew I was not meant to give them any alcohol, but I reckoned I would be allowed to if the commander himself was serving it with me. So, plucking up the courage to ask the question, I went to see him and invite him down for a call-round with the master at arms and a couple of other senior people to show them that there were no hard feelings and that we British were jolly nice chaps. 'Not like the Argies, Sir, who'd left them rotting away on South Georgia, without any decent facilities or even a change of clothes!'

The commander agreed unreservedly, and also agreed not to let on to them that they were going the following morning, because I had another wheeze lined up for them then! So that evening, straight after his broadcast, the commander and his 'selective entourage' appeared at the door of the 'three bears' den. Polly had popped one crate of beer into the fridge and had laid on a few nuts from the NAAFI, to which I had added a few bits and pieces from the galley in exchange for invitations to the chief cook and a couple of the chefs. Although none of the visitors could speak any Spanish, I managed to entertain everyone with my display of visual and drawing communication skills – all of which greatly amused the guests, who joined in the scribbling and hand-waving antics.

The commander could only stay an hour, and when it was time for him to leave I got the 'three bears' to say in almost perfect English, 'Thank you very much, Sir, for looking after us.' The commander was delighted with my show of hospitality, but he was not completely taken in by the excuse of a 'cocktail party', because as he left the mess he whispered in my ear, 'Don't let them drink too much, Yates, but make sure you show them which is the best side to be on!' So I did.

Although we were in a war and great losses had recently been suffered on each side, and we were in a state of extreme readiness, the commander knew that a bit of alcoholic PR would not do no harm, least of all to a virtual 'spare man' like myself and three harmless prisoners. What he did not know, though, was that in addition to the one crate that Polly had managed to 'lose' from the NAAFI beer cellar, there were another three hidden around the mess. Once the wardroom party had left, twenty other people of various ranks took their place for the *real* 'three bears' leaving run, including our next-door neighbour, No. 1 – with a gift of more free underwear and socks!

It was not difficult to get the 'bears' drunk, their lack of sea legs made them sway and wobble all over the place whenever they stood up to retrieve another tin, shake hands with someone or go to the heads. They were not the only ones wobbling, either, we were all glad of the temporary release from the 'two tins a day' routine, and made the very most of it. We knew we would not be getting fresh stocks of beer on board for some time, and after the strike on *Sheffield*, we also knew this might be our last 'leaving run' ever.

In the morning, the 'bears' den was not a pretty sight, and I was really glad I had had the foresight to get Chopper to bring down a nice big pot of tea and a large bag of hot bacon rolls. For the 'three bears' were not very happy, nor were their sore-headed keepers!

Just before lunchtime we met up with *Antelope*, and began transferring our human cargo, starting with our people and ending up with 'Nasti Asti' and then the 'three bears'. I had one final surprise in store for them. I had decided it would not be right to let them return home in the old clothes in which they had arrived. They deserved far better than that.

In their time on board, they had varied the clothes they wore on a daily basis, so that one set would always be in the laundry. One day they wore their own clothes, the next day they wore No. 8 trousers and *Antrim* T-shirts, and that day they just happened to be in their finest *Antrim* gear. They still did not realize they were leaving the ship when I started getting them ready. I made sure all their own shirts had gone to the laundry (and been ditched), then merely told them we were moving to another mess and would just be going for a little walk. We put on our jackets and I led them off for what everybody else on board knew would be their final tour of the ship – with a small detour via the hangar!

At the hangar, with *Antelope* over in the distance, they still did not realize what was happening. I quickly shook each of their hands and one of the Fleet Air Arm men escorted them into the helicopter. I was sad to see them go, because looking after them had been a real break from the normal routine, and we had had some good laughs too. But despite all the games and all the little tricks we had played on each other, as I stood watching Humphrey make her way over to *Antelope*, I knew that I had definitely had the last laugh. For I knew that, in a couple of days they would arrive at Buenos Aires – with their HMS *Antrim* T-shirts on!

CHAPTER TWELVE

Total Exclusion Zone

Having completed all the transfers, we immediately turned south again to join up with the main convoy, heading towards the total exclusion zone (TEZ). We made good speed in the relatively calm seas overnight, and by mid-morning had finally tagged on to the back of the latest group of ships, which included the hospital ship, SS *Uganda*. We felt pretty safe so far away from the Falklands, but we received a rude reminder that there was still a war going on when suddenly, at 1705, we heard the familiar 'click', followed closely by the claxon and the all too familiar 'pipe' of, 'Hands to action stations. Hands to action stations'. We did not stay 'closed up' for very long this time however, as it was only a precautionary measure to counter an Argentinian spotter plane that was apparently picked up on radar. Never coming closer than 20 miles, it was out of range, but it certainly kept us on our toes.

As we continued heading south, we were shown copies of the *Antrim* 'newsgram' that had recently been sent to all the families back home, through the *Antrim* Families' Association. Although we were sending letters home on every possible occasion, the powers that be had decided it would be good PR if the ship also sent back a communiqué, which might help to reassure our loved ones at home. The first signal-written text ran like this:

1.   IN SPITE OF ARGY PROPAGANDA ALL ON BOARD *ANTRIM* ARE FIT, WELL AND LIVING UP TO THE SHIP'S MOTTO 'ALWAYS READY'. *ANTRIM*'S CONTRIBUTION TO A MOMENTOUS MONTH IN THE NATION'S HISTORY HAS BEEN SIGNIFICANT AND WE ARE PROUD TO HAVE BEEN INVOLVED. WE ARE ALSO PROUD AND GRATEFUL FOR THE SUPPORT YOU OUR FAMILIES AND FRIENDS HAVE DEMONSTRATED IN YOUR LETTERS AND RECORD REQUESTS. IT HAS HELPED US CONSIDERABLY KNOW-ING THAT YOU HAVE ALL RESPONDED IN MOST SUPERB FASHION.

2. IN ADDITION TO A WIDE RANGE OF ARGY BASHING PREPARATIONS OUR ACTIVITIES HAVE INCLUDED A RUMBUSTUOUS CROSSING THE LINE CEREMONY (IN A TROPICAL DOWNPOUR), FUND RAISING FOR ANOTHER *ANTRIM* GUIDE DOG (PERHAPS TO BE NAMED GEORGINA), A RAFFLE AND BEARD GROWING COMPETITION; MANY OF THE YOUNG SAILORS ARE NOW WORZEL GUMMIDGE LOOK ALIKES.

3. SINCE LEAVING GIBRALTAR ON 29 MARCH WE HAVE STEAMED NEARLY 10,000 MILES AND HUMPHREY THE HELICOPTOR HAS FLOWN OVER 100 HOURS, 3 TIMES THE MONTHLY QUOTA. A PIGEON KNOWN AS PERCY TOOK UP RESIDENCE IN *ANTRIM* FOR NEARLY A WEEK BUT HE LEFT WHEN THE WEATHER GOT COLDER. WE HAVE SEEN ICEBERGS, SEALS, ALBATROSS AND PENGUINS AND HAD 2 ANTARCTIC TEAL DUCKS (DONALD AND DAFFY) ON BOARD FOR DELIVERY TO SIR PETER SCOTT.

4. TO CONSERVE FOOD WE HAVE REDUCED TO ONE MAIN MEAL A DAY WITH LUNCH CONSISTING OF SOUP AND HOMEMADE ROLLS NOW KNOWN AS BERGY BITS. THE WEATHER HAS BEEN REASONABLE ALTHOUGH A STORM FORCE 11 REMINDED US THAT THE SOUTH ATLANTIC IS A HARSH ENVIRONMENT. WE WERE PLEASED TO HEAR ABOUT THE ONE POUND A DAY EXTRA ALLOWANCE, BUT AWAIT CONFIRMATION OF RUMOURS ABOUT A 9 PER CENT PAY RISE. PLEASE DO NOT SPEND IT ALL BEFORE WE COME HOME. WE MISS YOU AND LOVE YOU. SEE YOU SOON.

Although there was some humour, it had obviously been written by an officer, and was not the sort of thing that most of us would have produced. But then I guess that was why an officer wrote it; certainly if it had been me the content would have been a little more realistic. Anyway to our families who knew no better, it was at least a sign that someone up top had cared enough to send them something – and in that respect, I suppose it did no harm.

Not yet in the TEZ, but close enough to increase our state of readiness, on Monday, 10 May we again went to full defence watches, with everyone sleeping fully clothed and other quick-reaction rules reintroduced. Our brief respite was over, and now it was time to get really serious again. But for one of *Antrim*'s men, this return to a much grimmer way of living was too much to handle, for one of the lads went berserk.

It was in the evening after supper, when the watch change had been completed and the ship had returned to its deathly quiet state. I had just taken three steps down the for'ard ladder heading for the bathroom when someone rushed to the bottom of the ladder and started clattering up it. This in itself was not unusual, as 'right of way' differences of this nature were always taking place. So I just shouted down the usual warning, 'Coming down, mate.' Normally, the second person on the ladder would back off. There was no rank involved, it was just common naval courtesy at sea.

On this occasion, it did not take me long to realize that this man was not going to back off for anyone – not even the skipper. Ignoring a second shout, he continued storming up the ladder, barged straight past me and shot out of the top of the hatch like a cork out of a bottle. Naturally, I was a bit annoyed by this and seeing that he was only an AB, I yelled at him, 'Oi, don't you even say "cheers, mate" when someone lets you up a ladder after they've got on it first?'

He was already breaking into a jog down the main passage, but he turned round with a raging expression on his face and screamed back, 'WHY DON'T YOU GO AND SCREW YOURSELF!'

Following the unusual rude display on the ladder, this outburst really caught me unawares, and as he disappeared from sight I thought I had better go and see what was the matter with him. So I started moving after him, and shouted out, 'Oi, you, get your arse back here now – and that's an order.'

But before I could run very far, the 'joss' came rushing by saying, 'It's all right, Rowdy. I'm dealing with this one already.'

So I let him get on with it and continued back down the ladder towards the bathrooms, thinking that would be the last I would hear of it – unless he wanted me to give a statement. But less than ten minutes later as I was returning to the mess, I bumped into the 'joss' again. Panting, he said, 'Rowdy, where did that bloke go to after he ran off?' I told him all I knew, but said I could not really guess where he had gone because once past the end of the main passage he could have gone anywhere – left, right, up or down. I then helped him and the RPO, who had also arrived on the scene, look for the man, who had clearly been in a very distressed state for some reason or another. The three of us scoured the ship and spoke to the bridge, the operation room and the section bases, but nobody had seen him. Under the circumstances there was only one thing that we could do, something that we had only ever done as an exercise before – conduct an Operation Thimblehunt.

Operation Thimblehunt involves every single compartment being searched for a suspect device or missing person, including locked areas, in the bilges, even inside the ship's radar masts. Not a single area is left unexamined. In exercises, it had actually been like a giant game of hunt the thimble: we had had to find a package that had been carefully hidden, often days before. But this was not an exercise and it was not a package. This was a hunt for one of our own men in the middle of the South Atlantic. It did not take long for us to realize that this poor man was so upset that he may have thrown himself overboard, for hunt as we did, nobody could find him anywhere!

Just about everyone in bed had had their sleep disturbed, but once the news got out that he could not be found, an irritable atmosphere was replaced by one of great concern. The situation was so bad that the whole flotilla of ships was briefly turned around to see if we could spot his body in the water, although everyone knew that nobody could survive long in those cold seas. In the ship's office a signal was even being drawn up to inform the authorities back home that one of our men had committed suicide.

Then to everyone's immense relief, the distressed AB was found, of all places, inside the captain's boat hanging from its davits high on the upper deck. I never found out what caused him to act as he did, but I think it reminded everyone that whilst we knew about the dangers that faced us outside the ship, in this war, as in any other war, there would also be dangers lurking in our own minds.

Fortunately, the following day was a very ordinary day at sea in defence watches, as we headed towards the war zone. It was a good day, for catching up on some of the events that had been going on further south and back home for most of which, as usual, we were grateful to the BBC World Service. At home, our latest carrier was being rushed through the builder's yard, and tension all round the country was building as our forces gathered for the next stage of the war. Clearly, some of what was said was propaganda, but from all the various news sources it was now quite obvious that we had gone way past any possibility of ending the conflict by political means. We heard that HMS *Alacrity* had shelled suspected enemy positions around Stanley, and that Sea Harriers and then the SBS had attacked the Argentinian trawler *Narwhal*. We also heard that HMS *Coventry* and HMS *Broadsword* had managed to shoot down a couple of Skyhawk jets and a Puma helicopter with Sea Dart missiles. *Alacrity* had also apparently sunk an Argentinian, Supply Ship with her 4.5 inch gun.

But as well as the good news, there was also bad. For we also heard that HMS *Sheffield*, after a forlorn attempt to tow her away from the TEZ had sunk. Seven days after her death, the burial at sea had taken place – of the still smoking Type 42 destroyer, and the 'Shiny Shef' was no more.

Back in defence watches, the monotony was beginning to bite as it had done before, broken only by the refreshing but all too quick meal breaks. The ship just plodded on at the same speed as the slowest in the group, in our own twilight but ever ready and highly tensed world. Despite the peace and monotony on board, however, elsewhere the action was hotting up again. Back home the *QE2* had finally sailed from Southampton with her cargo of Scots and Welsh Guards and Gurkha Rifles. When Barry Big Ball heard that they were coming down to join us he called out, 'Bloody hell, lads! There'll really be some bloody ears and noses getting chopped off now if we can't beat them before that bunch of savages get down here. Wild Scotsmen, crazy Welsh bastards, and a bunch of knife-slashing Gurkhas. Boy, I'm flippin' glad I haven't got to face that bloody lot!'

Local news was not quite so bright, however; as *Sheffield*'s sister ship HMS *Glasgow* had also been attacked and hit by a bomb – which had miraculously passed straight through the ship without exploding, or even killing anyone.

I wrote home:

I hope you are all well and having some nice weather to start the summer. It'll be another week before this letter goes off the ship, but I thought I should start writing now, as the last time I had a great rush trying to write about ten letters in one afternoon!

I'm keeping very well myself, but I'm afraid we're all getting very bored with all these days at sea (52 of the last 56). Nobody seems to have any work to do at the moment and people are just sitting around all the time reading books. I've lost count of the number that I've read these past few weeks.

I suppose after the excitement of South Georgia, this is all a bit of an anti-climax for us now. We unloaded our prisoners and passengers the other day – they went on a ship heading up to Ascension Island. Before my scrap metal merchant friends left, I swapped a pound note for a Uruguayan bank note. I don't think it's worth much, but it'll make a nice souvenir.

I believe all the prisoners we took will be flown back to Argy-land soon. It sounds crazy coming all this way, taking an island, capturing all those Argies, and then letting them go a couple of weeks later!

It seems the two governments are no nearer a solution, and all the time it's wrecking their economy and costing ours a fortune. There must be 100 different ships down here now, so imagine the cost of fuel and food for that lot.

The list of casualties came through from *Sheffield* the other day, and I'm sorry to say I knew four of them. Altogether, about twenty were killed – eight cooks, one caterer and eleven others. The Exocet must have gone into the ship and exploded near the galley, and by all accounts it was a lucky shot that caught them unawares.

The next few days were also uneventful, but we heard that ashore in the Falklands under a heavy bombardment from *Glamorgan*, a team of SAS had attacked the airstrip at Pebble Island, destroying all eleven Argentinian aircraft on the ground. Although two men were slightly injured, they were all eventually safely evacuated by helicopter. We wondered if Charlie was amongst them, and if so, what he thought of yet another ride in a 'pusser's chopper'!

We had been going so slowly that, the *Fearless* group caught up with ours, bringing the combined convoy total to twenty-nine ships! Apart from the extra feeling of comfort that the additional forces gave us, the best thing about the new arrivals was the chance to send mail home. So that night, as soon as I found out, I wrote home.

Did you hear about or see those two girls from Anglia TV who got back to UK yesterday? They were the two that we brought away from South Georgia. They even came down to the office once for a cup of coffee and a chocolate biscuit.

We heard today that our SAS friends had blown up some planes on the ground in Port Stanley. We're all pleased about that because, as you can imagine, our biggest threat comes from their air force.

I've managed to get a few 'presents' from the Argies: A helmet, a working shirt and a few cooks' T-shirts. The helmet is brand new, so it must have belonged to one of the conscripts. My mate in the SAS gave it to me for some extra food I gave him!

I hope you are not too worried about me at home. I feel pretty safe myself, and I had much sooner be on the *Antrim* than on one of our tankers. We all sleep in our clothes with our lifebelts and boots hanging from our beds, and we can all be in full action stations in three or four minutes, which is pretty good.

I think the whole thing will probably be over by the time you get this letter – that's what I hope anyway. Then we can all come away from this dark, cold place at the end of nowhere.

As we needed to top up with fuel, and it was finally safe to do so, *Antrim* refuelled with RFA *Tidespring*.

In the commander's broadcast on 16 May, we were informed that a further two Argentinian supply ships had been sunk by our Sea Harriers, and that *Alacrity* had landed a reconnaisance team of SBS on the banks of a place called North Falkland Sound, a fairly narrow strip of sea which divides the West and East Falklands like the ragged slash of a Gurkha's *kukri* knife.

Monday, 17 May, our fiftieth day at sea, marked a bit of a landmark in our trip. It was not that it was a particularly long time to be away from home, but this was fifty days *at sea*, when the normal stretch between ports, was fourteen days! Apart from a few ex-submariners, there was not a single man on board who could remember doing anything like this length of time.

We received reports that two Super Etendards had launched an Exocet attack on *Glamorgan* – but had been frightened off without releasing their bolts of exploding death. Whilst not exactly attacking in massed squadrons, this was clearly a sign that the Argentinians would still have a go whenever they could, trying to inflict a second *Sheffield* in revenge for their *Belgrano* and the other losses they were now sustaining. To us on board, it underlined yet again the need for razor-sharp reactions, because we did not know if the next attack would be directed at us.

The following morning we completed a swift replenishment with RFA *Stromness*, taking on some much-needed victuals and naval stores, as well as fifty members of the SBS. So with total numbers climbing back towards the 600 mark, rather than our normal 480, life was yet again pretty cramped and uncomfortable, with all the hot-bunking and groups of men sleeping in passageways that we had experienced before.

On the action front, things were also hotting up, as after the previous day's gentle little reminder, we again went to action stations – after the group had all gone to 'air raid warning red'. The colour-coded warning system was pretty well known to us before the war, but down here it was not just a means of enhancing exercise scenarios, it was for real. For a ship already in full defence watches and already closed up at action stations, there were two further warnings that could be broadcast to heighten even further the state of readiness in a battle group: 'air raid warning yellow – attack expected and air raid warning red – attack imminent'.

There were no pre-warnings, just the brutal yellow and red which, when broadcast, put the fear of God into us. Sometimes I wished they would not 'pipe' the warnings at all, and just take us to 'action stations' instead and let us get on with it. After all, the vast majority of us could not see any planes approaching from our enclosed positions on the lower decks. It only made us nervous when we knew there were jets coming in to kill us, and, unlike a soldier on the ground, we could not even tell which direction they were coming from. Dick Turpin summed it up quite nicely after this latest warning when he yelled, 'Oh bloody cheers. Thanks a bunch for letting us know we're all going to get blasted out of the bloody ocean – how the hell am I meant to get me bloody head down now you doughnut.'

In fact, the warnings were usually accompanied by some sort of follow-up running commentary which did give us some clues as to their positions, but 'coming in from the west' did not help when most of us did not even know which direction the ship was facing! Fortunately, the 'red', did not materialize into anything more serious than an alarm. But it certainly disturbed a few lads' sleep.

On the Wednesday we received news that chilled us just as much as the Exocet strike on the *Sheffield*. We heard that a Sea King helicopter had crashed on its way to HMS *Fearless*, with the loss of all twenty-one on board, including eighteen SAS. The news hit us like a giant mallet blow, especially when it became known that three of our former SAS troopers had been on that flight. Moreover, the crash had not resulted from enemy action, but from mechanical failure, probably brought about by a bird getting sucked into the air intakes. Our three SAS troopers had already have been in two helicopter crashes on Fortuna Glacier, and now they had been killed by an otherwise harmless bird.

Soon after these details were released, we received news which increased our already thumping pulse rate. The stage was set for the main assault on the Falklands, and *Antrim* was to lead the attack the following evening! We guessed it was coming, but now it had been confirmed. The level of excitement on board went through the roof. 'This is it, you men,' shouted Barry in his best John Wayne accent. 'Get your goddamn shithouse paper in your saddle bags and prepare to move on out!'

We did not have too long to dwell on the matter though, for the next 'pipe' announced that mail would close shortly – and this might be the last chance to send mail for some time. Scrambling for our writing pads, the ship must have been at its weakest state of readiness since the 'crossing the line' ceremony. For just about everyone stopped what they were doing and wrote a few short lines home, all realizing they could be our very last on earth.

As I sat alone in the catering office, I thought of my grandfather and the letter he must have written home to his parents the night before going 'over the top' at Loos in 1915. I was unsure of what I needed, wanted or was *able* to say even at such a critical moment in my life, for there were just so many things I wanted to tell my family – like how much I loved them, how, when they thought of me, they should always be brave and cheerful, and all the other things that young men say when they are going off to war. But in the end I could only bring myself to write these short lines:

Mail is going off in half an hour and we're hopefully going in to take back the Falklands tomorrow! By the time you get this letter it'll all be over anyway, but I wanted to make sure I got a letter in the post before we go. I'm really confident we're going to teach them a lesson.

I'm not feeling too scared, but obviously there's a lot going through my mind. I hope our ship does well when we go in, and I hope our lads ashore give them hell.

I'll write to you as soon as it's all over, and hopefully I'll have more time then – we were only told about mail closing five minutes ago!

Don't worry about me, by the time you read this, I expect I'll be on my way home.

CHAPTER THIRTEEN

Fanning Head

Somehow, despite the impending attack, I managed to sleep fairly well and, also surprisingly, I felt pretty calm on the morning of Thursday, 20 May as I went for breakfast then sauntered down to the catering office. I had been working down there for three weeks, and even in defence watches I was quite enjoying life back in a catering environment – rather than working in the galley or wardroom. My duties were exactly the same as on *Salisbury*, with the same mind-numbingly boring ledgers, but not with the same hard graft of hauling stores from all round the ship. To access *Antrim*'s provision rooms all we had to do was turn right out of the office door and there they all were – freezers, fridges, dry stores, the lot. We even had a mechanical lift up to the galley, so although storing ship was still extremely manpower-intensive, the rest of our daily work was not so physically demanding. There was, however, just one slight problem: with *Antrim* so tightly cram-stored for war, there was still a vast amount of food stowed in other parts of the ship – one of which was our 'bunker' of tinned vegetables up in the former senior rates dining hall.

I was an 'additional hand', but because of the extra people and stores on board I had been sent down from the galley, where my undoubted skills at chopping up meat and making 'Summer soup', whilst no doubt missed immensely, could easily be covered by other far more competent chefs. Normally the five of us all worked a day-work routine of 0800 to 1600, but during defence watches the chief caterer remained on day-work while the rest of us were split into two twelve-hour watches. Albert and I worked from 0700 to 1900 and Shiner and Dick from 1900 to 0700. That morning, straight after our breakfast of a bacon roll and a mug of tea, Albert and I went down to join the chief caterer, whilst the other two went off to bed for the day. We quite liked this arrangement, as it was far less disruptive than working the normal shorter rotational defence-watch routine. And although most of the time we could not actually see whether it was daylight or not, at least we could maintain some sense of day and night, and with twelve straight hours off, we were also guaranteed a reasonable amount of time in our beds – unless of course the ship's alarm sounded, for then it did not matter what sort of defence watch you were working because everyone had to close up at their action stations. So that morning, although Shiner and Dick had gone to bed, along with many other 'off-watch' personnel, nobody expected them to stay there until the next watch change.

Just as expected, as the morning progressed and the plans for the following day's landings were finalized, the word spread round that we would be going to action stations at 1300, ready to lead the attack force into North Falkland Sound. Still unable to make 'pipes' because of the ship's quietened status, news circulated that there would be four attack waves of vessels. *Antrim* would be leading the first, along with HMS *Plymouth*, HMS *Brilliant*, HMS *Broadsword*, HMS *Yarmouth* and HMS *Ardent*. The midday watch change and lunch complete, our attack wave went to action stations as we advanced towards the sound at 11 knots. The attack was under way.

At South Georgia, although the tension had been rising, it was not until Humphrey spotted the *Santa Fe* that we were forced to play our cards and attack. So we had not really had time to think about what lay immediately ahead. Moving ever closer towards the Falkland Islands, however, we had plenty of time to think about what was about to happen – and our thoughts were not very pleasant ! The talk was of our group being the attack guinea pigs, the ships to punch the hole that others would then try and burst through – or as Whisky Dave, the chief caterer so bluntly put it, when he heard this plan, 'Oh, bloody marvellous that. The bastards will be waiting for us with Exocets, and when they've used them all up, the rest of the bloody ships will be able to walk in unopposed!'

Being part of an attack in any ground, air or sea situation is not pleasant, but leading it offers a greater risk, or so it appeared in the minutes that ticked past after the alarms had sounded, as tension heightened even further. As well as all the usual user checks on guns, weapon systems, sonars, radars, damage-control apparatus and every other defence and attack mechanism, we were also paying very close attention to our own personal defence preparations. We user checked how we might react if a missile came through, what fire-fighting gear we could use, which way we could try to escape, and how we could increase our personal protection.

All these thoughts now ran through our heads, and although we had already practised drills over and over before, we ran through them once again. We were now doing everything possible to ensure our best chance of survival under any circumstances, and despite the extreme seriousness of the situation, some of the defensive measures taken were actually quite funny.

In order to put as much protective metal between themselves and the outside world, non-combatant lads were clambering into all sort of dark areas in the middle of the ship, hoping to improve their chances of survival. Men wedged themselves into heavy metal cupboards, in between office safes or next to heavy workshop lathes – anywhere they thought they would increase the amount of armour around their bodies. In the galley, the best positions were right in the middle, next to the large solid Hobart food mixer and the cupboards that supported the bread-roll making machine. In our position in the senior rates' dining hall, even our tinned vegetable 'redoubt' was being strengthened with extra layers of baked beans and tomatoes, so that it now resembled a Russian pillbox at the height of the siege of Stalingrad!

The other thing that added some much-needed humour to the situation was that, since our capture of South Georgia, the battle dress we were now wearing was becoming increasingly bizarre. For just like the Sioux after the Battle of the Little Big Horn, the big chiefs and little indians of *Antrim* were now also wearing the clothes of our beaten enemies. There were lads wandering around with Argentinian shirts, jackets, boots and all sorts. One certain killick caterer even had his Argentinian helmet on! But the humour did not just stop at what we were wearing. Some people went over the top, strapping rolls of bandages or water bottles to themselves to make themselves look like American GIs, and two men really used their imaginations to create battle dresses probably never seen in any battle before!

One of the 'booties', Spider Webb, had obtained from somewhere a brightly coloured stuffed parrot that he had stitched onto the shoulder of his flak jacket. To complete the picture, he had carefully painted small drips of white and black paint below the bird to make it look like it had been relieving itself down his back!

That sort of thing, coming from a 'booty', or even a lowly matelot, was understandable, given our warped sense of humour. But for me the one that really took the biscuit as we attacked the Falklands was our commander's battle dress. He was wearing something that surely was not included in the courses at Dartmouth. Produced by the master gunner's people, it was an oddly shaped metal helmet to which had been attached two cow horns. As a result he became known as 'Hagar the Horrible'!

It might sound crazy that at such a time he should act like this, but it was just the sort of thing that kept morale on board as high as it undeniably was, even though most people were also terrified at the prospect of what might lie ahead. It certainly kept my morale up, and I will always remember the first time I saw him coming round to inspect our tinned vegetable redoubt.

'Ah Leading Caterer. Where did you get that hat from?'

'Sir, I won it in a raffle at South Georgia. Where did you get yours from Sir, steal it from a Viking museum?'

There was also a much darker moment, when news spread round the ship that a second lad had cracked. This time I did not witness the incident, but I could just picture the distressed state the lad must have been in when his remaining thin wire had snapped. Fortunately he was calmed down before he had a chance to do himself any harm, and I believe he spent the next few hours doped up to prevent a reccurrence. But again it sent the message around *Antrim* that we had to try and fight our own internal enemies as well as the ones waiting for us in the skies ahead.

Already at full action stations, as we moved closer and closer to the Falklands we knew that the next warning of attack would be in the form of a 'yellow' or 'red'. And sure enough at 1520, the ship's broadcast beat out the message we had all been dreading, 'Click – AIR RAID WARNING YELLOW – AIR RAID WARNING YELLOW – TASK FORCE COMING UNDER ATTACK FROM TWO MIRAGES AND TWO ENTENDARDS.'

We blinked at those around us and our hearts beat faster and faster. Hairs stood like porcupine quills on the back of our necks, and some even felt physically sick. There really were forces out there which were coming straight for us to try and blast us out of the water and wipe us off the face of the earth.

The operations room gave a running commentary of events, which kept us well informed, but also increased the level of anxiety in the 'blind' decks below. Those without their fingers on buttons, controls, machinery or triggers instinctively looked from side to side to check their damage control and survival equipment – or their fastest bolt hole. In the tinned vegetable redoubt, four of us huddled in our own little cubbyholes with our eyes closed in the semi-darkness, our minds trying to track the movements of the air attack in our tensed-up heads.

This attack was beaten back by Sea Harriers from the defensive umbrella of the carrier air protection, (CAP). So the immediate danger was over, but we knew our pulses would probably not stop racing until the attack was over, however long that might take – which nobody could really hazard a guess at.

The Argentinians did not launch any more attacks that afternoon, and our small force of ships was left to continue unimpeded towards the islands. Darkness came, and with it a reduced risk of counter attack, and at 1920 the next stage of the operation commenced when *Antrim* and *Ardent* broke away at 29 knots to enter North Falkland Sound itself.

By this time we had had supper, and although we were still closed up, some of the men took advantage of the perceived lull to catch a few winks of sleep. I stayed awake, not just because I was not particularly tired, but also because I did not want to spoil any sleep I might be able to grab at my normal time overnight – thereby keeping my body-clock in the best shape I could. From our action messing station in the redoubt, just as in South Georgia, we took it in turns to drift round the ship and top up urns of hot drinks, although now there were no No. 3 biscuits or other snacks, because they had run out long before. But we were able to do our bit to keep spirits reasonably high amongst the massed huddles of spread-eagled men, mostly indistinguishable owing to their filthy coverings of full anti-flash.

With all the tension and waiting around, it was clear that things did appear to be going according to some sort of plan. We were still moving steadily forward with *Ardent*, and then at 2130, Humphrey started flying our recently embarked SBS troops ashore to reconnoitre Fanning Head, where an Argentinian stronghold was said to be positioned, with clear strategic views over the northern entrance to the sound.

As our 'local' midnight finally approached it was clear that things were really hotting up and that the next day would probably, for one reason or another, for good or bad, be a day we would never forget. And it was not just the prospect of a bloodthirsty battle that was on everyone's minds as the galley clock ticked past 2359. For as the DSO, my old rugby-playing colleague from Yeovil, said, adding to the somewhat light-hearted theme of this closing day, 'I hope tomorrow is a good day chaps, because it's my ruddy birthday!' 'At least my hair's still the same colour as when we left. Have you seen the state of the supply officer's hair? His has turned almost completely grey since we left Gibraltar!' The supply officer was not alone in succumbing to that drastic transformation, for a few others were also showing visual signs of the stress we were now under.

Friday, 21 May was only about a minute old when *Antrim* again went to action stations as a precaution against the next stage of the assault. As soon as the alarm stopped blaring, the commander, still in his Viking helmet, broadcast to the ship's company his last message to his men. 'We are now 9 miles from Penguin Island at the entrance to North Falkland Sound. The ship is silent and dark and we are heading into the sound with *Ardent*, travelling at 29 knots.' He then went on to read a last brief signal that had been received from London at 00.03. 'THE

EYES OF THE WORLD ARE UPON US. BE STRONG AND BOLD AND MERCIFUL IN BATTLE.'

Even now, the image of that incredibly tense scene just north of the Falklands, and those few short words from our homeland are enough to make my whole nervous system tremble like plucked harp strings. For with this signal, and the commander's own more personal last words of encouragement, we knew this was it – kick-off, curtain up, show time. HMS *Antrim* and HMS *Ardent*, and then the rest of our attack wave and the other three waves, and then as much of the might of the British armed forces as we could muster were ready to roar out of the Southern Ocean and start reminding the Argentinians and the entire world that this proud nation would not stand by and let others pick at the remaining bones of her once mighty empire. For now our nation's declining fortunes were ready to be thrown into dramatic reverse – and turn the course of history on its heels once more.

All of this had kept the adrenalin pumping and, despite the late hour, I was not feeling very tired. However, a little later exhaustion did finally overtake me, so at about 0100 Albert and I left the other two to keep tabs on things while we got our heads down for a while. Despite everything that was going on around us, I even had a pretty good five hours' sleep – in fact I did not even realise that the 4.5 inch gun at the other end of the ship had been blasting away for much of it!

I vaguely remembered experiencing the muffled sounds and vibrations that echoed to our position, but with so many doors and hatches closed between for'ard and aft, even the rotten smell of cordite had not been enough to wake me up. The first time I really knew something had been going on was when I bumped into the tired, blackened figure of my leading writer mate, Jimmy Riddle, as he came off watch from his shell-loading action station in the for'ard magazine at 0600. 'Bloody hell Jimmy,' I called out when I saw him. 'What the hell have you been up to?'

He did not believe me at first when I told him I had been asleep and had not really heard anything, but once he realized I was not joking, he updated me on events that had taken place during the night. Apparently, once the SBS had got themselves into good positions ashore and we had got close enough ourselves, they had signalled the Argentinians to see if they would like to surrender, but received only gunfire in response. So *Antrim* had bombarded the target area with NGS for two solid hours, firing nearly 360 rounds of high explosive 4.5 inch shells.

SBS thermal imaging reports indicated that the accuracy and rate of firepower had completely decimated the Fanning Head anti-tank and mortar stronghold and caused numerous fatalities and serious injuries.

Once the barrage had stopped, the SBS had moved in for the kill and inflicted further casualties. Jimmy said he thought we had knocked out about 140 Argentinians, but more importantly we had destroyed their only position overlooking the chosen landing sites. And now, with Fanning Head clear of defenders, the way was clear for the next stage of the attack.

CHAPTER FOURTEEN

Bomb Alley Day

After the Fanning Head defenders had finally been beaten into submission by the SBS, further troops were landed ashore from *Antrim* and *Ardent*, and the next waves of ships began taking up positions in an area of the sound called San Carlos Water at 0630.

Because of the advanced clocks in the task force, 0630 was 0130 in local time, and so we still had almost five hours of autumn darkness for the attack force, under the comparative safety that it provided, to get into full position and start landing the major contingents of assault troops. Once it became light, at about 1100, we knew that some form of enemy air attack would be likely.

Having successfully knocked out the Argentinian defences, the attack force now had to inject our own. But a few anti-tank weapons and mortars would be no match for the air attacks that were later envisaged, so a whole package of different defence mechanisms had to be quickly installed. Some of the weaponry was already familiar to us matelots, but others were quite new. We were told that several Scimitars and Scorpions and 105 mm guns were being landed ashore. We could hazard a guess at what they might look like, but talk of a Rapier air-defence system had most of us completely baffled. But as long as it did what it was designed to do, we knew we would be more than happy.

On board *Antrim*, once all our troops were ashore, our priority was to prepare the ship even further for the air attack which we all knew must be inevitable. Everywhere was now fully resecured for action after all the night-time activities, so all most of us could then do was either catch some sleep, sit around playing cards, read books or write letters. At about 1000, Albert and I did a quick tour round the ship to check the tea and coffee urns, and found the mood comparatively up-beat. We knew the Argentinians would have a go later on, but at least we would have a lot of ships nearby to assist us, and the CAP flying overhead to fend off the counter-attacks. In fact most people had actually calmed down a lot from the previous night, and were now relatively confident of seeing the rest of the day out safely.

137

At 1050, as the sun slowly rose above the horizon, the entire landing group yet again went to action stations to increase our readiness for the daylight raids that would surely come very soon. It took less than two minutes to achieve this highest state of readiness on board, after which we all sat around with our hands on radar screens, machinery, weapons, or books and cards.

HMS *Ardent* was positioned at the entrance of the sound as our 'goal-keeper', a position nobody envied, while the rest of the group took up positions in San Carlos Water to provide support cover for their troops, who had already been landed ashore. At 1145, with full daylight now upon us, Albert and I, itching to see what was going on ashore before lunch started, took a quick trip up to the hangar. The first thing that struck us when we stepped out of the last darkened hatch was the amazingly clear blue skies and the very peaceful scene about us. The air was cold, but crisp and still. The water was like a millpond. We chatted for a while with some of the Fleet Air Arm lads, then went on to the back of the flight deck to view the amazing panorama around us. Some of the ships were easy to recognize from their shapes, sizes and positions in the water. Some we could only make out by the class of vessel. Probably the easiest to pick out was the P&O cruise ship *Canberra*, with her enormous mottled white superstructure. We could also see the two specialist assault ships, HMS *Intrepid* and HMS *Fearless*. Scanning the 4 or 5 mile wide sound we could also pick out several army landing ships and civilian container vessels, all still ferrying men and machinery ashore. Fussing round the supply and landing vessels were the warships. We could not pick them all out because their distances ranged considerably, but we knew we were in the immediate company of at least HMS *Argonaut*, HMS *Brilliant*, HMS *Plymouth*, HMS *Broadsword* and HMS *Yarmouth*.

With the weather so calm and the scene so tranquil, we could have stayed up there much longer, but suddenly at 1200 on the dot the other ships' sirens started to drone and the first of many dreaded warning broadcasts was made. 'Click – AIR RAID WARNING RED – AIR RAID WARNING RED.' We were still hurling ourselves into the tinned vegetable 'redoubt' when the rest of the 'pipe' was made, 'RAID DETECTED FORMING TO THE WEST OF THE FALKLANDS.'

Our previously calm dispositions were abandoned as we again checked our safety contingency plans. What if we get hit over there? How will I get out of the 'redoubt'? Where can I find a fire hose? Which way will I go to get out of this compartment? Will there be a compartment left to get out of? For the first time during the war, I started to wonder what it would be like to get hit myself, what the shock and pain would feel like, where I would get hit, where I would prefer to get hit, and where I would prefer not to get hit. I tightened the chinstrap on my helmet, licked my increasingly dry lips, took deep, deep breaths and braced myself to do what my grandfather had done at Loos before. And although he was long gone, I felt his spirit beside me in the redoubt, and it whispered in his broad old Scottish tongue, 'Ye'll be a'right son. Keep ahaud a'yersel an ye'ell be fine.'

So this is what it feels like I thought, to be waiting below the parapet for the whistles to blow and for your chances with instant death or terrible wounds to be taken. This is what he went through as a 23-year-old in the autumn mud of northern France in 1915, and that I must now face as a 24-year-old in the freezing seas of the deep South Atlantic.

The operations room commentator broadcast his 'sitreps' as often as there was fresh news of the attack to report, but for all the talk, so far there had been no action. The drum-rolls of tension beat on and on and on as we waited in our positions. At 1205 a 'yellow' was broadcast. At 1235 it escalated to 'red', and the group actually came under direct attack for the first time. The commentator excitedly reported that two Argentinian A4 fighters were attacking *Argonaut* with rockets. Suddenly our own 4.5 inch gun cracked into action, firing 'chaff' and shells to deter and counter the A4 attack. Below decks, the rotten-egg smell of cordite confirmed that we were now in a life and death struggle. *Antrim* increased her speed, and with all the other warships began manoeuvering fast in the relatively tight confines of San Carlos Water. Although the sound was not rough, the speed and tight cornering now started to roll the ship from side to side as she banked to port and starboard on her constantly snaking evasion course.

We felt like rats in a barrel running round and round in crazy spiral patterns to avoid the farmer's stick. And this was only the start, for the raids kept on coming. At 1255, another 'yellow' was broadcast. At 1315 as the jets screamed ever closer, the alarm was raised to 'red'. Ten minutes later we fired 'chaff' again, closely followed at 1326 by three Sea Cat missiles, more 'chaff', and then our 4.5 inch gun again. *Argonaut* had had her dose of rough medicine, now it was our turn. *Antrim* was their next target, and the next entry in the rough diary that I kept was: 13.30 Fired Sea Slug. HIT.

The attacking jet had hit us! Sitting in the 'redoubt', taking notes as the battle progressed, we could clearly hear the loud 'swoosh-swoosh' as our two Sea Slug missiles were fired from the launcher. Then we felt something like a giant mule kick us up the stern of the ship, followed by some horrendous crashing and exploding sounds, only a few yards from where we were sitting. Immediately, the operations room broadcast that we had received a direct hit aft, and that the aft damage control party should investigate at the rush.

We could hear the sound of hatches and doors being rapidly opened and shut, and soon after, more men, some in fearnought suits, came rushing aft from the midships section base to provide additional support – including the commander, still in his Viking helmet. In the 'redoubt' itself, we took the only course of action we had been trained to perform, running the backs of our hands over all the rearmost decks, bulkheads and deckheads, checking for hot spots that would reveal a fire in an adjacent compartment. Whilst three or four did that, the rest ran out fire hoses to prepare for any boundary cooling or actual fire fighting that might be required. There was no panic in our actions. We worked hard together in our little team to do what we had been trained to do under those circumstances, just like performing another drill – only this drill had a bit more adrenalin in it! With no further damage control news coming from the operations room for a while, we stood next to our hoses and fire extinguishers waiting for someone to tell us what had hit us and where, and how many men we had lost. Thankfully, verbal reports from the assorted damage reconnaissance teams did not take long to filter through to our position, which was just the other side of the bulkhead from the one which appeared to have received the strike.

One of the teams came charging through an adjacent door to let us know what was going on. In a panting voice, the initially unrecognizable anti-flash-hooded man yelled, 'Listen in lads. We've been hit by a large four foot six inch bomb back aft. Looks like it's come in through the Sea Slug launcher doors and passed straight through the magazine. It did not go off, but it did cause a lot of damage and the unexploded bomb is still on board in the aft heads. Recce parties are still combing all the adjacent compartments to check for casualties and the full extent of the damage. So far, miraculously, we don't appear to have lost anyone, or had any major fires break out. But when you eventually get to see the damage back there yourselves, you'll realize what a close thing it was. We think we'll probably have to evacuate the rear end of the ship to try and make the bomb safe, but for the time being stay where you are!'

We fired loads of questions, most of which he answered. Then he left us to brief other groups further for'ard. Just as he departed, the phone rang. It was the chief caterer, Whisky Dave, on the line from down below in the catering office. 'Hi, Rowdy! What was that bloody great bang, mate?'

'Chief,' I replied, 'We've been hit by a bomb in the Sea Slug launcher doors. It passed through the magazine and is now lying unexploded in the aft heads.' There was no response, so I shouted a little louder, 'Chief, did you hear that? We've got an unexploded bomb on board.' Still there was no reply. Then I heard the sound of his phone hitting something hard a couple of times, the more distant sound of the metal office door being wrenched open, and what could only be Whisky Dave pounding up the ladder, wrestling open the hatch at the top and clambering out of the compartment.

Like everyone else on board, he had calculated the risks of being hit, and where would be the best place to shelter. Off South Georgia, when there had been a submarine threat, he had found a safe haven as far above the water line as possible, but here in the Falklands with threat coming from the air, he had thought it wiser to stay down below the water line in the catering office. The thinking was quite reasonable, but what he had not banked on was getting a bomb in the stern, especially one that had entered the Sea Slug launcher door, which led to the enormous Sea Slug magazine, which in turn ran almost half the length of the ship and backed straight onto the catering office!

Whisky Dave was not the only one to be disturbed by the news of a direct hit on the magazine and the unexploded bomb in the heads. As a 'sitrep' 'pipe' was eventually made from the operations room to confirm the state of play, several other men made their way forward through doors and hatches at a great speed. We did not have much time to think about what the consequences of the bombing might have been just at that moment, for as all this was going on, the raids continued, in what was now becoming known as 'Bomb Alley'.

Less than 10 minutes after the strike, some joker made a 'pipe' to say, 'The aft heads are now out of bound – no shit!' And then Albert and I were spared to go and do a quick walk round. We had only got as far as the midships section base when the ship was attacked again. This time, without the cover of our 'redoubt', we dived into the ship's office to join the sprawl of unrecognizable bodies curled up next to the safes and filing cabinets. Although we could hear that we had been hit again, it did not sound so loud this time, or as close. Leaving the office to move on through the ship, we were approached by one of the chefs from 3N mess, Swampy Deadmarsh. 'Here, lads! Where can I get a Y piece from? I need it to rig up some extra hoses back aft.' A Y piece is a bit of brass fire-fighting equipment that allows two hoses to be run off one hydrant or a through-bulkhead connector. Knowing there was one quite near the 'redoubt', I directed Swampy down the port side of the ship past the galley to where he would find one.

'Just outside the senior rates' dining hall it is,' I cried out as he rushed off to find it, and we went into the midships heads. Standing there chatting about how lucky we were that the bomb had not gone off, we heard the 4.5 inch gun pounding away again, and small-arms fire from up top somewhere, then we felt and heard the 'smack,

smack,smack' of cannon shells hitting us – some of them not very far away.

'Bloody hell,' I screamed. 'I'm getting the hell out of here quick! Come on Albert. Let's get back into the "redoubt"'. We ran back towards the dining hall, to find a group of men attending to someone who had been hit in the last attack. It was Swampy, who had just been removing the Y piece from the bulkhead when a cannon shell ripped through the ½-inch ship's side and the resulting shrapnel tore a small chunk out of his leg.

The first-aid party were already looking after him, so we were just going to jump back in amongst the tins of vegetables, when a couple of the lads showed us the damage that just one small cannon shell had caused – and how many layers of metal it had cut through before coming to rest somewhere in the back of a cupboard in the middle of the galley. 'Bloody hell,' I said. 'If that's what just one small cannon shell can do to half-inch sheets of steel, what will it do to a few boxes of beans?' From that moment on, all the men in the "redoubt" joined the rest of the first-aid party and other non-combatants a little further aft in the junior rates' dining hall, next to the compartment with the un-exploded bomb in it, to adopt a very different style of defence.

With the air-sea battle having raged almost non-stop for an hour, the operations room commentary was starting to be of more assistance to the 600 men on the lower decks. For as the raids came in across the low hills surrounding 'Bomb Alley', they were screaming out, 'ATTACK COMING IN FROM PORT,' or, 'ATTACK COMING IN FROM STAR-BOARD.' This let those of us down below know which side of the ship to get away from, and the survival tactic we used was quite simply to charge backwards and forwards across the dining hall and into the passageway furthest away from the attack direction. The speed at which we could cover these short distances was incredible, as might be expected under those 'stay and get killed' circumstances. As we lay flat on the deck in one passageway, the attacking 'pipe' would be made, and we would all explode from the deck like sprinters out of their blocks, and dash for survival to assume the same prone position in the oppo-site passageway in the least possible time. There were often collisions, and I well remember one occasion when the wardroom chief cook was slightly slower out of his blocks than the rest of us and someone ran straight over his back!

In between the attacks we also started to receive verbal reports and other buzzes of the damage inflicted so far, and it did not make good listening. Our Sea Slug system was out of action, and the 4.5 inch gun was of little value other than for firing chaff because of the speed of the attacking jets and their ranges when sighted. The Sea Cat missile systems were also not proving very effective, and of course we could not use our Exocet system because there were not any of their ships to fire at. So our main form of defensive weaponry were the two 20 mm Oerlikons – one of which had jammed – plus a few SLRs, all of which had been firing almost continuously since the attacks first started.

As if the feeling of being 'sitting ducks' was not bad enough, we had picked up a number of serious casualties on the flight deck, where Humphrey had also been strafed. We had also taken hits in the tiller flat, 3P and 3N messes, the wardroom heads, plus other areas of the ship, with further casualties. At only 1400, the situation was not looking too bright on board, and there were a lot of very pessimistic eyes peering out from some of the dirty anti-flash hoods that Albert and I saw around the ship.

All this time, I still believed that I would come through, and whilst my blood pressure and pulse rate must have been right off the scale, I was not so frightened I was unable to function. Instead, I experienced a strange sort of slow-motion calmness – just like in a really tough, physical rugby match, when you know it is nip and tuck but you are still taking the blows and the tackles. I would not say I was extremely confident or enjoying myself, but it was certainly an experience to remember. Throughout this harrowing time, amazingly enough, I still managed to keep my little rough diary running to record the events as they transpired through that seemingly endless day:

1405	Air raid
1420	Air raid
1445	Air raid
1520	Air raid – Two Mirages shot down by Harriers
1555	Three planes hitting HMS *Ardent* 10 miles from our position – two shot down by Harriers
1715	Air raid warning 'red' – Argies attacking HMS *Brilliant*
1730	Fleet sirens heard
1735	Two A4s destroyed – one by *Brilliant*'s Sea Wolf, one by Harrier
1740	Three Mirages tried to attack Canberra but turned away (chickens!)
1745	HMS *Argonaut* beaching

1750	*Argonaut* requested a tow!
1751	Fired at an attacking Mirage – *Brilliant* hit it
1800	Last raid formed (end of five and a half hours' battle).

After one of the raids a 'pipe' was made for a first aid party to go to the gun deck platform (GDP)'at the rush'. Knowing that this meant we had taken more casualties, and as I was visiting a midships compartment not far from the GDP at this time, I decided to go and lend a hand. I made my way up through the various hatches into the wardroom cabin flat, passed through one of the airlock doors and was about to step outside the second door, when I heard the Oerlikons spring into life as someone near the guns screamed, 'There she is over there. Take cover. Get the fucker.' Before diving back through the two airlock doors I just managed to catch a glimpse of the evil black shape hurtling towards us at over 450 miles an hour. After that, I did not hang around, and took cover back inside one of the central wardroom cabins. Once it was safe to venture outside again I did so, but by that time I found that the three casualties had already been moved to the sickbay or wardroom, so I just collected a couple of small spent shell-casings as souvenirs and returned below again before the next raid burst over the hills.

Returning to the main passage outside 1G1 mess, I came across one of our Chinese laundrymen very distressed, being escorted by one of the first aiders. He was not injured, but his helper told me, 'He was down near the tiller flat when that got hit, and he was badly shaken up.' He had been given a shot of something in the wardroom to calm him down, and now Dixie Deane was taking him down to recover in 3N chef's mess, which they thought, being below the waterline, would offer a greater level of protection than some of the other places around the ship. The move to 3N mess did not improve things either, because he had no sooner lain down on one of the middle bunks, when another raid strafed the port side of the ship and punched a number of holes not far from where he was trying to recover from his last attack.

In amongst all the raids, and the terror of coming under constant attack, we were annoyed by a broadcast by the BBC World Service. Normally, the BBC had kept us invaluably informed of events, not only at home but also down in the South Atlantic. However, during a lull between two of the raids, a crackling transmission was picked up, telling the world that a large air-sea battle was taking place and that several ships had been hit, some by unexploded bombs. It went on to say that the reason the bombs had not gone off was because the Argentinian pilots were flying too low!

Imagine our feelings, having just survived over a dozen air raids and a bomb strike in our magazine, to hear one of our own side letting the enemy know how they can improve their attacks! Fortunately, for the rest of that day at least, the Argentinians either did not appear to have picked up the BBC broadcast, or if they did, they were not paying any attention to it!

At about 1830, once it had become apparent that no more raids were coming in, I decided to pay a visit to the bridge, just as I had done at South Georgia. I passed groups of excited men, as before but what was different this time was the scene that greeted me when I finally stepped out on to one of the bridge wings. For looking around me I counted *Broadsword, Brilliant* and three other warships in 'Bomb Alley' with smoke pouring out of them from various places. *Argonaut* was now beached close to the shore and not looking good at all.

As I stood there open-mouthed, one of the seamen, Billy Cotton, called across, 'If you think they look bad, take a look through these over there at the entrance of the sound.' I grabbed the large, black rubber-cased binoculars and brought the distant image of HMS *Ardent* into view. She was sideways on with her bows facing to the right and her quarterdeck to the left. She was in flames and exploding repeatedly. It was a terrible sight to behold; one of our own ships so badly damaged, quaking in the water as each eruption in her bowels signalled a further stage of her inevitable death throes. I could see some men climbing into life rafts alongside her in the sea. I could also see other men valiantly trying to quell the fires that were so clearly raging about her tortured superstructure.

There were many others that I could not see: those below decks, who as I looked on from my safe position 10 miles away, were fighting for their lives in compartments below the water line where the doors and hatches had been buckled shut, and whose only hope of survival was to stop the freezing water from erupting from every jagged blast, shrapnel hole or split pipe and engulfing them. My mind raced back to our training exercises and how we had struggled to stem the torrents of cold liquid steel – how frightened we had been when the water had lifted us so high off the deck that our ears had touched the deckhead. But on HMS *Ardent* I knew there would be no sadistic chief stoker to scream, 'Water off, stand clear. Open the door – Let's do it again properly, shall we?' For nothing could save the men who had already lost their lives, or were now losing their fights for survival, on that brave 'goalkeeping' ship.

With the air attacks over for the day because of encroaching darkness, we now had to try and get rid of the bomb from our aft heads. Much of the ship aft of midships had already been placed out of bounds since the bomb had struck. Now, a specialist team was hurriedly convened to make the bomb safe and to cut it free from its web of tangled metal, deck-tiles, deckhead panels, twisted pipes, shattered doors, urinals and toilet pans. While this dangerous work went on, another team started cutting a suitably sized hole above the bomb in the flight deck, ready to lift it out and drop it over the side. For those of us not involved in any of these critical tasks, our role was very simple – remain closed up in defence watches, but stay for'ard of the midships cross-passageway just in case the bomb went off! Not that even that threat had stopped Albert and me from continuing our ship's tours because just before they started cutting the hole in the flight deck, we both went and stood briefly on the 'bump' it had created! However, not everyone looked on the bomb-disposal operation so light heartedly, for having a live 4 foot 6 inch 1,000 pound bomb cut out of your belly while you are still awake is not a pleasant experience, and a lot of men were extremely worried. There was no chance whatsoever of abandoning ship before commencing this operation, so we all just had to hope and pray that the bomb did not have any booby traps, and that our brave friends below knew what they were doing and had steady, dry fingers.

We later found out that the bomb had been one of a batch that the UK had sold sold to the Argentinians some years previously!

During the bomb-extraction process the other main concern of the ship's company was the lack of food as, having no access to the main galley or storerooms, lunch had had to be abandoned, and supper could also not be prepared and served as usual. The vast majority of men had not had anything substantial to eat since breakfast, over twelve hours before. Pleas were made to try and knock up something in the small wardroom galley, but this idea was rejected on the grounds of mini-mizing all power requirements and fire risks during this hypersensitive period. So apart from the intermittent and slow supplies of tea, coffee and soft drinks, most people just stayed hungry, with their stomachs also aching from the fear of what might happen if the bomb exploded and ripped us apart in the water. The lack of food did not worry me at all; I just kept focusing on how I would help fight any resultant fires and floods, and ultimately how I would make my escape to the compar-ative safety of the outside world, even though I knew the freezing seas would almost certainly kill anyone within two minutes of entering the water.

The bomb-extraction process ran smoothly, and at almost 2230, with an A frame and lifting gear rigged above the hole on the flight deck, a 'pipe' was made for everyone not involved in the lifting operation to move even further for'ard – a command that did not need to be repeated! With everyone in rearranged positions, and every conceivable hatch and door shut to reduce the impact of any explosion, the lifting operation commenced, as we all took and held deep, long breaths in our filthy, sweat-soaked anti-flash hoods. Fortunately, the lifting operation also went reasonably well, and within thirty minutes the bomb had been lifted clear of the disintegrated heads and up through the flight deck to a position where it balanced in its strong cradle, ready to be slung over the side. At this point, a signal was suddenly received telling us not to touch the bomb *at all*, because it might be fitted with an anti-tamper device.

'Too bloody late, mate,' one of the bomb-disposal team cursed when he heard this news. 'We're chuckin' the bastard over the bloody side in a minute!'

And then, with the A frame rigging adjusted and checked, the ship was manoeuvered tightly to starboard so that the deck angled as much over to port as possible, easing the task of unleashing the bomb when it was in position above the water. A running commentary was given, and once the bomb was actually released into the depths, a muffled cheer roared round the ship. We all heaved a massive sigh of relief. The immediate threat of being belatedly blown out of the water had been eradicated. The time was now past 2300, and it had been a very long time since we had entered 'Bomb Alley'. As a result, even with the prospect of an emergency meal, most people not on watch went straight to bed, or just crashed out where they lay – physically and mentally exhausted after a day that none of us would forget for the rest of our lives.

CHAPTER FIFTEEN

Licking our Wounds and Losing More Ships

I awoke on the morning after 'Bomb Alley Day' to find that *Antrim* had retreated through the night towards a safer position to the east of the Falkland Islands. The intention now was to link up with a repair ship and get a few much-needed large metal plasters for our wounds. We needed more than just a few plasters for our wounded, however; although we had not actually lost anyone or suffered too many casualties considering the number of attacks, the list of injuries did not make pleasant reading:

CPO Terry Bullingham	Permanently blinded in both eyes
RM Colour Sergeant Gordon Kendall	Severe shrapnel wounds in the shoulder and liver
PO David (Fitz) Fitzgerald	Shrapnel wounds
SM D. R. Shenton	Shrapnel wounds and burns
Lt Cdr Ian Stanley	Shrapnel wounds
Cook Alan (Swampy) Deadmarsh	Shrapnel wounds
SM C. A. (Nobby) Clarkson	Shrapnel wounds
RO(T) S. V. Bigsby	Shrapnel wounds
MNE J. N. (Pincher) Martin	Shrapnel wounds

Despite the terrible wounds suffered, *Antrim* as a whole had undoubt-edly got off lightly, for had the bomb gone off – or even taken an alternative path – it could so easily have been a very different story. All the other near misses that were recorded could also have inflicted far more serious casualties. We all know, even the seriously wounded, just how lucky *Antrim* was. The poor men listed were our fated allotment of battle victims for the day. Of Terry, the other five hundred or so on board that day can say, 'There but for the grace of God go I,' and none of us will ever forget the sacrifice he and the others paid, and continue to pay, on our behalf.

Apart from our own list of casualties and structural damage, good and bad news also filtered on board about the other details of the battle. The Argentinians had lost at least three helicopters and thirteen fighter bombers, plus numerous men in the air and on the ground. It appeared that our side had also lost three helicopters, but only one RAF Harrier. However, our most significant losses were at sea, where HMS *Ardent* had been sunk and HMS *Argonaut* badly damaged and left with an unexploded bomb on board. HMS *Brilliant* and HMS *Broadsword* had also been damaged.

Total British fatalities for the day were reckoned to be around twenty-seven, and the Argentinians many more. We realized that not only *Antrim* but also the entire task force had been lucky. It was abundantly clear that if just a few more bombs had gone off, or been more closely directed, then the end result could have been very different. With more of the warships out of the way, the Argentinians could have focused their attacks on the landing and support vessels. Then they would have been able to take pot shots at the rest of the lesser combative ships. It would have been like shooting crocodiles in a tank. The landings and every other operation in the South Atlantic could have been put in jeopardy. As it was, luck and fate played into our hands that day, and the initial landings were successfully made. From that platform the reconquest of the Falkland Islands could begin in earnest, but it was a close-run thing.

In the morning we listened as usual to the BBC World Service, and for the first time I started to wonder what it must have been like for our families and friends back home, listening in to their radios, watching for every television news flash, waiting for newspapers to drop through their letter boxes, or the postman to call, or the phone to ring with some terrible news. I now know that my own family and friends were a lot more worried than I was. At least I knew how the war was progressing, where the ship was, whether it was still afloat and whether I was still alive or not. They could not know any of that. The worry of it must have been an enormous burden to bear – particularly for my father, who had been suffering for some time with heart disease. He was a bit of a worrier anyway, and I now had real fears of what his blood pressure would be like.

At 1200 we finally met up with the main carrier group, and after lunch we conducted ammunition and fuel replenishments, both of which, after our exploits of the previous few days, were in almost desperately short supply. I crept up onto the upper deck with my camera during the transfers and managed to take quite a few photographs of the supply ships, our battle damage, and some of my friends who looked surprisingly upbeat considering the battering we had taken only the previous day. The photographs also show that we were still wearing our anti-flash, and although it was very cold, the sea was almost flat calm.

Along with the fresh supplies, we were surprised to receive and transfer mail – a sweet gift that most of us thought we might never see again. Of course the mail was quite old, and there was not much of it, but it was still good to see the handwriting of our loved ones and friends again, and then to focus briefly on scribbling hasty replies. I managed to churn out four or five responses to Jackie and others. To my family I wrote a fourteen pager, part of which I reproduce below.

You will have heard about the battle in North Falkland Sound yesterday. The first five minutes I felt shocked and very cold, but that feeling soon passed and then I felt OK. I kept thinking that Dad and both Grandads had gone through similar stuff and that I had to get through it somehow.

I kept myself as busy as possible, helping out wherever I could. The people who were most shocked were the ones who cowered in corners and panicked. I kept saying to myself, 'They're not going to get me,' and it worked well.

It's funny, but after the bomb landed, I felt even better – hardly afraid at all. I thought then that if a big bomb like that had hit us and not gone off, then it must be 'our' day. We could not use the back-end of the ship for the rest of the day, and when they eventually cut it out and dropped the bomb over the side you could have heard a pin drop.

We're now heading away from the Falklands to rejoin the main task force to refuel, rearm and get patched up. I doubt if we'll be used in any attacking forces again because of the damage to our missile systems, but we'll probably have to stay around as air defence for the carriers.

I'm telling you everything that happens, so that you'll know the truth about what's happening, and know that I'm not worried about anything. Anyway, it should all be over by the time you get this letter in the middle of June, and because of our damage, we'll be one of the first ships to go home.

And to think, only half an hour before it all started I was on the upper deck having a look at the Falkland Islands for the first time. They look just like Scotland, all green hills, but no trees. When the Scots Guards get down here they'll feel at home in this countryside!

My mate from Henley and I are going to organize ourselves a party when we get back, so get the flags out of the attic ready. He did well yesterday, in fact all the young lads I saw did well, it was just a few of the older people who cracked up a bit. I must say though, that all the officers I saw were working hard. I went for a walk on the upper deck a little while ago to look at the damage. It felt good to be alive – I can tell you.

As for the casualties, their next of kin were notified by signals almost as soon as they were hit, so it's as I said to you in an earlier letter, 'no news is good news'. I expect I must have lost friends from other ships. I only hope there weren't too many.

I've enclosed the page from my desk diary as a souvenir for you; one of my other souvenirs I was wearing a lot of the time yesterday – my Argy helmet!

I can now thank you for all the letters and parcels you've sent so far. It was just like the Christmases we used to have when I was little. I had thirty-two letters and parcels altogether, and it made me a bit homesick and nearly brought a tear to my eye.

I could do with a couple of pairs of long woollen socks – I've got some socks already, but they are short and nylon.

I hope they are classing this affair as a war back home now, instead of just a conflict. If this isn't a war, I don't want to be in a real one!

It's no use telling you not to worry about me because I know it must be hard, but I am OK, and I'm still confident we're going to beat this lot, and I know I'll be back soon.

We spent the next day under the apparent protection of the main carrier group again, but we were given two heart-thumping reminders that there were in fact no real safe havens in these waters. At 1150 and then at 1710, the nerve-jangling 'pipes' of 'AIR RAID WARNING YELLOW' were once more broadcast to the fleet. The first time, the enemy did not come close enough to endanger the group, but on the second occasion we closed up to action stations in the fastest time ever, then fired our rockets at an attacking aircraft, without actually hitting it. So after a day comparative relief and relaxation, we were given very firm reminders that this war was not over by a very long shot. In the evening, to re-inforce this stark message, we received the awful news that our third ship, HMS *Antelope*, had been severely attacked, and later the following day blown completely in two like a massive exploding firework. Fortunately, most of the ship's company had managed to get off before the last massive explosion, but she still lost two men and suffered a further five casualties. Ten Argentinian aircraft were also claimed as being destroyed, but most of us agreed that we could not afford to go on losing ships at this rate – the Royal Navy at the time only consisted of fifty or so frigates and destroyers, and now in the space of only twenty days we had lost three of them!

'Shitty death,' roared Frank Carvelli when he heard this news in the mess. 'At this bloody rate we'll have no flippin' ships left at all by the end of the week! Surely we can't go on taking bloody punches like this?'

Late that night, even with the increased protection of darkness, our the day was still not over. At 2255 there was a massive explosion. We did not know at the time what had caused it, but dreading a surprise submarine attack and loss of yet another ship, we reacted accordingly. No ships were lost that night, but we later heard that the explosion had been caused by one of our Sea Harriers exploding shortly after taking off from *Hermes*'s carrier deck, with the loss of yet another pilot.

The next day, 24 May, we were still hovering around in the main carrier group, and came under Argentinian air attack – this at 1405, when our CAP Harriers claimed to have shot down three Mirages and chased the others away. We closed up at action stations in a new record time, shaving fractions of seconds off our previous day's best time, and shredding even more brittle nerve endings. Back aft in the 'redoubt', we cursed the attacks and the loss of sleep, and voiced our concerns over the way the war was going. News from ashore did not appear to be too bad, but out here at sea, stuck below decks in large ready-made steel coffins, we were all feeling as if we were perched on the very narrowest of knife edges.

I again wrote home that night, and although my words express the optimism I still felt, the early signs of guarded desperation and despair are there too.

We haven't seen much action since leaving North Falkland Sound, or 'Bomb Alley' as they now call it. We are with the main task force at the moment, who stay well away from their aircraft, although yesterday one of them came within 40 miles of us, which meant we closed up to action stations. Today we are sailing towards South Georgia again to get some repairs done, which should give us about a week of safety and a bit of time to relax.

We hear that our troops are doing well ashore, and it can only be a matter of time before an airfield can be built and the RAF can come down and give us a hand. Yesterday the Argies lost another six planes and three helicopters, and we heard the sad news of the loss of another of our ships, HMS *Antelope*. The damage was caused by an unexploded bomb like ours which, because of a split mercury fuse, went off when it was moved. Bad luck that.

I feel kind of excited all the time; I sleep very well each night, no trouble there, but during the day I get this feeling of excitement. It's funny, but I feel much better when we go to action stations – then I seem to be able to think a lot clearer.

Their air force was reckoned to be about 240 strong and our Harrier force only about 25, and with losses of about 60 to 40 in our favour, they simply can't go on sending raids like they have done in the past.

We received a personal signal from the 'big chief' in London last night, to say that the battle in North Falkland Sound was the largest air-sea battle since the last war, and that we had achieved a substantial victory in gaining a good beach-head for our troops.

We did not have a funeral service for crews of the *Sheffield*, *Ardent*, or any of the other poor men who have lost their lives, but we all pass on our deepest regrets to their families back home.

I've made a 'HOMEWARD BOUND' stamp out of lino to use when we're on our way back. When the day comes, I'll send you a card with it stamped on the back. Hopefully it won't be long now.

Antrim had by now 'rafted up' with a repair vessel from the Fleet Maintenance Group (FMG), but stuck on the high seas there was very little that the FMG could do with our badly battered back end, so only superficial work was undertaken – just enough to improve our sea-worthiness and habitability. Without any Sea Slug, and with several other weapons systems put out of action, we knew we would be unable to play any significant part in the war for the foreseeable future. While these facts cheered up many on board, it left several others feeling frustrated that we still had not done enough. It is crazy really, because up until then *Antrim* had done more than her fair share of fighting, and those like me who yearned for even more must have been getting punch-drunk or battle-fatigued. It did not matter that we had already come under attack over fifty times; we were still ready to take on more – just like an old boxer who does not know when to hang up the gloves.

And then, as if the damage repair assessment news had not been bad enough, things became worse. We lost yet another two ships, and many more poor unfortunate men. Quite some distance away from the Falklands, with our FMG team tied up alongside, our hearts and minds were nonetheless still very much with our colleagues who were closer to, or actually on, the islands, and the 'pipes' that were made through the day brought more bad news with each broadcast. Firstly we heard that the Argentinians had launched one of their biggest raids so far, and that there had been losses in the air on both sides. Then we heard that HMS *Broadsword* and HMS *Coventry* had both been hit by Skyhawks and that, like *Antrim* a few days before, *Broadsword* had received an un-exploded bomb on board. Her helicopter which was still on her flight deck, was totally written off. Unfortunately the news from *Coventry* was not as good, it soon became clear that we were about to lose our fourth ship in three weeks.

The next news we heard was that the Argentinians had again launched an Exocet attack. This time they had hit the *Atlantic Conveyor*, with the loss not only of much-needed helicopters and many other vitally important heavy equipment that would have made quite a difference in the land battle, but also men. Little wonder then, that on 25 May – Argentina's independence day – I closed my diary with just one line: *'Morale for the first time was noticeably lower amongst the ship's company.'*

I often think back to those days and wonder how we coped when we were taking such alarming casualties. I suppose what really mattered was that we kept hold of ourselves individually and worked together as one big team, not just on *Antrim*, but in the fleet as a whole, not forgetting our comrades landing ashore and flying endless sorties in the air.

CHAPTER SIXTEEN

Task Force Ferry Boat

By 26 May, we were on a compass heading to meet up with the *QE II* north of South Georgia, and thankfully, after the last frantic few days, the day was relatively quiet for us. Moving further east, we were still licking our wounds, but to the west, cloud cover over the Falklands was very low and there were no recorded raids. The news of the *Atlantic Conveyor* also did not appear to be so bad, as it was reported that, although she had been badly damaged and had lost several men, attempts were being made to tow her back into the comparative safety of 'Bomb Alley' from her earlier, more exposed position. As a result of all this news, morale was noticeably better, and once the commander had worked his verbal magic during his evening broadcast, spirits were even higher. There was no ranting and raving, just the clear, calm words of a man who knew how to get the best out of his men and keep their spirits up when events around them did everything to bring them crumbling down. At the end of a pretty traumatic week, it was just the pep talk we needed, and his 'Keep your chins up, boys' speech lifted everyone.

I took advantage of the quiet period to write a few more letters to Jackie, other friends and girlfriends, and of course my family:

Mail is going off this afternoon onto the *QE II*, so I've taken this chance to get a letter written. We have been away from the main fleet for a couple of days, patching up the damage from the battle of the 21st. We were all shocked to hear of the loss of our fourth ship, HMS *Coventry*, which took our place after 'Bomb Alley', so yet again we have had a lucky break.

All our casualties are said to be coming along OK on the *Uganda* but we heard that a CPO has lost the sight in one eye and possibly two, so we are all doing lots to raise money for the fund which has been set up to aid their relatives.

After lunch on the 27th we finally met up with the large black and white shape of the most famous civilian ship afloat anywhere in the world, the *QE II*. Now that we were in a comparatively safe position, crowds of us poured onto the upper deck to see the ship we had all heard so much about, and yet most of us had never seen. The reason for meeting her was quite simply to save her having to go any closer to the TEZ, and allow her to transfer some of her embarked forces across to us for eventual passage to other ships heading towards the Falklands. Maintaining stationary positions about 3 miles apart, the transfer of men, equipment, and some more mail commenced – but it did not run as smoothly as planned!

Standing up on the flight deck with other men, I watched as the *QE II* liberty boat came across with her first load of troops. As she started to come alongside our quarterdeck I could easily see the packed ranks of green-clad men, eagerly waiting to commence their part in the war. But for the first man across, there was to be no war at all, because, not listening to the advice of our seamen, he failed to wait until the craft was securely alongside, he jumped across, missed his footing and (very loudly) broke his leg! Although it looked quite painful, it brought about a bit of a cheer from the naval audience hovering on the flight deck above. 'Oh, bloody good ho, that'll teach the stupid, cocky pongo [army] bastard,' someone muttered, just loud enough for us alone to hear. The 'pongo' must have felt stupid, especially when he was carted straight back to the *QE II* again.

The rest of the men finally made it on board safely, including their commander, Major General Jeremy Moore. They had certainly learned from their colleague's mistake, for they treated every naval command, and every inch of *Antrim*'s deck, with the utmost respect. In total, thirty-two wardroom-class personnel and forty-four other military passengers came on board, so it again became a bit cramped 'down below'. But our inconvenience was not half as bad as that experienced by the soldiers, for after their long cruise on the *QE II*, the tightly packed, wartime conditions on board *Antrim* came as a real shock. They just could not believe we had to live like this in peacetime, let alone during a war, and even though they were tough soldiers, we could tell that they were beginning to look on us with the respect that can only be gained when one has proved oneself in battle. And for the first time, I think we all knew we could now really call ourselves Falklands War veterans.

We now made our way back to the main carrier group, in effect playing just about the only role left open to us, that of task force ferry boat. But having overcome some of our 'punch-drunkenness', most of us were now quite happy to be playing this more peaceful non-combatant role. It gave us all a chance to practise our battle stories on our wide-eyed, greenhorn audience, and also take them on tours of the battle-damaged areas, especially the aft heads. Back aft, although the wreckage had been cleared away, it was still very easy to see where the bomb had struck and blasted her way inside, bounced around the heads, and smacked the underside of the flight deck like a boxer's jaw-crunching uppercut.

Whenever they saw this impressively destructive sight, no matter what rank they were, they stood there staring open-mouthed. 'You mean nobody got killed in this lot? Jesus Christ almighty, you boys were bloody lucky. You must have been absolutely crapping yourselves!' To which their guides would normally reply, 'Yeah, we were a bit, but the raids were still coming in thick and fast, so we did not have too much time to think about the unexploded bomb. I suppose you're right though, it could have been bloody nasty if it had gone off and blown the ship apart down the middle!' Battle-hardened matelots were quickly learning how to appear cool and blasé.

We met up with the assault ship, HMS *Fearless* or, as we liked to call her because of her peculiar flat-ended shape, *Rearless*. Being closer to the TEZ, transfers of personnel, stores and mail were soon completed, *Fearless* taking on our soldiers and outgoing mail, and us taking on some stores, two prisoners and more mail.

The commander's broadcast on 28 May updated us on the events of the past two days. On the Falklands, the Argentinians had apparently attacked the shore positions at 'Bomb Alley', killing several ground troops, for the loss of only one of their raiders. Despite this setback, our troops had started to break out from the beach-head and were now making their way across East Falkland. An attack had also been launched on a place called Goose Green, where a large force of Argentinians had been holed up in their Flanders-style trenches. Despite some losses on our side, it sounded as though their defences were proving little match for the attacking force from 2 Para, who were very much men of the last quarter of the century rather than the first!

The commander rounded off his broadcast with some light-hearted news of the Pope arriving at Gatwick Airport, where he had descended the steep narrow aircraft steps and stooped down to kiss the black tarmac. 'Yeah, I'll kiss the bloody tarmac too when I get home,' I yelled out. 'But I won't be heading off to the nearest God-shop after I've done it like that old bible-basher! I'm going for a bloody pint of Guinness first, then a Kentucky Fried Chicken, then a shag!' Needless to say, the Catholics amongst us in the mess tried hard not to laugh at this obvious insult to their leader.

I again found the time to scribble a letter home.

Last night we had some more mail come on board, and one of your letters was dated 30 March – so that's been kicking around for nearly two months!

We are moving back to South Georgia today to act as guard ship for the stores ships and tankers, so I think that's our part in this war over with. The only problem is we've probably got a few boring weeks at sea doing nothing. Last night the weather broke again, and the seas are running high. Today it's the same, so I think I'll get my head down for a rest this afternoon! We heard yesterday that 2 Para had captured Goose Green and taken 500 prisoners! So the situation must look pretty hopeless for the rest of the Argies in the Falklands.

Two more prisoners came on board us yesterday (the last one we had was Astiz). I saw them being searched, and they looked a proper scruffy pair. One of their pilots our boys picked up last week has been talking a lot, and said they were told there would be hardly any resistance awaiting them at the Falklands, and that all the pilots who did not return had been 'redeployed' to other airfields! (Redeployed to the drink we say.)

On Sunday, 30 May, we made our way back to South Georgia, and as we were now fairly established as the task force ferry boat, rumours were rife that as we could play no further active part in the war, we might be in the next group to head for home. It was certainly a nice thought. I personally knew enough about rumours – and the war by this stage – to realize, that whilst we could still float and fight with even limited weapon systems, we would not be going anywhere just yet. Nonetheless, some sweepstakes were started on the date when we would be going home, ranging from five to twenty days' time. Surely not, I felt, not with the war still going on – unless they needed a good, strong escort ship to shepherd any weaker, more battle-damaged vessels back I thought it might be worth an outside bet on starting to return home on the 20 June.

News from the Falklands centred on the progress of our troops ashore as they advanced ever closer to Port Stanley. Precise positions and tactical manoeuvres were unclear to us lower-deck novices, but it was apparent that having suffered a few setbacks the previous week, things were now looking much brighter. As I turned in for the night in my increasingly battered old blue nylon sleeping bag, for the first time I started to think about the war actually coming to end – and surviving. This was an incredible thought, because only a few days before it had looked as though none of us on *Antrim* would survive, or many of the other ships either. Now it felt as if the end of the war might be near. That night, after downing my two tins of beer from the fridge, I slept like a log.

The next day we received further mail and stores air drops. Their arrival heightened the increasingly positive mood on board, which the commander later added to by announcing that the land forces had now completely surrounded a 12 mile perimeter of Port Stanley. Yes, I thought, the war really might be over soon.

June arrived with the news of the loss of yet another Sea Harrier. Then came the better news that we had shot down one of their Hercules transport planes and were making further ground advances all over the islands. However, further sad news came in that the abandoned *Atlantic Conveyor* had finally sunk.

We arrived back at South Georgia on the 2nd, and found a very different scene to the one we had left on 1 May. East and West Cumberland Bays were full of great supply ships at anchor, and Grytviken itself looked to have quadrupled in size since the day Shiner and I had raided the BAS hut and taken its beer! Now that we were in a much safer environment, defence watches were relaxed and some of the lads were even allowed to go ashore to stretch their legs around the old whaling station. It was freezing cold, and there was a lot of thin drift ice in the bay, but it was good to gaze at a friendly shore again, and later when five of us got the opportunity to visit one of the 'STUFT' vessels for a 'food recce', it made the day even better. Just before darkness fell at around 1500, the chief caterer, Shiner, Slinger Wood, Banjo West and I piled into the ship's boat for the short trip across the bay to the much larger civilian ship, *Saxonia*, nestling below one of the island's steep, jagged, snow-covered cliffs. On arrival alongside, we had to scramble up the long wooden-slatted rope ladder like a troop of performing monkeys to the main deck, which towered about 25 feet above us. We were quickly whisked off for an introductory tour of this very un-familiar ship – starting, of course, with their crew's bar!

Although it was on a ship, the bar we entered was more like some-thing ashore in seaside town, full of pictures and posters and plaques. There was low lighting and music, and men sat on high stools supping pints of beer. After so many weeks of our own ship's sparse, secured-for-action conditions, this sight was a wonder to our eyes. When the drinks started to flow, the wonderment increased even further, for once we had drunk more than two cans, we realized that we were not going to be rationed. It felt good to experience our heads filling with that long-forgotten heavenly, relaxed floating sensation. However, as the chief caterer reminded us, we were on board to look at the food stores to see what we could use on board *Antrim*, particularly frozen items, which were now very low.

So leaving Whisky Dave behind in the bar to continue his 'liaison duties' the rest of us were led down a lengthy maze of passageways and stairways (not ladders as on *Antrim*), to an enormous compartment deep in the ship's hold, where our guide announced, 'Here you are lads – our main freezer. It's minus twenty-six in there, mind, so make sure you do your jackets up before you go in.' And he was not joking; it really was like the South Pole inside their freezer. Within a couple of minutes we could feel our faces hardening and our toes numbing inside our boots.

As in Grytviken, Shiner and I had a list of items we needed, so as we found boxes of frozen meats and vegetables, we pulled them onto empty pallets ready for transferring across to *Antrim* at the next available opportunity. Moving about was the only thing that kept us warm enough to think straight; our brains seemed to be numbing, as well as our limbs. Having downed a couple of pints, a couple of the lads now felt the 'call of nature' and asked to head back to the accommodation area. As we were the senior men down there, Shiner and I agreed to split the work party, and allow Shiner to nip away with Slinger for a fifteen-minute break. When they returned, Banjo and I would go up.

With just the two us of left down in the freezer, the workload doubled, but we did not mind because the extra activity helped to stem the ice-cold tentacles stabbing the inner extremities of our bodies. The only snag with working harder though, was that we forgot all about the time, until after nearly half an hour had passed it suddenly dawned on us that the others still were not back.

'Cheeky bastards,' I muttered to Banjo. I bet they're up in that flippin' warm bar drinking with the chief caterer.' How true that was we found out a another twenty-five minutes later when we staggered back up through the strange ship. We got lost a couple of times, and by the time we eventually made it back to the bar we were really angry. We opened the door to find Shiner, Slinger and our guide sitting on warm bar stools knocking back large tumblers of rum! After a while, Banjo and I managed to see the funny side of it and got on with knocking back the drinks, with me repeating over and over again, 'Cheeky bastards, bloody good kids in harbour eh – leaving your bloody mates freeezin' to death down there in that bloody igloo – you bunch of bastards.'

We did not stay much longer in the bar. First we could not, because the ship's boat had been booked for 1900 to take us back across the harbour. Secondly, because after barely surviving on only two tins of beer a day for so long, we became drunk easily. This must have made for interesting viewing as we made our way back to the boat, down the ladder that now seemed to be 200 feet long and was swaying around like a cow's tail! How we ever made it down to the boat in one piece, I will never know, nor how we made it back across the harbour without all drowning, for during our brief stay on board the sea had picked up and was now sending small waves lapping over the side of the gunwales!

In the morning, not surprisingly, none of the 'food recce' team was looking or feeling too bright. But the somewhat cavalier mood of the day was soon brought to an abrupt end later on when the list of HMS *Coventry*'s fatalities was posted on all the main noticeboards. Near the top I saw the name of my old mate Slammer Dawson from my run ashore in Gibraltar.

I could not take it in at first, but I quickly sobered up and stood there staring at the scrap of white signal paper that bore his name and those of nineteen others who had been lost when their ship was blasted by the Argentinian jets. Dodger Long, the other killick caterer from that crazy day in Gibraltar, joined me at the noticeboard. Strangely enough, my brief letter home that night made no mention of it, I suppose to hide the painful truth from my family – and ultimately from myself.

> The weather yesterday was terrible, with force eight and nine gales, a big swell and very cold. One thousand, four hundred prisoners have now been taken, and our boys are only 12 miles from Stanley, so the end must be very near now. If so, we should be back home sometime in July.

I did not sleep very well, thinking of Slammer and his mates on the *Coventry*, and all the other ships that had been lost, and of the guys in the air and on land who had lost their lives. So this was what it felt like to lose your mates, like my father and grandfather, who had lost so many of theirs – and Slammer was not even someone I had grown up with or a brother, husband, son or boyfriend.

In the morning there was better news, because mail was coming on board again, mail was the only thing that helped to maintain any sort of sanity. The letters may have arrived out of order and two weeks late, but they certainly did the trick. In addition to our normal barrage of family and other parcels and letters, we received a lot of 'fan mail' from various other sources. There were masses of unaddressed letters from randy girls offering themselves to us on our return, from caring grandmothers and from ordinary citizens across the length and breadth of the country. They even came from young school children, like the one I received, simply addressed to 'A sailor in the task force':

> Good day Sailor
> I hope you are safe
> And the Task Force win
>
> Joke
> What's big, black, ugly and dangerous?
> A crow with a machine-gun!
> Thomas Jeffery – aged 7

Support like this, from someone so young and so far away, was really touching. And as *Antrim* finished her stint as task force ferry boat, we all knew we had absolutely everyone at home rooting for us – even a totally unknown seven-year-old.

In 1G1 mess, we also started receiving the first letters back from of a 'pen pals' competition we had started soon after hearing the news that we were going south. I had been in these contests before. They were not only fun, but quite often we would end up with some pretty neat girls. If they were not up to our standards, their pictures would end up on our 'gronk board'. The idea of the competition was for each contestant to pick out three girl's names from the 'Pen Pals' section of *Navy News*, then write to them to see who got the most, and then the best, replies. Points were scored for the degree of success in this initial stage – and extra bonus points were awarded if you could prove that you had met one of the girls, made love to her, or if you brought a pair of knickers back! One or two men on the ship even ended up marrying their pen pals.

CHAPTER SEVENTEEN

South Georgia Guard Ship

On Saturday, 5 June, we returned to South Georgia in the semi-official capacity of South Georgia guard ship. It had been clear for a number of days that we were not going to be patched up in time to re-enter the fray before the war ended. Feeling certain that we would be leaving for home in the very near future, this task sounded just the job for an old war veteran like *Antrim*, especially as we had led the attack that retook the island in the first place. As we were now a guard ship, however, we had to have something and some-body to guard the *ship* with, and as most of our major weapon systems were out of action, the decision was made to form a rifle party on the upper deck. The announcement of its creation was made on daily orders, and rather than take any seamen gunners or marines from their other action stations, the note asked for volunteers with some rifle-handling experience.

I used to shoot a .22 air rifle at home with my grandfather, and later-on in the Sea Scouts I had joined a rifle club and gained my marksman's badge, so I went down to see the chief gunnery instructor. As it turned out there were quite a few volunteers, but once the ones who could not be spared from other parts of the ship had been weeded out there were only four of us left. As I was the senior member of the bunch, I was put in charge of the new HMS *Antrim* Rifle Company.

As a result my action station changed. Instead of carrying urns of tea around the ship, I was now leading my little band of heroes high up in the superstructure of the ship in the flat area, just aft of the secondary bridge position. Every time we went to action stations after that, the four of us, with some young sub-lieutenant standing to the side with a pistol, had to charge up to our position, form a line and prepare to shoot the Argentinian jets out of the sky like grouse on a highland moor. That was the plan, and we were undoubtedly the finest and bravest shots the

British armed forces had ever known, but disappointingly the Argentinians must also have got wind of our call to arms, for they never attacked *Antrim* again, and despite hundreds of practice rounds, we never fired a single shot in anger! However, it really bolstered our egos – especially mine, for now, instead of having to say, 'I carried tea urns round the ship during the war', I was able to boast, 'Oh, I was in charge of a rifle party – but I don't like to talk about it!'

The following day was our seventieth at sea. Although we were actually based in and around Cumberland Bay, but as we were not tied up alongside, it still counted as being at sea. Seventy days is an awful long time to be at sea, and the tally-marked chits all round the ship bore witness to a consecutive run that none of us would have guessed at when we left the dockside at Portsmouth. While it was very quiet and already a little tedious, being at South Georgia did offer us the chance of dispatching and receiving fairly regular mail drops, so my letters started to take on an almost casual air, like the one I wrote home that evening.

> Well here I am, 'safe as houses' in sunny South Georgia, where it's a lot colder than our last visit. Today we sailed out of Cumberland Bay and had to dodge small icebergs, and at the entrance to the bay is an enormous 'berg' about the size of St Paul's. The weather is calm, but we can really feel the winter settling in down here.

With the very next mail drop came a real surprise – my B13 notification for advancement to acting petty officer catering accountant! I knew it was long overdue, but when Jimmy Riddle finally handed me the note, it really knocked me back. 'This'll be something to write home about', I called out, ' being promoted in the field!'

'Yeah, it's great news, Rowdy, Jimmy replied drily. 'When are you putting your barrel on, mate?'

'Putting on a barrel' means celebrating some kind of good news with the purchase of a barrel of beer. Down here, however, with beer rationing in place, this would be difficult. However, I did still have a couple of crates of illicit South Georgia beer from the BAS hut raid, so I replied, 'Tonight, in the mess at 2000 – pass the buzz round. I'm still sticking a barrel on, no matter where we are, or what bloody beer rationing is in place!'

And so yet another 1G1 mess party was hastily organized. We had trays of food, a couple of guests, a bit of music, a few games and a few extra crates of beer, plus some bottles of wine 'borrowed' from the wardroom. Like the hoard that Shiner and I had discovered, the Argentinian wine had been liberated from the BAS base in South Georgia.

But life on board was not just one long succession of parties and drinking. There were also several occasions when tempers flared down the mess decks and fists flew, and bones were broken. One of those such occasions happened somedays earlier in 1G1 mess, when Chopper Cox and I got into a stupid argument over something (what it was, neither of us could remember the following week). The war of words became louder, then blows were exchanged. Most of the others in the mess at the time made themselves scarce so as not to become 'witnesses to the act', but thankfully Barry and Frank stayed behind, and pulled us apart when we both ended up on the deck and the blood started flowing!

The fight had come to an inconclusive end, but one thing that was not inconclusive was the damage we had caused to each other, for within half an hour we had both (separately) reported to the sick bay. 'That's strange,' the sick-bay attendant said when I went in with a badly swollen left hand, 'Young Chopper was in here two minutes ago with a nasty crack in the face. Must have fallen down the same ladder as you, eh Rowdy?'

Unless things really got out of hand, that was the way such incidents were normally dealt with on board, especially under those wartime circumstances. Neither of us got into trouble, and we shook hands and made up a short time later. The mess was far too small to carry any grudges. One thing I did carry though, was a badly broken knuckle which left me unable to open my left hand properly for the rest of the trip, and still looks crooked to this day.

Feeling decidedly and noticeably hungover, I received a big shock at 0900 the next morning, when Jimmy rang down to let me know that I was on the captain's table at 1000! Thankfully, being in relaxed defence watches, I did not have to clamber into my best No. 1 uniform or polish my boots. Jimmy said, 'Just make sure you have a shave and tidy yourself up a bit – oh, and keep your anti-flash on as well.' So, making my excuses from the catering office, I rushed up to the mess, dragged a razor across my three-day stubble, straightened my filthy anti-flash hood, and made my way up to the captain's cabin. I subsequently wrote in my diary:

CAPTAIN's TABLE
1000

I marched in as Leading Catering Accountant Yates, dressed in full anti-flash gear. The captain (Brian Young) was dressed the same. We stood there facing each other for a few moments, then we both started to laugh. Normally when a person is promoted, everyone is dressed up to the nines, but here we were dressed up like scarecrows! I marched out as a petty officer (aged twenty-four years) and promptly changed my badges of rank and moved my kit from 1G1 mess, next door to No. 5 petty officer's mess.

Straight after moving my gear into my new mess, I wrote another quick letter home, for dispatch via a ship with the strange name *Wimpey Seahorse*.

> Just a short line to let you know of my promotion! The form arrived yesterday, and it's backdated to 1 May because it's been kicking around in the post for over six weeks! My actual rank now is acting petty officer catering accountant, but the 'acting' bit is never verbally used, and I'm just referred to as a PO caterer.
>
> I haven't come down from the clouds yet. This has been a big boost for me. It's only taken six years and two months to get to PO, which isn't bad. I've moved messes, but only next door to No. 5 petty officer's mess. There are thirty-four POs' in there, and I think I'm about the youngest. I'm borrowing all sorts of PO's kit, because we don't hold any on board.

Unfortunately, whilst my own day had gone very well indeed, 800 miles to the west, in the Falklands, things had not gone quite as planned, for late in the afternoon we started hearing reports of yet more Argentinian raids and yet more strikes on our ships, this time our old partner HMS *Plymouth*, and the much less familiar landing ships, *Sir Tristran* and *Sir Galahad*. As always, first reports were very hazy, but later the commander let us know that, just as on *Antrim* and several other ships, the bombs that fell on *Plymouth* had failed to explode, and that *Tristran* had got off fairly lightly. However, he went on to add that the news from *Galahad* wasn't so good, and it sounded as though a considerable number of Welsh Guards had been lost. At this stage of the war, we were conditioned to hearing bad news out of the blue, but the words 'considerable numbers' added an extra shudder to the thought of what must have happened to our army colleagues. It certainly took the edge off the euphoria I had felt over my promotion, and despite the fact that I was now sleeping in a mess square as a new joiner, I still managed to get an early but restless night, unable to get the thought of the brave guardsmen off my mind, who had perished so far away from their green valleys of Wales.

Late the following night we were patrolling quietly off the coast when the ship hit something in the water with a loud *smack*. Like a lot of others, I was rushing to my action station, when a 'pipe' announced that we had 'only' hit a small iceberg! 'Bloody hell,' cried Sharkey Ward. 'The flippin' *Titanic* got sunk by an iceberg. Some bleedin' war this is – the Argies can't sink us down here, so the bloody icebergs are trying instead!'

Over the next two days we took on stores from RFA *Stromness*, and stores and mail from RFA *Regent* and we were able to make up some of the deficiencies we were experiencing. But there was still not enough food or beer to relax either state of rationing, which was frustrating considering the massive amount of gear *Stromness* had on board.

Now that suitable spares had arrived, the decision was taken to start changing the badly worn barrels on our 4.5 inch gun. As things stood, they were about as much use as an old poacher's catapult after their efforts at Fanning Head and during the air attacks, and there were plenty of people who doubted whether this task could be performed successfully at sea without dockyard cranes and assistance, but our gunners, engineers, seamen, flight crew and Humphrey proved them wrong, because by the end of the first day the first barrel had already been lifted out!

We heard that the QE II had returned safely to Southampton. It had not been as much of a 'cruise' as the southern voyage. Then she had carried hundreds of fit and healthy men, and now she was returning with hundreds who had lost their ships or mates, and nearly their own lives too.

On Saturday, 12 June, work on the barrel change continued apace and the troops ashore appeared to be forging ahead at a place called Mount Longdon, but the good news was completely outweighed by the terrible news of a land-based Exocet strike on our sister ship, HMS *Glamorgan*, which had taken over our role in the main task force when we had been crippled. This was yet another lucky turn of fate for *Antrim*, but the news hit us like another massive hammer blow below the belt. We all had mates on board the '*Glamorous Organ*' and the suspense as we waited to hear if they had survived was almost unbearable. When the list of fatalities did eventually come on board just a few short hours later, some of my worst personal fears materialized, it appeared that all the casualties were cooks, the same lads I had been ashore with in Gibraltar, and one cook in particular, Jock Malcolm, whom I knew very well from my days at RNAS Yeovilton.

The barrel-change operation was completed the following day, and there were pats on the back for all those involved in the extremely tricky procedure. However, for some people there was a downside, for with our 4.5 inch gun back in action, we could expect to return to the Falklands – especially as our sister ship had now been taken out of the game! But while we wondered if we would rejoin the fray, the news from the Falklands became increasingly good, and it was looking very much as if the islands would be recaptured in a matter of days, if not hours.

In his broadcast, the commander informed us that a battle was now raging on a place called Mount Tumbledown, primarily between the Scots Guards and one of the better Argentinian units. In a slightly more exaggerated Scottish voice than usual, the commander said, 'And they'd better be one of their better units too, because with my Scots Guards breathing down their necks they'll need every ounce of courage they can muster!'

So, as I had jokingly predicted some weeks ago to my Scottish father, the Scots Guards were now in the thick of it, and somehow with them on the scene I felt that the Argentinians surely could not last much longer – what army ever has, with hordes of men in skirts coming screaming across the field with their red hair and wild looks and their pipes skirling away promising a grisly death to all those who stand and fight against them. And I thought of what my father would be saying at home. 'The Roman's could not beat us, and nor can anybody else, son!'

For the next day, Monday, 14 June, we were all just 'treading water', waiting for the news to be announced that the war was over, but as the hours ticked by no such news arrived. Darkness fell and we still could not believe that the enemy had managed to hold out for yet another day, when their position must have been so obviously hopeless. But at 1815, a 'pipe' was made: 'The captain will speak to the ship's company in five minutes' time.' This must be it, we thought – they must have surrendered. Five minutes later, with the suspense at absolute bursting point, the skipper made one of his infrequent but most important announcements. 'Y'hear there, captain speaking. I am delighted to announce that we have just received the wonderful news that our troops have finally taken Port Stanley.' I think he went on to add a few words of personal congratulations, but nobody could hear the rest of his 'pipe', such was the noise as we roared our approval of this fantastic news. We leaped up and down and danced jigs and shook hands, and grabbed each other and raised our mugs of tea or tins of beer; and we grinned ecstatic wide grins. We would soon be going home – alive.

A bad snowstorm raged across South Georgia the following day, but no amount of white-outs, rough weather or biting cold could dampen our spirits, because we knew the war was as good as over. We still had to keep a vigilant eye out for any stragglers, but the mood on board was full of confidence and success and victory – real victory, because beyond our wildest and most unexpected dreams we had done it, and 'Lucky *Antrim*' had survived against all the odds. It truly was, an incredible achievement.

CHAPTER EIGHTEEN

We Want to Go Home

The next news we wanted to hear, above all else, was when we could go home. But there was little news at all from anyone and no mail at all. The mood after the initial euphoria can be summed up by the comment I made in my diary, 'We're all bored stiff.' We did, however, receive some stores from RFA *Fort Regent*, and in the World Cup in Spain, England beat France 3–1, which upset the commander and all the other Scots on board, who always cheered for England's opposition, no matter who they were.

Antrim assumed a new role when she was appointed as the Queen's Harbour Master South Georgia. Whether this 'honour' was meant to impress us we were not sure, but it did not – as Bagsy Baker so quaintly put it, 'Oh great, bloody marvellous that. Do we all get Blue Peter badges as well? Why don't they just cut the bullshit and get us out of this bloody shithole.'

We did hear in the commander's evening broadcast that the Argentinian leader, Galtieri, had been removed from power, but that was about it. There were many buzzes flying around about when we would be heading home, but the commander could not confirm any of them.

The tedium of performing our 'harbour master's' role was thankfully broken on 18 June with the arrival of mail. In the four bags that were dragged into No. 5 mess were thirty-two letters and parcels for me. As on previous occasions when mail arrived, most of the ship's company stopped what they were doing and congregated in the mess decks for the arrival of the mailbag carriers. Being in a larger mess now, I had to wait slightly longer as the mail was thrown or passed across the mess square, but once the last sack had been emptied, I crept off to the catering office, where I could digest the contents in relative privacy.

After the excitement of the mail-drop had settled down, we began almost watching the hands of the clocks tick slowly round. Each day there was less and less to do. The commander and other officers tried their best, but they all knew we were only interested in one particular bit of news – our approval to go home. However, there was some good news over those two days; we heard that *Canberra* had sailed north with over 5,000 prisoners, and the neighbouring Sandwich Islands were now back in British hands. We also heard (although again the Scots were not impressed) that England had beaten Czechoslovakia 2–0. Considering myself half-Scottish, I could sit on the fence during the ensuing arguments in the mess. With a war in the bag and one of our teams doing all right in the World Cup, we could sense that the people back home must be feeling pretty good right now – especially as they were also starting to experience some decent sunshine. What more could they possibly ask for, apart from their soldiers, sailors and airmen to come home from the war.

People tried all sorts of things to boost morale during this very low period. For instance, one of the quartermasters on the bridge, Scrumpy Appleton, decided that the early-morning 'call the hands pipe' was far too boring, and got the whole day off to a depressing start with its monotonous, 'Call the hands, call the hands, call the hands.' Sometimes some bright spark would liven it up a bit by calling out, 'Wakey, wakey rise and shine. You've had yours, now I want mine.' But Scrumpy felt he could go one better. He was renowned on board for mimicking famous people's voices. One morning we would be woken up by Barry White, another time it would be Muhammad Ali. On other occasions we would have Tommy Cooper, or Frank Spencer. At that unearthly hour of the morning, Scrumpy's 'pipes' did the trick and we would often wake up with a smile on our faces. Probably the best morning was when the ships company had the unique privilege of being shaken from our beds by Sir Winston Churchill himself, in a speech which ran something like this: 'A very good morning to you, men of the mighty British warship *Antrim*. Hands off cocks, get on your socks, and get on with the war – which we shall never lose, because we will carry on fighting the Argentinians in the streets and in the houses, and in the hills. And if this proud nation survives for another thousand years, people will always say – *Antrim* was our finest ship!' Scrumpy had a few tins bought for him that day!

Another means of boosting morale was to organize competitions and raffles, one of which carried the unusual prize of a good soak in the skipper's bath! He not only had an accommodation suite that was as big as two or three junior rates' messes, but he also had a large, white enamel bath. There were other smaller richer prizes on offer, but after so long without a decent back scrub and soak, the thing that most people wanted was that half-hour in the skipper's bath. I think it was a young stoker who won the first prize, and he bragged for ages of how he had enjoyed the sheer luxury of lying in the famous bath – soaping himself down with a fresh bar of Imperial Leather and sipping a glass or two of something (which was also part of the prize). Most people were really jealous when they heard his mouth-wateringly descriptive tales, but one person who was not, was Barry, who had to clean the bath out afterwards. As he said, 'A stoker's greasy arse is a lot bloody dirtier than a naval officer's bottom!'

When the different types of entertainment failed, we all resorted to the time-honoured habits of just reading endless books, writing hundreds of letters, or polishing our 'war trophies'. At the start of the trip, there had been a rush to produce dog tags out of old coins, but now, with that essential task complete, men all round the ship were into far more advanced cutting, grinding and polishing operations. For they had captured spoils of war to clean up and mount on wooden plaques, or bullet and shell cases to shape and shine until they shone like the best exhibits in a fancy jeweller's window. I spent hours, – no, days – cutting down my 4.5 inch shell case, burnishing and polishing it inside and out until I could almost shave in it. It was only a straightforward flat-topped design, but I must have used gallons of Brasso on it. Others, though, were not satisfied with simple designs like mine; they carved intricate patterns and letters into the top of their shell cases which, just like mine, would only end up on some windowsill holding a lanky busy lizzy or other unwatered pot plant.

One person whose ideas did not go completely to plan was our chief caterer, Whisky Dave. He obviously got this name, because of his love of the 'water of life'. In Gibraltar where it was dirt cheap, he had bought a gallon bottle – which he later discovered would fit exactly into the cleaned-out centre of a 4.5 inch shell case. So the huge bottle of whisky stayed in the catering office for his nightcap before he got his head down. Whisky Dave made a point of saying, 'You see this bottle here lads? When it's empty I'm going to get it mounted in the finest shell case that caterer's currency will buy, and on the front I'm getting "Drunk in the Falklands War 1982" put on it.' Sadly this dream never materialized. One afternoon Albert lived up to his nickname of Albatross by smashing the bottle! At least it was empty when he broke it.

I had plenty of opportunity to finish replying to all the mail I had received. One of my letters conveys frustration of that time.

The weather is really starting to get bad down here at South Georgia. The other day a massive iceberg drifted up against the ship and we had to up anchor and get out quickly! It gets light at about 1100 and dark again at

1700, but I haven't been on the upper deck for ages, and it's now a very strange world we are living in – we could even be on Mars for all we know. The worst times for us are when we don't get any mail for two weeks, in the second week of which we get really fed up and bored silly.

Still no news of when we're going home yet. Lots of the other ships are going back, but we seem to have been forgotten. I often wonder if it's got something to do with our captain and admiral Woodward not getting on with each other. When we left Pompey, the Admiral was on board, but after we left Gib he transferred to *Glamorgan* because he and our captain did not see eye to eye. Since then we've been put in charge of the group that took South Georgia, and we nearly got sunk by a submarine. And then we were the ship in charge of all the landing operations and air defence in North Falkland Sound, and again we nearly got sunk. Both times we have received hardly any mention in the press, and Woodward has tried to grab all the glory. At South Georgia it even came out that he sent the signal to the Queen, when in fact it was our Captain!

At Bomb Alley, he must have expected to lose a couple of ships, and guess who was the second ship in – us! The first ship in was *Ardent* and we all know what happened to her. So all in all we don't like this Admiral Woodward one little bit. I hope his tactics get ripped to shreds when he gets back, he's very lucky to have any fleet left at all.

The Royal baby was born yesterday, and although we were pleased, it angered us that we never got a mention on the World Service last night. I expect it'll be all 'baby news' in the press now, and us poor lot will just get left down here in this dump to rot away merrily! I'm sorry for having a bit of a moan, but we are getting really fed up with the way our ship has been treated. We've got 480 not very happy officers and crew at the moment.

I wrote again the following day.

Mail is going off again tonight or tomorrow, so I thought I would take advantage and get a letter in the post to you. Today we had one mailbag delivered, but it was just filled with paperback books, so a false alarm there, as we had been expecting some real mail. Still no news about going home, but quite a few other ships are starting to make the journey north. Also a lot of the troops in the Falklands are going home too, leaving just a garrison and a few ships to protect the place from further invasion.

Today I've been cleaning down some paintwork in the office. It's amazing what a difference it makes when the walls are washed down and all the lampshades are scrubbed. Normally we just slap another coat of paint on the walls, but we haven't got much left on board.

I was really becoming bored now, because for the third day in succession I wrote home, again, not mincing my words.

Mail arrived yesterday. I read about Corporal Hardman from Larkhall. My sympathies go out to his family. I also heard that one of my cousin's school friends was killed. I don't remember his name, but I think he was on the *Coventry*, along with one of my old mates, POCA Steve Dawson. I lost a few old pals, and it still seems strange that we were all ashore together only thirteen weeks ago in Gib – having a great time.

Glad to hear the weather is good at home, it's almost too cold to go out here now. The blokes who actually work on the upper deck have to get dressed up in full cold-weather thermal clothing – some of which is electrically heated!

Antrim and *Endurance* have both sent signals to Woodward asking what plans he has for us regarding going home etc. And all that useless idiot has to say is that as long as there appears to be an enemy threat, a military presence will be maintained – not even a direct mention of us at all!

We are now the longest-serving warship down here in the South Atlantic, and a few people are even wishing we had been hit a few more times, so we would have had to go back! I don't see it like that personally, as I know how lucky I am to be alive, but this hanging around down here is absolutely soul-destroying. I've never felt or known anything like it before. We could be a ghost ship as far as he sees us.

I try to stay happy and keep up a smiling image, but it is really hard. You'll never know how much we look forward to our only real lifeline – the mail deliveries. But for those, I think we would all go stark raving mad.

Although I've painted a fairly black picture of what the mood was like on board since the surrender, it was not all gloom and doom because, matelots being matelots, there was always a party being arranged somewhere. One was belatedly to celebrate my promotion. I was given a 'call-round' to 3E seamen's mess, inhabited by forty-six men, which for a 'call-round' spelt 'very dangerous' – especially for a brand new PO caterer stupidly carrying boxes of fruit and biscuits!

A normal 'call-round' in that, the largest of all *Antrim*'s messes, was bad enough, but when I encouraged even more hospitality by 'bearing gifts', that was just asking for trouble! No sooner had I deposited the boxes in the mess square and sat in the 'host's chair' than at least twenty tins were piled in front of me. Others kept appearing until I totally lost count of how many were presented in total. There was absolutely no way I could drink all that amount – they knew it and so did I – but I gave it a go! I can actually remember knocking back the first five or six pretty quickly, then playing darts until I could no longer hit the board then I could not count all the empty tins piled in front of me because they were too high, and then I do not really remember much at all, other than the fact that when I eventually came round the following day, one of the seamen yelled out, 'Oi, shoot-through! When are you coming down the mess to finish off your beer – you've still got a dozen tins left!' No wonder the entry in my diary just says, 'Slept well again tonight!'

Apparently, I had tried to sneak off on a number of occasions after going to the heads, but each time sentries posted outside made sure that I did not 'get lost'. Eventually, I just passed out in 3E mess and slept in one of the 'gulches', where nobody would catch me if they happened to visit the mess in the night.

Finally, on Friday, 25 June, the news came through that we were in the next group to go home.

CHAPTER NINETEEN

Homeward Bound

The next day I wrote: 'For the third and final time we left South Georgia to head for the main task force.' And it felt really good when we eventually swung away from the bleak, storm-ravaged, snow-covered rocky South Atlantic outcrop. I do not think I truly realized the part that this awful place had played in my life until I left it. Many years later I read about Sir Ernest Shackleton and the whaling industry. It was only then that I was able to compare *Antrim*'s and our other ships' achievements against those of our heroic predecessors; it is a very humbling comparison.

I returned to the island many years later on another warship, but it was not until I met a former occupant of the old whaling station when writing this account, that I heard the best description of the place where they used to process the great leviathans of the sea, and where Shackleton, and Felix Artuso, and another few men lie permanently frozen at rest. For one day in August 2001, during a brief stop-over at a tiny hamlet called Brae in the Shetland Islands, I met an incredibly interesting and lucid old gentleman called Jimmy Balfour, who had lived at the Grytviken whaling station for several years in his youth. These were his words:

SOUTH GEORGIA
A place of freezation, fantasion,
and the continuation of hell and damnation.

After one day's passage we met up again with the main task force, and our captain went across to visit Admiral Woodward on his flagship, HMS *Hermes*. We never heard what they discussed, but we could hazard a few guesses. However, we did not dwell on old scores too long, for we also received more mail, which eradicated nearly all negative thoughts. Not that it stopped me venting some of my less than complimentary views about the admiral when I replied.

> I'm feeling over the moon! Three days ago we were finally told we could go back with the next group. Woodward wanted us to stay down here, but the 'big chiefs' in London overruled him and said enough is enough. So it seems he really did have it in for us on the *Antrim*. We are now with his ship, *Hermes*, after leaving South Georgia for the last time on Saturday.
>
> We don't know when we'll be home, but you'll be told a few days before we arrive, and as long as we keep heading north I won't worry too much when it is. I could either fly off at Ascension Island or go all the way back to Pompey on *Antrim*, and would prefer the latter option so that I can enjoy the 'cruise' on the way back.
>
> Oh, how I'm looking forward to some sunshine again. The weather at South Georgia was getting really bad before we sailed. I went up on to the bridge and looked out into the bay, and all I could see was icebergs floating around the ship. Even though we're only 700 miles away from there now, the weather is a lot milder. It's still too cold to go on the upper deck, but at least there's no ice on the decks now.
>
> I think this mail will go off by plane from Stanley to UK via Ascension Island, so it could reach you in about ten days. It's our ninety-second consecutive day at sea today, so only another eight days to go.

The next day we entered North Falkland Sound again and went down to Port Howard, where the helicopter picked up a civilian passenger. Then we headed out again via the positions we had held on the 21 May. At 0925 we crossed over the war grave of HMS *Ardent*, and the padre called for a minute's silence, then said a prayer or two. The last time I had seen the *Ardent* was as a burning hulk from the Bridge on the evening of 21 May.

As we left the Falkland Islands we received a signal from Admiral Woodward, which read:

FROM ASCENSION TO SOUTH GEORGIA AND ON TO SAN CARLOS YOU WERE VERY MUCH IN THE FOREFRONT OF OPERATIONS, THE SUCCESS OF WHICH RESULTED IN BRITISH REOCCUPATION OF ALL THE ISLANDS. THIS, TOGETHER WITH YOUR SWIFT RECOVERY FROM BOMB DAMAGE, ALLOWING CONTINUED OPERATION IN THE TEZ AND OFF SOUTH GEORGIA, WON WIDE ACCLAIM. BZ [Bravo Zulu – Well done] AND A HAPPY RETURN HOME.

As we finally headed north, we heard that the passenger we had picked up, was in fact the captain's nephew, who had gone to work on a farm in West Falkland for his 'gap' year. What a year and what a return journey home, for we quickly hit a storm force ten and the poor young lad was as sick as a parrot! Mind you, he was not alone. There were a few 'war veterans' who did not feel too good – including me! I might now be a war veteran, I thought, but I had yet to conquer seasickness!

The weather soon improved, however; after cutting through the storm we were again in calmer, and now noticeably warmer seas – so warm in fact, that for the first time in ages it was mild enough to venture onto the upper deck. Most incredibly of all, we were able to take off our shirts and expose our bleached white, thinner bodies to the approaching equatorial sun. I could not believe just how pale-faced we were. Apart from Sharkey Ward and a few of our other 'naturally tanned' mates, the rest of us looked just like archetypal British holidaymakers ten minutes after stepping off the plane in Majorca! I took my camera to the upper deck with me, and the human white glare factor was so bad I almost had to use a lens filter!

On 3 July we met up with some of our relief force, HMS *Southampton* and her tanker. We were really pleased to see them, because it was a further sign of progress in our journey north. After taking on fuel and stores, we waved the south-bound group farewell, glad we were not going with them.

The next day we had a Sunday routine at sea for the first time since any of us could remember, and as the temperature was increasing with each nautical mile, most of our relaxation time was spent sunbathing on the upper deck. Not that everyone rested; that day *Antrim* also conducted a 100 by 1 mile relay around the ship!

On ships with enough clear upper deck space, running has always been a major means of maintaining at least some basic level of fitness, weather permitting. On *Antrim*, a pedometer had been used to calculate that a man would have to run seven and a quarter laps of the upper deck to complete a mile. So with a team of 100, a constant relay of men of all ranks and fitness levels attempted the pretty gruelling challenge – at least I found it pretty gruelling, after so long without stretching my legs properly.

Receiving the baton from a shattered Chopper Cox, I felt great for the first lap, with loads of lads cheering me on and the adrenalin surging through every muscle and sinew. Then reality kicked in and the effects of such a long period of inactivity made themselves felt as I became more and more light-headed. Only eight years before I had run for my school in the county championships at 110 metres high hurdles and 400 metres but that day I managed only six minutes, twenty-five seconds for the mile, and I felt awful as I finally handed over the baton to Rattler Morgan.

Tuesday, 6 July was our 100th day at sea. Between spells of rubbing in lots of baby oil I wrote my last letter home.

I'm feeling really very well now that we are back in warmer seas again. We left the Falklands last week after paying a visit to Port Howard. We did not actually go alongside, but our helicopter went in and picked up a civvy passenger and some mail. Then we sailed out of North Falkland Sound for the last time, and the ship went very quiet as we went through 'Bomb Alley', as we all thought back to 21 May and the day most of us were lucky to see the end of.

We then went over the war grave of the *Ardent* and the 'still' was piped as the padre said a prayer for those who were lost. I can still picture her now, as I saw her from the bridge that day. She was burning badly, listing to one side, and explosions kept ripping her apart.

After leaving 'Bomb Alley' we said goodbye to the Falklands and headed north – straight into a raging storm! It was the roughest weather we had had since we arrived at South Georgia, and I felt a bit 'woozy' for a couple of days. Then as soon as the storm ended, the sun started shining again and that's the way it's been ever since. Today looks like being a real 'scorcher' as we are near latitude 17 degrees south. Tomorrow we reach Ascension Island and the first leave party of 140 men fly off to the UK.

Hopefully, we'll get in on the day of the World Cup Final, Saturday, 17 July. You'll be able to see the ship from either side of the harbour entrance, but if you want to see the 'battle scars' they are on our port (left) side, and you'll have to watch from Gosport. The crew will be lining the decks when we 'go in' but I doubt if I'll be there as I haven't got my full PO's uniform yet.

Well, with all the excitement of going home, it seems funny that today is the 100th consecutive day at sea. And of course we're having our little celebration party. Eleven days to go (I hope), and then it'll all be over. A month's trip to Gib that turned into a voyage of 8,000 miles to fight a war on the other side of the globe!

We arrived at Ascension Island early the next morning and transferred the advanced leave party ashore for their onward flights to the UK. There had been some drawing of lots to decide who would go home early, but not for me. As I had written home earlier, there was no way I was going to miss the experience of entering Portsmouth harbour, even if I would not be able to join my mates out on the deck for Procedure Alpha, because I did not have a suitable uniform.

The excited group left the ship in their 'civvies'. The rest of us stood around on the upper deck shouting and waving, with our freshly made banners proclaiming 'SLIB' (second leave is best), and 'HALF TRIPPERS'. When they were all ashore, and no doubt supping RAF NAAFI beer in the airport departure lounge, the remaining 340 of us stored ship with some much needed basic items, and also some long-forgotten delicacies, such as fillet steak, strawberries, melons and pineapples.

We sailed from Ascension Island at 1030 next day. It was blistering hot under the clear blue tropical sky. Although it felt great to be on the way home, as we left the island I spared a thought for the ship I had last seen only a short distance away all those weeks ago – HMS *Sheffield*. As the island disappeared into the distance, I was sure I could sense her ghostly shape in the mirage that was formed by the wispy shimmers of heat-mist that rose slowly from the warm turquoise seas, where so many of her crew had last basked in the sunshine.

We 'crossed the line' again but not ceremonially as before, for ships only invite King Neptune on board on their way into his watery domain, not when leaving it. Then we passed the coast of my father's Second World War stamping ground, Sierra Leone. As my father had predicted, it was raining – not that we minded much, because the heat of the last few days had been getting almost unbearable. I had only been able to lie on the deck after laying down a sheet of cardboard and a towel, and even then it was like sunbathing on top of a baker's oven!

The days were being crossed off now with increasing excitement, and some men had even produced charts with hours to go instead of just days. On 11 July we had the last Sunday routine, and we knew for certain that we could say, 'We'll be home at the end of the week.' After fighting a war so far away, that was an amazing milestone.

Soon after passing by the popular tourist island of Tenerife, there was a medical drama; one of the crew developed an acute appendicitis that required immediate evacuation to the nearest hospital, on Madeira. The poor lad did not look too good when they slung him into Humphrey. One of the crew soon cheered him up a little when he yelled out above the roar of the rotor blades, 'Never mind, mate. Think of all that madeira you'll be drinking when you come round from the operation. Save us a bottle, will ya?'

Another milestone was reached when we passed our last real land-fall, Gibraltar. All we had to do was cross the Bay of Biscay and we would be home again! The air of expectancy now felt like all the mail drops we had ever had, all the good news broadcasts, plus every Christmas, all rolled into one. There was now virtually no work of any kind to do on board, other than basic day-to-day operational tasks, and this final leg, without the cramped conditions of the past months, really did feel a bit like a cruise.

The Bay of Biscay was its usual turbulent self, but I managed to keep my stomach in place – with a bit of extra lying down on the upper deck. We could almost taste our homeland now, and there were other sure signs that we had less than 400 miles to go, for the colour of the sea had returned to its deeper, darker blue-green, and at last, in the evenings, we could start picking up Radio One again.

We had always had the BBC World Service, which had kept us informed of news, current affairs and sport, but there was rarely any decent music to listen to. Now we could tune our mess radios in to hear the latest records – which all sounded so different from when we had left. The music felt fresher, and more alive, and Radio One seemed to be in tune with our spirits, with a series of up-beat titles with which we now became increasingly familiar, such as the Steve Miller Band's 'Abracadabra', Captain Sensible's 'Happy Talk' and Dexy's Midnight Runners', 'Come on Eileen'.

As we left the Bay of Biscay and the sea calmed sufficiently, parties kicked off all around the ship, as we knew that the next day we would finally see our homeland again. Not long after the parties had started, there was added excitement when *Antrim* came into range to receive television pictures! They were very fuzzy at first, and the sound was irregular and crackled, but it was there on our screens, where it had not been for so long. Although the images rolled and flickered and came and went, most of the TV screens were left on as the parties went into full swing and our coming home celebrations started in earnest.

There was quite a one organised in No. 5 mess, but there was really only one place I wanted to be that night, so I almost bit Jimmy's hand off when he knocked on the door and said, 'Fancy nipping next door for a few tins, Rowdy?' I made my apologies to my new mess, but I was not alone, because there was a general movement of men all over the ship that night, as people took up invitations one after the other in every throbbing 'nightclub' on board. Normal white lights were turned down low, and multi-coloured flashing lights turned on. Everywhere one walked, one could hear matelots singing, laughing and partying.

Back in my spiritual home, the 1G1 mess party was in full swing when I arrived at about 2100, and a great cheer rang out as I walked through the old familiar door, dressed differently from the rest now, in my white-shirted PO's night clothing, instead of the more recognisable blue-piped square rig that they wore. But it did not matter what we looked like, or what rank we were, or what colour, or what accent we had, or what rows and fights we had had. Tonight we were all 1G1 mess brothers together again – brothers who had lived so tightly together through a time in our lives that none of us would ever forget.

The stories we told that night were all ones we had told before, but they were told even more outrageously than ever before, and everyone screamed with laughter when the much-repeated punchlines were revealed. We talked about the runs in Bremerhaven and Oslo, and the final run in Gibraltar, about the chicken-eating race and all the ships that were there, and all the tricks we played on the Yanks. And there were games played that night too, crazy games that we had not played for ages, not one of which involved an uckers or crib board or a sticky pack of cards. Some games had already been played by the time I had arrived, but the main events were saved for when the endless supply of tins had taken their desired effect and our mouths and bodies were ready to receive the punishment specially saved for such occasions.

There was a chefs' sumo wrestling contest, that involved the men with the biggest 'beer bellies' using no other part of their bodies to force their opponents off a designated area. And there were the more traditional games too, like Indian arm-wrestling and cream cracker eating races, and contests to see who could fit a whole Mars bar in their mouth sideways in one go. And of course there was the odd drinking race, where sometimes the undersides of the tins were 'spiked', and the beer not only went in the racers' mouths, but also sprayed the entire mess. Then there was a 'blowing-up-a-Durex-on-your-head' competition, and Barry rounded the evening off by performing his amazing party piece of sticking fifty-two two-pence coins up his foreskin. You cannot beat those two games to round off a party!

Nobody cared what they did or what they looked like, or what bad things had happened in the past, or why Woodward seemed to have had it in for us. We knew we had got one up on them all and we would be seeing our own coastline the next day, and that thought made the roars of laughter increase with every new story or stupid game and drunken stumble, or every lurid description of what we were going to do when we got ashore.

The parties went on very late into the night, and most ended in a more sombre mood for those still left standing – or rather sitting, huddled around the small square tables that occupied central positions in almost every mess deck. And although some of the slurred conversation was about sincere, comparatively sober, reflections, in one of the mess decks, 3N, the mood suddenly changed when Shiner Wright, appeared to have had just one morose reflection too many. While the balance of his very drunken mind was disturbed by the lateness of the hour and the stillness of the early dawn, for want of a better word, he 'flipped'. But being Shiner, he did not just 'flip' like any normal person. He had to put on a special show for the whole of 3N mess, with a drunken rampage. As Bomber Mills explained it the following day.

As usual, he and Little Taff were the last ones still pissing up at two in the morning, then Taff crashed out and left Shiner cleaning the rest of the fridge out on his own. But you know what he's like when he gets a few wets down inside him – he gets all depressed and starts muttering to himself like a bloody nutter. Tommy Docherty remembers telling him to put a sock in it and get to bed, but apparently he just carried on talking to himself like he was having a conversation with someone else at the table.

Anyway, the next thing anyone knew was when Wiggy Bennett was woken up by someone shining a torch in his eyes. Then, when he realized it was Shiner with that bloody great stainless steel torch he used to carry around. He told him to bugger off and get to bed, but instead of doing that he started tapping him on the head with the torch – with a blank, vacant look in his eyes. He had really lost it then, and after waking up Wiggy he went on to to shake Tansy Lee and Hutch, who also told him to bugger off and get to bed. But then he made a big mistake, because he tried shaking Big Taff – all Taff did was punch him in the gob!

Then Shiner went completely loopy and started chucking tins around everywhere – waking nearly everyone up, and that's when Tommy went off and got the bloody scab lifters and the killick reg, because he'd really lost the whole plot.

The next morning, everyone had filthy hangovers. In every mess deck, there was an explosion of empty tins sweet wrappers, beer-stained clothing, and greasy old steaming boots – most of which had lost their partners – covering each deck to a depth of almost 6 inches!

Those who managed to make it through for breakfast were greeted by a scene of comparative destruction, for the chefs had clearly got other things on their mind, and little 'clean as you go' work had been done. The counter that I saw when I staggered through at 0745 was covered with all sorts of dregs from the trays of beans and tomatoes and eggs. And it was also possible to see where some men had to leave their trays on the side because the spinning image of a great dish of scrambled eggs was just too stomach churning for their fragile constitutions.

Deciding to stick with just a 'bacon butty', because I also doubted if I would keep anything more elaborate down, I discovered why the counter was in such a shabby state. Half the morning watch were away giving statements to the Joss and the doctor, and the other half were talking about Shiner's rampage.

It was also a sorry tale. Even though old Shiner was not one of the most outgoing men on board, and certainly did not win any popularity medals in the catering office, he had served through the same war as the rest of us and been through all the various ups and downs, I felt a little sorry for him when I saw him being carted into Humphrey's big belly, strapped tightly into a stretcher with a crazy, distant look in his eyes.

We had finally reached the coast of Devon and Cornwall and could see in the distance the outline of Plymouth and Devonport. Now that we could relate to the counties and ports along the south coast, we knew that there was less than 200 miles to go, and as we completed our 'guz' transfers and picked up speed to 25 knots, we could almost count down the individual miles along the inlet-strewn shoreline. We had passed HMS *Cambridge*, Torquay, Lyme Regis and Seaton, and then the ship slowed down again as we approached Portland Bill for our very last transfers of the entire trip – which included the last delivery of mail. For me this included an incredible fifty letters and parcels – including the woolly socks I had asked my mother for weeks before!

Such good progress had been made over the past few days that we knew we would definitely be off Pompey early in the evening. We also knew that our families and loved ones and everything else would only be a few yards away. This knowledge prompted one of the most obvious questions the entire voyage home: 'Why can't we bloody well go in tonight instead of tomorrow morning?' But it was fairly easy to see why we could not go in early. Everything had been planned so precisely for the next day although what exactly 'everything' meant we could only guess.

With the Portland transfers complete, the grand old warhorse *Antrim* cast aside all fears of exhausting her remaining fuel reserves and wrecking her sorely tested gas turbines, and made a dash for the line, now less than 100 nautical miles away. I have been on ships before and since that could move through the water, but that afternoon *Antrim* was like a giant powerboat, cutting a sharp gash through the calm seas and leaving a massive boiling cauldron of white churning water in her wake. It was even difficult to stand up, as the slightest ripple kicked her briefly to port or starboard before the bosun's mate corrected the course and kept her heading straight and true, past Swanage and Bournemouth, and further on towards the looming Needles lighthouse on the western tip of my old holiday haunt, the Isle of Wight.

Reading what seemed like an endless supply of letters, I was unable to wrench myself away from the upper deck for any of those last few miles, and I felt sure that even if all the engineers below had suddenly abandoned their posts, *Antrim* would still have found her own way home from there – just round the coast a little, past Blackgang Chine, St Catherine's Lighthouse, Ventnor, Shanklin, Sandown and White Cliff Bay, and then finally slowing right down to crawl past the first of Lord Palmerston's forts to our allotted anchorage at that most famous of all anchorages, Spithead – just 3 miles from the entrance to Portsmouth Harbour and home.

And then *Antrim*'s exhausted engines were finally called for no more. In the morning the tugs would come out and tow us in the last few yards if the engines did not feel like responding to the captain's last call for 'slow ahead both engines.'

There were very few men below now; this was not surprising considering they had just finished an 8,000 mile voyage, and home was just a few short yards away. 'Over there, look! There's Billy Manning's funfair and Southsea seafront, and look, over there, that's HMS *Dolphin* and the hospital at *Haslar*.' We felt like pinching ourselves to make sure it was all real. Some of the men were even claiming they could see empty milk bottles on their front door steps!

CHAPTER TWENTY

Lucky *Antrim's* Homecoming

I did not party too heavily that night. Some did and it showed, but I knew I would want to savour this final day of the trip, when the sun would rise for the last time for us at sea, and the ship would finally touch dry land again, one hundred and eleven days after the drunken morning we had left Gibraltar. Another reason that most of us did not party very much was that we had to suspend our mess celebrations and to receive an honoured guest on board: not anyone particularly important just an admiral – a good one, but all the same just an admiral.

After meeting the skipper and the other officers, Admiral Fieldhouse (or 'Fieldmouse' as we called him) was then escorted on a quick 'morale-boosting' tour of the ship, which all went strictly according to plan until he entered the infamous Admiral-insulting lion's den of No. 5 petty officer's mess. For here, in our huddle of thirty-four cross but polite petty officers, was one at the back who was even more angry than the rest of us, and was not quite so polite! The admiral gave us some 'well done chaps' stuff, and then cracked some officer-type joke about why we could not go alongside that night'. That was the cue for the short one at the back to heckle him with some of his own brand of humour. 'Cheers, Sir! We just love staying at sea another night when we can wave at our families on the beach.' Although he was not reprimanded, his comment was not well received.

However, just after 'Fieldmouse' had departed, spirits were lifted a little when the last daily orders of the trip were distributed. Listed on the front page in clear bold letters, were words several of us thought we would never see again:

0730   Storeship fresh provisions – 20 hands

0830   Weigh anchor

0845   Hands fall in for Procedure Alpha

0900   Commence final passage into Portsmouth

1000   Due alongside north-west wall jetty

1015   Embark families and first leave party

O/c   Leave commences for second leave party.

Very early in the morning, before all the stores arrived for the lunchtime buffet meals (for a possible 2,500), I nipped into the senior rate's dining hall to eat two bowls of cereal for breakfast, and also drank a wonderful pint of fresh cold milk. Then I joined dozens of others on the upper deck, with their mugs of steaming tea, and their minds already far away with their families and girlfriends, who we knew must be craning their necks ashore, less than 2 miles away. We were still bitter at not being allowed to get alongside the previous day, and by the visit of Admiral Fieldhouse (no matter how well intentioned it was), but unlimited beer and sleep had helped to quell some of the rage we felt, and at least we knew for certain that it was not the skipper's fault. So with the sun continuing its ascending arc across the midsummer sky, we bathed in its heat and looked repeatedly at our watches as the minutes and seconds ticked slowly by – as slowly as a snail across the shadow of a sundial.

There was no shortage of volunteers to assist the fo'c'sle party raise the anchor; although no real manhandling was involved, there would have been no shortage of strong hands available if the powerful capstan machinery had broken down. There was also no need for a 'pipe' to announce, 'Hands fall in for Procedure Alpha', because most were already there, and had been there since wolfing back their own bowls of cereal and fresh milk and climbing into their proudest No. 1 uniforms. I felt a bit sad and alone when the last of the lads had left the mess. I sat on my own with my short memories of this place and much longer ones of the mess next door, which all my mates had also left to take up their allocated position on the starboard waist, just outside the wardroom. I sat still and alone for the first time for a very long time.

I felt the ship get under way again, and then heard the first blast of her sirens as they exploded into voice to echo the roar of the other hooters and whistles that came from the flotilla of small vessels which were escorting us into the harbour. *Antrim* sounded proud, and her men on the upper deck must have felt proud too. I dearly wished I could have experienced the full atmosphere of the homecoming as they were doing.

I thought quickly about donning someone else's No. 2 uniform, but it would have been hard to find one my size; I did not have a proper hat either – it was really frustrating. I left the isolation of the mess to walk along the equally deserted main passage, climb the steep ladder to the wardroom, where I knew nobody should be around, and where I also knew I would find the largest scuttles on the ship. I knelt on one of the softly covered perimeter seats and peered out of a scuttle to see a long line of my mates formed up outside, all laughing and joking, and waving and blowing kisses with wide sparkling eyes. I changed scuttles a couple of times, then found a good one with a clear view of the scene outside. I felt like a goldfish behind the thick glass, but I had perfect views of the eastern tip of the Isle of Wight and Palmerston's follies, the Solent forts, and the hundreds of small boats, and the clear blue sky of our homecoming day.

Suddenly I heard footsteps coming up the ladder, and someone entered the wardroom. Getting ready to make some excuse, I was relieved to find it was only Barry in his half blues. 'I didn't have a jacket that would fit, Rowdy', he said, 'so the chief steward told me to stay inside and get the wardroom ready for the reception. Want a drink, mate?'

'What a jolly splendid idea old boy. I'll have the largest G&T you can squeeze into a tall glass – and go easy on the ice will you – it ruins the gin and affects me war wounds, don't you know!'

Peering out of the scuttle, I could now see Southsea looming into view, and the screaming crowds who appeared to be massed along the length of the 3 mile seafront. Even behind the glass, I could still hear their screams above the sound of the ship's sirens and hooters – and above the sound of the Irish Ranger who was now playing his pipes on top of the 4.5 inch gun – the same gun that had silenced so many at Fanning Head.

Barry returned with the drinks on a brightly polished silver tray, dipped his head slightly and said, 'Thank you for fighting our war for us – here's a drink on the house from a grateful nation, old boy.' We raised our glasses towards the portrait of our queen, then raised them to ourselves, and exchanged our own congratulations, before downing the tall drinks in two lovely long gulps.

'Jolly well done old chap. See you at the *Antrim* reunion in twenty-five years' time?' asked Barry.

'Yes, I'll be there, old boy,' I replied. 'I expect I'll be a millionaire by then, of course, but it'll be jolly nice to meet all the chaps again and talk over old times. Yes, damn fine idea, old boy! I'll definitely put that date in my diary for 2007 – and if I am worth a penny or two by then, I promise to buy every one of them a drink too, old boy.'

I poured the next round from my old wardroom bar, and did not forget to 'chit' for the drinks either, just as the chief steward always used to remind me. Only these drinks were not charged to just any of the officers. 'Mind if the commander picks up the tab for these old boy?' I called out.

'Not at all. I'm sure he had be absolutely delighted to get all our wets in today, old chap!'

And so we knelt side by side and raised our glasses again – to the queen, to the commander, to ourselves, and then to our mates outside – who were now shuffling from side to side and gazing inside at the two grinning goldfish. They also knew that we were charging our rounds of large drinks to the commander's mess bill, because we kept holding the chits up to the scuttle to prove it! We did not get drunk though, because we were already drunk. In fact everybody on board was drunk at that wonderful moment – drunk with sheer joy as the ship finally reached the large orange navigation buoy and swung slowly to port to begin her last course. We were so close to the shore now that we could almost smell the delirious crowds. My hands were trembling, and my pulse thumped like a large Victorian steam hammer.

Then the excitement turned to outrageous humour as *Antrim* yet again got into an admiral's bad books. This time it was not 'Woodworm' or 'Fieldmouse', but Admiral Tippet. Among all the small craft keeping us company were a couple of naval launches with senior officers on board. He was on one of these that breezed into view between us and Billy Manning's funfair. As he came alongside our bridge, he raised his fluted glass of freshly poured champagne to our officers, who were high above us on the starboard bridge wing.

Never missing a chance of making a fool of anyone, Barry and I roared back together, 'Three cheers for Admiral Tippet', and raised our drinks against the glass towards him. But, we also raised two fingers of our spare hands. We were sure we caught the Admiral's attention, because he turned sharply to one of his entourage and pointed in our precise direction before his launch kicked the water and sped off to take up a friendlier position on the other side of the ship. As he did so, no doubt enquiries were already underway to try and establish who the two rude midshipmen were who were gesticulating from *Antrim*'s wardroom. As *Antrim* continued her passage, the level of noise intensified so much that even the glasses in the wardroom bar started to tinkle in tune with the roar outside. We had heard that earlier ships had had fantastic home-comings, but Portsmouth, Southsea and Gosport had never seen anything like *Antrim*'s return before – not even for an aircraft carrier. One explanation was that it was a Saturday in the middle of July, the first day of the school holidays when the entire south coast was packed with its first wave of holidaymakers. There was hardly a cloud in the sky, and excitement was also running high because that afternoon the World Cup final was taking place in Spain, between Italy and West Germany before 90,000 people – and the bars were already checking their barrels for the onslaught of thirsty drinkers the game would inevitably bring. So *Antrim's* homecoming was different, and special, the very best – the best that anyone there would ever remember.

We could now see that every possible vantage point was absolutely choked with cheering and sun-tanned bodies of all shapes, colours and sizes. Bands were playing, loud music was blaring out and flags were waving, as families, girlfriends and a multitude of others stood on tiptoes, seemingly transfixed by the sight of *Antrim's* majestic and lucky return from the jaws of death. And there were holidaymakers too, thousands of them, who stood in their coach parties and jammed the promenades, or sat on rows of beach towels waving buckets and spades and little sandcastle flags that they flapped madly. No matter where they had come from, they were now experiencing part of this war at first hand.

From all four corners of the British Isles they came, and even from across the water. It did not matter where they came from, for they welcomed us as if we were the finest conquering heroes of their lives. And we all felt like conquering heroes too. As we passed between HMS *Dolphin* on our port side and Henry VIII's Round Tower to starboard, even behind the thick sheet of glass, Barry and I, now joined by 'the Albatross', felt we could almost reach out and touch the multicoloured pincushion of outstretched hands. The people were going wild. We passed the 'Still and West' on our right and the Gosport Ferry on our left, and then the Isle of Wight Ferries on our right. And then we saw, in the distance, larger, more familiar ships – and their sirens blew and their crews cheered and cried, like all the others who were now crying. And I felt warm tears of joy trickle down my cheeks too.

We crept alongside the Hard on the Portsmouth side, and passed the row of old drinking haunts we had frequented so many times at the start and end of our runs ashore: the Victory, the Keppel's Head Hotel, the Lady Hamilton and the Ship Anson. To our right, behind some tall Georgian buildings, we could see in the distance the lofty wooden masts of that most famous ship of all time – Nelson's flagship, HMS *Victory* – and much closer to us, the dockyard entrance named in his honour, Victory Gate. When we saw it I think we all knew that we had won a great victory too. We had maintained the victorious record of the Royal Navy, and we knew we could walk through those gates as victors too.

We saw the first of many grey naval vessels as we slid further into the dockyard, preceded now only by our two tugs, with their enormous fire hoses jetting into the sky. Some of these ships looked fine and were covered in new grey paint. Others did not look so fresh, and it was clear that they had been down south with us and had not seen a good paint job in months. Like *Antrim*'s, their sides bore the unmistakable signs of long, hard weeks at sea and battles, which had resulted in large orange streaks of rust, patches of roughly welded metal and enormous sheets of black tarpaulin over holes that were too big for anyone to patch at sea. As we turned to let the tugs gently nudge us alongside, we saw a ship further away that had suffered even worse damage – our sister ship, *Glamorgan*, with the remains of her hangar covered in dark sheets and ropes above the galley where so many of my mates had met their premature ends.

But now was not the time for sad reflection, because we could see *Antrim*'s very own welcome-home party on the dockside of our allotted berth. There must have been over 5,000 of them all told – laughing, crying, screaming, cheering people that we knew belonged to us, and whose wide banners we searched for names. We could not believe that they could all be for us. Another large band played on this dockside too, and the drunken Irish Ranger tried to match them with his pipes, but he failed miserably and sat down on the gun instead to wave and cheer with the rest of us.

Then I saw my three banners, enormous things, easily the largest there. My mother had sewn large white sheets together, and my father and brother had painted in large bold letters:
'LUCKY *ANTRIM* – SOUTH GEORGIA AND FALKLAND ISLANDS, WELCOME HOME DAVID'; 'COME IN D18 – YOUR TIME IS UP'; and 'WELCOME HOME – POCA DAVID YATES'. And there, holding the long sticks that supported the banners, were my family: my parents, my brother and sisters, and other relations too, all trying to spot me amongst the ranks of uniformed men outside – unable to notice my grinning face and wildly waving arms inside the wardroom goldfish bowl. Then someone did spot my mop of curly hair and pointed me out to the others. My eyes blurred as we all saw each other for the first time in almost five months. Now they finally knew for certain that I had returned safely, just as I always said I would.

Then the 'pipe' was made, 'Three cheers for the families and friends of HMS *Antrim*.' The whole ship trembled with the triple chorus of thunderous cheers, as the people on the dockside went completely wild, and cameras flashed and flashed, and young babies howled in the confusion.

After so many hundreds before, the final 'pipe' of the trip was made. 'Hands will fall out from Procedure Alpha and prepare to come along-side. HMS *Antrim*'s ship's company – ho. Ship's company, turning for'ard, diss–miss.' Then it was our turn to go absolutely crazy, and the lads outside threw their hats in the air or tossed them ashore, and danced up and down and screamed at their loved ones only a few yards away. Now that the ship had fallen out from Alpha, Barry, Albert and I could join them, and we burst through the wardroom door to force our way through the uniformed throng to wave to our own families. We could almost touch them now. Delirious seamen and many other helpers struggled to arrange the large ropes that would eventually secure us at last to our native shore.

The noise inside the ship had been loud, but outside it was unbeliev-able – like the continuous roar of an express train through a tunnel, or a cup-final crowd when the score is 3–3 with five minutes to play. I split up from the others, and squeezed my way for'ard as they made their way aft. We were all waving our arms like the winners of the World Cup final itself – only this was much, much better.

It took some minutes to secure all the large ropes to the dockside bollards, then the crowds ashore parted like the Red Sea to allow two mobile cranes to draw into position and swing the gangways across. As soon as they were dropped in place, the crowd surged forward again. But they were still not allowed to cross the rope barriers, until the gang-ways themselves had been secured to the side of the ship. The tension during these last few minutes of separation was almost unbearable. At last the captain appeared from his position on the bridge wing and composed himself, ready to be the first of *Antrim's* men to hold his loved ones again.

With everything now in place, and the roar rising to fever pitch again, an elegant-looking lady was finally given the all clear to be the first of the crowd to climb the steep narrow gangway and fall into the arms of her husband – our skipper. There was another enormous cheer as Captain Young became the first *Antrim* man to kiss a woman on the lips since the ship had left Gibraltar. We all knew our turn would be next, and for some, like me, we did not have to wait long. My eldest sister had tired of queuing with everyone else and had wriggled to the front of the crowd and somehow sneaked under the barrier. Then she by-passed 5 yards of solidly packed people, side-stepped the security attendants and leaped up on to the gangway – to be the first of my family to touch *Antrim's* deck. We met a few yards aft of the for'ard gangway and cuddled each other tightly as we waited for the rest to join us.

We did not really know what to say, other than, 'Are you OK, and are you glad to be back?' It was impossible to say much else because of the noise and crush as the people poured over the gangways. Eventually, though, groups of people started to move away from the starboard waist to allow others to come on board, and then, almost twenty minutes after my sister arrived, the rest of my family made it on board too. I cuddled

my mother tightly and shook hands with my father in the same movement, then I gave him a warm cuddle too. Then it was the turn of my
brother and another sister, an aunt and cousins, and many others.
Again, we could not say much because of the drive to get the rest of the
5,000 on board. It took some doing, but linking hands, we eventually
made our way to the other side of the ship, where at least we could stand
in a small group together. After a few words there, I took them slowly
through the doors and down the ladders towards the mess, but it was
absolutely mobbed in there too, so we just had to keep moving through
the ship wherever the crowds took us – as if we were on an endless
conveyor belt.

At the start of the tour I managed to show them 1G1 mess, and
although it was virtually impossible to venture inside, they could at
least have a quick look and see the cramped conditions in which I had
spent most of the trip. Then we passed by the NAAFI and the main
galley, and on to the hole where the cannon shell had come through and
taken a chunk out of Swampy's leg. He just happened to be standing
there pointing to the same area, with his own relieved family standing
about him. Then, through the tightly packed corridors, we made our
way back into the bright sunshine of the upper deck. It was as packed
as the rest of the ship, but I managed to show them some of the other
bullet holes and the enormous hole in the Sea Slug launcher door where
the bomb had scored its bullseye and very nearly blown *Antrim* apart.

On the flight deck we finally got some reasonably free space to
stand and talk, but what can you say when you cannot believe you are
home, and have survived – and when so many of your mates have not.
I answered their questions as best as I could, but it was impossible to
explain everything at that time. I think they realized that, too, and they
kept hugging me and asking when could I get ashore. 'We've got a little
surprise for you up the road!' I told them I needed to get changed, and
wanted to get some things in town, so we agreed that I would meet them
at my aunt's house in about two or three hours. But before they left, there
was something I desperately wanted to do. It was the first item on my
'list of things to do ashore': to touch solid ground again. So after waiting
a short while in yet another queue, I led them all back down the aft
gangway, onto the dry land I had craved for so long. When we had
found enough space to stand together, I knelt down and kissed the
tarmac. I was finally ashore on dry British land again.

CHAPTER TWENTY-ONE

Home Again

After another round of hugs and kisses, I escorted my group to one of the waiting buses that would take them back to their cars, then went back up the gangway to stand and wave them off. Back at the mess, I managed to get inside, but it was still packed and a rare old party was going on. I felt slightly embarrassed that I was not part of it, but I shook hands with lots of the families, friends and beautiful girls. I wished that my own new girlfriend was there too, but she was still working in her hairdressing salon. I knew I could not see her until after she finished work and I had attended a 'welcome home' party. Before doing any of that though, I wanted to tackle the next three items on my 'list of things to do ashore' – taste a lovely cool pint of Guinness in a pub, get a decent haircut, and eat some juicy Kentucky Fried Chicken. Not far from Unicorn Gate, I knew a street where I could do all three within 100 yards.

I could not spend much time ashore that weekend as I had to be back on board to cover the duty that Shiner should have kept. So I only carried a few war souvenirs. The bag was not really heavy, but as I hurriedly made my way towards the dockyard gate, it certainly felt it. I also noticed that I was feeling very tired, and that the ground seemed to be moving under my feet like the decks at sea. I realized that it would take a bit of time to find my land-legs again. I must have looked like Popeye as I swayed from side to side with my wide-legged gait.

I soon passed the last of the ships tied up alongside in the large non-tidal basin, showed my battered old ID card at Unicorn Gate, and stepped back into 'civvy street' again, only 100 yards from the first destination on my list – the Royal Standard.

Leaving the glaring sunshine, I stepped into a world I had at times thought I would never see again – a real British pub, where the walls were covered in plaques, a jukebox blasted out more unfamiliar tunes and the air reeked of tobacco, perfume and beer. Then I knew I was truly ashore again. I dropped my grip on the floor, and before I could open my mouth, the landlady called out, 'You just got back have you, luv?

Here, what do you want? The first drink is on the house. You deserve it. Well done, luv.' I could not believe this act of kindness from a total stranger. I had been in the Royal Standard once or twice before, but I did not know this woman.

I ordered a pint of Guinness and thanked her profusely. My eyes were filling up again so I turned away from the people who had not been where I had been, and who had not missed a pint of Guinness in the way that I had. I kissed the rim, took one small sip, then a second larger gulp, then drained the glass in a third movement and held my arm out for a refill. I took my time with the second pint, still feeling the motion of the sea under my feet as I gazed at the rows of ships' photographs and plaques that adorned every spare bit of wall and beam space. Strangely, one of the plaques I first saw was my old ship *Salisbury* – a type of vessel that, if still in commission, might have provided better air protection down south. I knew that she was now a rusting hulk somewhere, and would soon be sunk as submarine target practice. Surrounding her plaque were others in various shapes and sizes, with names ranging from the famous ones of the Second World War, to some I had never heard of. I saw many names from the distant past, such as *Hood*, *Rodney*, *Vanguard* and *Belfast*. There were also more familiar ones from my brief time in the navy, names like the ones that had served with *Antrim* in the Falklands War: *Argonaut*, *Arrow*, *Brilliant*, *Broadsword*, *Endurance*, *Exeter*, *Fearless*, *Glamorgan*, *Glasgow*, *Hermes*, *Intrepid*, *Invincible*, *Leeds Castle*, *Minerva*, *Plymouth* and *Yarmouth*. There were probably other plaques up there, and certainly some of our submarine friends too, but those were the ones that caught my eye. And then, amongst those brightly coloured ship's emblems, I saw the plaques of the four ships that had not returned from the South Atlantic, and the reflecting rays of sunshine from outside picked them out like spotlights: *Ardent*, *Antelope*, *Coventry* and *Sheffield*. So I raised my glass to each of them in turn, downed the rest of the pint, thanked the landlady again and rushed out into the street before my eyes welled up again.

The next place on my list was just up the road a short way – a first-floor hairdresser. Like a lot of men on board, I had let my hair grow since hearing the news that we could return home. Now it really was in desperate need of a good trim. And although I knew I was seeing my own hairdresser later, I did not want to ask her to do it, I was hoping we might have other things to do!

I did not wait long to be called forward from the row of deep comfortable chairs by a girl who looked as though she had just stepped out of a fashion magazine. 'What can I do for you, luv? A good wash and cut is it?' As I had my hair washed, and took my position in the high swivel chair, I tried to explain why the mop was in such an unkempt state – that I had been down in the Falklands, and that various men had been shearing it with blunt electric clippers. She asked if it had been cold down there, and if I had lost any mates. I replied yes to both, without venturing into too many details. I was too interested in getting my hair back in proper shape again, and also looking at her, as she glided around me, with her scissors snipping away. She not only looked fantastic, she also smelt heavenly too, and the wonderful aroma of a beautiful woman was bliss after the months of smoke-filled messes, diesel, cordite, matelots' deodorants and other unattractive ship's smells.

Whilst she worked, I listened to Radio One blaring in the background, and told her how much I had missed the charts while we had been away. I did not recognize any of these new tunes, but as she finished off I made a mental note to get some new cassettes for the car, as clearly my old Roxy Music, Police and Queen tapes were now far too outdated. I would have to go out and buy some ABC, Culture Club and Kraftwerk instead.

The cut over, I said, 'Great. That's brilliant – just what I've been looking forward to.' She charged me £3, but I gave her a fiver and said it was worth every penny. Then I skipped back downstairs to head for the last item on my list – a Kentucky Fried Chicken. Apart from sex, Guinness and a decent haircut, this mouth-watering fast food had been in my mind more than anything else – even more than fresh milk, daily papers, live TV and the smell of flowers and an autumn bonfire.

'Six pieces, double chips, large coleslaw and a large coke please, to take away,' I said in a speech that I had rehearsed over and over again so many times that I even knew how many letters it contained: sixty two. I felt like grabbing the first bit of golden chicken right off the young girl's tongs as she lowered it into the bag, but I waited patiently for her to complete the order. She finished adding things, folded the top of the bag and passed the order across with a distinctly American, 'Thank you, Sir, enjoy your meal.'

'Oh I certainly will,' I replied.

I did not know the time of the train I needed to catch to get to my aunt's house up the line, so my next plan was to go to the station, buy a ticket and eat the Kentucky on the platform or in a carriage. However, the smell wafting up from the bag was just too much, and I had only managed to walk a couple of hundred yards before I took a seat on a park bench, tore the bag open and wolfed back the first chicken portion. I devoured a second piece, then half a pot of creamy coleslaw and a few chips, before I stood up and continued on my way towards the station – my free hand just occasionally dipping into the bag for odd little bits of juicy golden treasure.

I did not have to wait long for the train, and had just enough time to complete my meal before clambering on board for the twenty-minute ride to my aunt's . Once the train pulled away, I sat back and gazed at the passing scenery, as all the things I had not seen for so long rolled past the window like the panorama of an enormous cinema screen. Everything seemed so new, all the bright little cars, lorries and buses, and all the houses, shops and factories, and then the schools and fields and hedgerows – with my beloved butterflies fluttering in the light summer breeze. I saw people going about their daily lives, and small land birds darting across the sky – things I had never really noticed or appreciated before. I felt so alive, it was like being born again, this time with the sun streaming through beneath a massive double rainbow.

Leaving the train at the small halt of Rowlands Castle, I walked up the little hill to my aunt's large modern country house. It was easy to pick out because of all the flags and balloons in the front garden. In the drive, my gleaming white Ford Capri was waiting for me with its own 'welcome home' banner slung across the tinted windscreen. I brushed it with my hand as I walked past almost in a dream – still unable to believe I was back again. Before I could reach the door, it swung open in welcome. There were all the faces I had seen earlier, plus many more relations and friends, and I felt like an astronaut home at last from the moon.

My aunt had laid on a massive buffet and there was a large punch bowl of elderflower champagne (which even my teetotal father drank – and enjoyed). My mother had made a fantastic 'welcome home' cake. I was not very hungry, but I politely nibbled at a few things and took a thin slice of cake as I passed from room to room, chatting to everyone about my experiences and the changes I had noticed since my return. I had left Portsmouth at the end of a cold winter. Now it was midsummer, and although I had twice crossed the equator, I had seen an awful lot of cold, barren seas in between.

Between conversations and repeated handshakes and cuddles, I kept looking at my watch to see how time was progressing, because I had promised to pick Jackie up at Havant station at 8 o'clock. I had broken the news to my parents earlier by letter that I would not be able to be at home with the family for very long that day. I had made some excuses about ship's duties. The news did not go down too well when I reminded everyone that I needed to leave at about 7.30, as clearly the party was set to run as long as I could stand up. But the naval uncle who had originally taken me to join *Antrim*, realized the priorities that were running through my mind when he said, 'Oh let him go, you lot. He looks like he needs another haircut, and I'm sure he'll be wanting to show this new girlfriend his war wounds – wherever they are!'

After kissing and shaking hands with everyone again, I gingerly stepped into my beloved 'passion wagon' and strapped myself into the soft, furry brown rally seats. I could not find the ignition slot with the key at first, then I stalled the engine, but after that I slowly crept out of the drive and waved to everyone as I nervously edged forward in second gear. It was only a few miles to Havant, and would normally have taken only ten minutes or so, but today it felt just like the first day I had ever driven on my own – worse in fact, because not only was I finding the car strange to handle, I was still trying to take in the new surroundings. The combination almost brought me to an abrupt halt on more than one occasion!

In Havant, the first major built-up area I came to, the strangeness of the outside world became almost unbearable and I nearly stopped the car and walked the rest of the way. But I soon joined a traffic queue, so I was able to gather my senses a bit and recover a little of my road confidence. This was awful, I thought – everything felt and looked so strange and even smelt different; and now driving my own familiar car was really weird too. I wondered what it was going to be like when it came to touching a woman again. I was afraid I would not know what to do, and would have to start all over from scratch.

As the car gradually made its way to the station I kept looking at all the people walking by on the pavements, many of them semi-clad females in short skirts, with beautifully tanned bare legs. Some strode along on their own, others tugged infants or pushed babies' buggies. But all of them, to my female-starved eyes, looked absolutely divine. Then I saw Jackie trying to make her way through the shoppers on the far side of the road. I wound down my window and called out, 'Excuse me, luv. Can you tell me how to get to the railway station?'

She did not recognize me at first behind her dark glasses. Then she looked more closely as I stuck my head right out of the car, and screamed, 'Dave! Wow! It's you! I did not recognize you in a car – and you're late, too!' I hadn't noticed the time, but I was slightly late. Not that it mattered, because within seconds she had run across the road and dived into the passenger seat beside me, planting a massive kiss on my cheek as I tried to move the car a few inches further forward in the slowly-advancing queue.

As soon as I could, I pulled over into an empty parking space and we greeted each other in a more appropriate way. Forgetting the passing shoppers and the yelling children and everything else going on outside, I squeezed her so tight I thought she would pop out of my arms and through the window. We kissed long and hard, and I could feel the frustrations of the past four months starting to ebb from my body. The embrace almost developed into something far more explicit there and then in the middle of Havant High Street, but fortunately we recovered enough of our clothing and composure to refrain from taking our desire any further. It was the first time that Jackie had been in the Capri with me, so as I drove off to look for somewhere to be alone with her, she looked around, and tried out all the different knobs and buttons, and the radio and cassette player – all the time squeezing my left hand whenever it was free, or my leg when it was not. She looked really lovely sitting next to me, small and thin, just as I remembered her, with just a flimsy blouse on and something she called a ra-ra skirt.

Jackie still lived with her parents and sister, who were all at home, so she said we could not go round there. She also could not risk upsetting or worrying them by staying out all night in some bed and breakfast or hotel. So she suggested, 'Why don't we just spend a quiet evening together in this lovely new car of yours. I know a great place we could go to on Hayling Island – just next to the funfair it is, but it'll be lovely and quiet at this time of night.' I did not ask how she knew it was nice and quiet – I did not really care at that moment. Crossing the short narrow bridge to Hayling Island, we made idle chitchat about things that had happened to us while we had been apart. We still did not really know each other very well, but we talked about stuff we had written to each other about. She also asked me lots of questions about what it had *really* been like down there, but I was still not in the mood to give her or anyone else any full answers, so I just rattled off the same sort of replies I had been giving all day. 'Yeah, it was pretty cold sometimes. We were lucky the bomb never went off. Yeah, I just could not wait to get back.'

As we reached the seafront, Jackie told me to head along the coast road for about a mile or two, to where we could see the spinning wheels of the funfair. Sure enough, in the distance I could see the distinctive shape of an old fashioned looking amusement park with a bright, flashing big wheel, noisy dodgems and rows of different stalls. We drew closer, and a feeling of *deja vu* came over me as we passed near enough to smell the hot dogs and candy floss, and hear the familiar sounds of the whirling waltzers and a spinning carousel.

Backing onto the funfair was a large stretch of gravel-covered land that spread from the road to the sea, and around the edge of this rough car park were clumps of green and yellow gorse bushes. There was one particularly inviting clump that Jackie pointed out for me to head towards. As I did, the conversation changed rapidly from talk of war to talk of love – or more precisely lust. It's a wonder that we even waited for the car to stop amongst the gorse bushes before the words turned into actions. No sooner had the Capri come to a gentle halt, than our hands were working feverishly on each other, almost tearing our clothes off in our frantic attempts to end the long months of frustration.

Some time later, we gazed across the Solent at the Isle of Wight, but it reminded me of being back in 'Bomb Alley' the evening after we had been bombed and strafed, so I did not look across the 4 mile wide expanse of water for long. The hills on the Isle of Wight reminded me too much of the hills that the Argentinian jets had emerged from.

And as we lay there in silence, apart from the sound of Del Shannon's 'Runaway' coming from the fair, my thoughts went back in time and my eyes started to moisten again. Because although I was home again on dry land, and now in the arms of a girl to whom I had just made love, my mind was still back in the cold expanses of the South Atlantic. When I became too quiet and distant, Jackie wiped my eyes with her delicate little red-nailed index finger, held me tightly and whispered, 'Don't worry. Don't be embarrassed. You must have been through a lot of hard times – I'll help you to recover.'

For some time after those words of comfort, I just lay there, deep in thought, with all the memories of the past few months and then this most incredible day of my life. And there in my white Ford Capri on Hayling Island seafront, I thought of all my mates from the *Antrim*, and what they all must be doing at this time – in cars, trains, fields or soft beds. Then I thought of all my dead mates, and the rest of the 250, who were not so lucky as us and would never drink pints of Guinness again, or have decent haircuts, or eat Kentucky Fried Chicken. Or ever feel a beautiful woman's touch against their naked skin as most of us were doing this first evening ashore.

But my sombre mood suddenly lifted, as, just loud enough to hear, from one of the stalls at the funfair came the familiar sound of a coin-operated laughing sailor like the one I had heard when I was a little curly-haired boy. I joined in with the laughter and cried along with my earliest childhood naval memory, and my salty tears trickled down my cheeks. Now a much older, curly-haired laughing sailor had finally come home again.

Glossary

AB	Able seaman – equivalent of an army lance corporal
Aft	At the back of the ship
Afternoon watch	1200–1600
Argies	Argentinians
Beer boat	A junior rates' organization for distributing beer with their mess decks
Beer bosun	The person in charge of the beer boat
Bows	Front sides of the ship
Buffer	The chief bosun's mate
Bulkhead	A wall within a ship
Buzzes	Rumours
Call the hands	The 'pipe' made to wake matelots up
Can man	The canteen manager
CAP	Carrier air protection
Captain's table	A tall wooden lectern in front of which matelots stand to receive awards
Caterer's currency	Normally Gold Blend coffee and chocolate biscuits, used to bribe
CPO	Chief petty officer – equivalent of an army warrant officer (second class)
Dit	A tale or story
Dog watches	The hours between 1600 and 1800 when matelots play sport and cards at sea
Drinks chit	A common, but illegal, document for recording junior rates' mess beer issues
Fearnought suit	Heavy woollen fire-fighting clothing
First watch	2000–2359

Flat	A small deck area or passageway outside a compartment
Fleet chief	Equivalent of an army warrant officer (first class)
Forenoon watch	0800–1200
GIs	Gunnery instructors
Goffa	Any non-alcoholic cold drink
Good ho	A good thing or event
GMD	Guided missile destroyer
Greeny	An electrician
Gronk Board	Noticeboard for displaying pictures and other lewd female memorabilia
Gulch	The narrow space between a row of triple-tiered bunks
Heads	Toilets
Jimmy	The first lieutenant
Killick	A leading hand – equivalent of an army corporal
Ladder sliding	Descending a multi-runged ladder between decks without touching any rungs
Leading hand	Equivalent of an army corporal
Limers	Orange or lemon powder, originally issued to prevent scurvy
Main Drag	The ship's main passageway
MAA	Master at Arms. Ship's head of police
Mess deck	The compartment containing a matelot's mess
Mess square	Communal area within a mess deck
Middies	Midshipmen
Middle watch	0001–0400
Morning Watch	0400–0800
NAAFI	Navy Army Air Force Institution – the little corner shop on board
NBCD	Nuclear biological chemical defence
NGS	Naval gunfire support
No. 1s	Best naval uniform
No. 2s	Second best naval uniform

No. 3s	NAAFI No. 3 biscuits
No. 8s	Working clothes
Nutty	Sweets and chocolates
Pig	An officer
Pipe	A ship's broadcast or tannoy announcement
Plate layer	A Steward
PO	A petty officer – equivalent of an army sergeant
Pongoes	Any member of the army
POMA	Petty officer medical attendant
Pusser	The ship's supply officer
Pusser's grip	A fawn-coloured naval holdall
QM	Quartermaster
QRRNs	Queen's Regulations for the Royal Navy
RA	A matelot who lives, or who is rationed ashore
RAS	Replenishment at sea from another vessel
RAS (A)	Replenishing ammunition
RAS (L)	Replenishing liquids – fuel, water etc
RAS (S)	Replenishing stores
RO	Radio operator
Scab lifter	Any sickbay staff
Scran	Food
Scupper	A drain
Scuttle	A ships window
Ship's office	Pay, administration and records office
Steamy boots	Non-slip working boots
Stoker	Marine engineering mechanic
Store ship	Replenishing stocks of provisions or any other stores
Vertrep	Vertical replenishment by helicopter at sea
Wafu	A member of the Fleet Air Arm
Writer	A ship's clerk or administration assistant

Naval Cook's Glossary

D ear reader,
   In addition to the previous glossary, I also felt there was a requirement for another one – purely to explain the terms used to describe some of the food and drink consumed at sea. Thank you Ben.

AB Biscuits	Arse Blocking Biscuits – successors to ship's biscuits
Babies Heads	Tinned Steak and Kidney Puddings
BITS	Beans in Tomato Sauce
Bitsa Soup	Made with bits of this and bits of that
Black Death	Rum
Blood Pumps	Ox or Sheep's Hearts
Cackle Berries	Eggs
Cheesey Hammy Eggy	Cheese, ham and fried egg on toast
Chicken Pie Surprise	Chicken Pie without any chicken in it
Chicken Shit	Sweetcorn
Choggie Nosh	Chinese Food
Colon Collapser	Vindaloo
Commanche's Bollocks	Tinned Tomatoes
Corned Dog	Ex Argentinian tinned meat used for all dishes
Cow Pie	Steak Pie
Dark and Stormy	Rum and Coke with ice
Dead Fly Cemetery	Currant and Syrup Flan
Dead Fly Sandwiches	Garibaldi Biscuits

Dockyard Slide	Butter or Margarine
Dockyard Tortoises	Steak and Kidney Pies – served upside down
Dogs Bollocks	Tinned Potatoes
Elephant's Dicks	Haggis
Elephant's Footprints	Deep-fried Spam Fritters
Excreta a'la Kontiki	French Garlic-Kidneys on Toast
Farter Starters	Baked Beans in Tomato Sauce
Frog in a Bog	Toad in the Hole
Frog in a Log	Sausage Rolls
Frogs Spawn	Tapioca
Gash Bag Weights	Haricot Beans
Germoline Sandwiches	Deep-fried Spam Fritters in a Bread Roll
Golden Soup	Made with only twenty-two Carrots
Green Grenades	Heineken Tinned Lager
Hawaiian Wedding Cake	Steamed Rice and Pineapple Chunks
HITS	Herrings in Tomato Sauce
Irish Mixed Grill	Roast Potatoes, Boiled Potatoes and Jacket Potatoes
Italian Teabags	Ravioli
JC	Gin drink sold in Gib by the Gallon
Jockanese Hand Grenades	Scotch Eggs
Jock Roast	Mince and Tatties
Jewish Hand Grenades	Individual Pork Pies
Leg of Liver	Joint of meat requested by new joiners
Lepers Hankies	Pizzas
Little Dogs Willies	Tinned Baby Carrots
Limers	Orange or lemon powdered anti-scurvy drink
Loop the Loop	Soup
Mad Dog's Spew	Sandwich Spread
Meat and Two Veg	Something matelot's birds like for breakfast
Mermaid's Piss	Vinegar

Nicky Lauder's Dick	Austrian Smoked Cheese
Nicky Lauder's Ears	Pork Scratchings
Pigs in Blankets	Sausages in batter
Piss Strainers	Kidneys
Plaz Ninia Na Plotto	Russian Grilled Kidneys on Toast
POM	Mashed Potato Powder
Pot Mess	Meat and anything else stewed in a large Mess pot
Rats Coffins	Cornish Pasties
Rat Packs	Emergency Ration Packs – used in the field
Red Grenades	McEwan's Tinned Beer
Red Lead	Tinned tomatoes
Ruby Murray	Curry
Sea Dust	Salt
Shit on a Raft	Sauted Kidney on Toast
SHITS	Spaghetti Hoops in Tomato Sauce
SITS	Spaghetti in Tomato Sauce
Skinheads on a Raft	Baked Beans on Toast
Smeggers	Semolina
Snake and Pygmy Pie	Steak and Kidney Pie
Snorkers	Sausages
Spithead Pheasant	Kippers
Summer Soup	Made with summa this and summa that
Tartan Breadcrumbs	Requested by new joiners for covering Scotch Eggs
Tiffies Toenails	String-grated Parmesan Cheese
Train Smash	Tomatoes, Baked Beans, Sausages and Eggs – all mixed together
Underground Chicken	Rabbit
Wicked Chicken	Grouse
Wooly Beef	Lamb
Yellow Peril	Smoked Haddock
Zeppelins in the Clouds	Bangers and Mash

Naval Nicknames

Not an exhaustive list, but certainly one that may give the reader some idea of a matelot's mind in allocating nicknames. Some of the names you will recognise from old school lessons, books, stage, film or television; whereas others originate from further back in the mists of naval history – when, although sharing the same birthday as Lord Nelson, I wasn't actually serving in the mob at the time!

Daisy Adams
Derby Allan
Andy Anderson
Scrumpy Appleton
Arnie Arnold
Bill Bailey
Stan Baldwin
Bagsy Baker
Barny Barnes
Bertie Bassett
Basher Bates
Soapy Bath
Cec Beaton
Dinger Bell
Wiggy Bennett
Chuck Berry
Blacky Blackman
Blakey Blake
Danny Boone
Welly Boot
Botty Bottrell
Ziggy Bowie
Buster Brown
Robbie Bruce
Rab Burns

Rab Butler
Mary Campbell
Nick Carter
Charlie Chaplin
Charlie Chester
Nobby Clarke
Cas Clay
Manny Cohen
Smokey Cole
Jumper Collins
Chuck Conners
Billy Connolly
Gary Cooper
Billy Cotton
Chopper Cox
Chris Cross
Tony Curtis
Danny Daniels
Jim Davidson
Steve Davis
Dickie Dawson
Slammer Dawson
Happy Day
Dixie Deane
Willy Dick

Tommy Docherty
Tom Dooley
Dougie Douglas
Duke Earl
Crash Evans
Bungie Edwards
Arthur English
Doc Findlay
Florrie Ford
George Formby
Frankie Fraser
Froggy French
Jack Frost
Digger Gardener
Gibbo Gibson
Johnny Giles
George Graham
Dolly Gary
Jimmy Green
Jimmy Greaves
Nobby Hall
Billy Halliday
Tony Hancock
Chats Harris
Harry Harrison

Ticker Hart
Will Hay
Gabby Hayes
Pusser Hill
Jack Hobbs
Dick Holder
Tab Hunter
Jacko Jackson
Jesse James
Danny Kaye
Spider Kelly
Billy Kidd
Killer Kilpatrick
Boogy Knight
Larry Lamb
Burt Lancaster
Shady Lane
Tansy Lee
Dodger Long
Pincher Martin
Swampy Marsh
Tex Marshall
Perry Mason
Stan Mathews
Bertie Mee
Bomber Mills
Dusty Miller
Mitch Mitchell
Monty Montgomery
Keith Moon

Pony Moore
Rattler Morgan
Mo Morris
Ozzy Mosely
Spud Murphy
Ruby Murray
Paul Newman
Hilda Ogden
Olly Oliver
Nosey Parker
Pedler Palmer
Wacker Payne
Polly Pearce
Fred Perry
Blue Peters
Lester Piggott
Pip Piper
Pansy Potter
Pricky Price
Alf Ramsay
Blood Reed
Jim Reeves
Jimmy Riddle
Robbie Roberts
Albert Ross
Sammy Samuels
Artie Shaw
Simmo Simpson
Sammy Small
Smudge Smith

Snowy Snow
Stevie Stevenson
Jimmy Stewart
Jed Stone
Nobby Styles
Buck Taylor
Shirley Temple
Tommo Thomson
Topsy Turner
Dick Turpin
Whisky Walker
Wally Wallace
Max Wall
Sharky Ward
George Washington
Soapy Watson
Spider Webb
Banjo West
Knocker White
Oscar Wilde
Bungy Williams
Wilky Wilkinson
Tug Wilson
Slinger Wood
Shep Wooley
Shiner Wright
Rowdy Yates
Brigham Young

Then of course there are the national or regional nicknames that may be applied instead of, or in addition to the other names:

Jock
Mac
Tam
Taff

Paddy
Mick
George
Scouse

Jan
Yorky

Index